Y0-CPB-656

The Russian Parliament

The Russian Parliament

Institutional Evolution in a Transitional

Regime, 1989–1999

Thomas F. Remington

Yale University Press

New Haven & London

Published with assistance from the Kingsley Trust Association Publication Fund established by the Scroll and Key Society of Yale College.

Set in Adobe Garamond type by The Composing Room of Michigan, Inc.

Printed in the United States of America by Sheridan Books, Chelsea, Michigan.

Library of Congress Cataloging-in-Publication Data

Remington, Thomas F., 1948–
    The Russian Parliament : institutional evolution in a transitional
regime, 1989–1999 / Thomas F. Remington.
        p.   cm.
Includes bibliographical references and index.
    ISBN 0-300-08498-6 (cloth : alk. paper)
    1. Russia (Federation). Federal'noe Sobranie.   2. Russia (Federation).
Federal'noe Sobranie. Gosudarstvennaya Duma.   3. Representative
government and represenation—Russia (Federation) I. Title.
JN6697 .R46   2001
328.47—dc21

                                        00-011938

The paper in this book meets the guidelines for permanence and durability of the Committee on Production Guidelines for Book Longevity of the Council on Library Resources.

10 9 8 7 6 5 4 3 2 1

Contents

Tables and Figures

FIGURES

Preface

In the final decade of the twentieth century tumultuous political change occurred in Russia. Both the Soviet regime and the Soviet state collapsed. In Russia, largest by far of the fifteen newly sovereign successor states, drastic political and economic reforms launched at the beginning of the decade were stalled by the end. Boris Yeltsin's abrupt resignation as president of the Russian Federation on New Year's Eve 1999 left to his successor, Vladimir Putin, a state gravely weakened by maladministration, corruption, and mistrust. The promise of a democratic Russia became one of those unfulfilled hopes for which Yeltsin sought the forgiveness of his countrymen in his resignation speech. Many Russian and Western observers questioned whether the notion of "democratic transition" had any relevance whatever to the changes in Russia's state structures since the fall of communism, seeing them as varieties of power grabs. In the economic arena, as Thane Gustafson notes, analysts tend to treat Russia's economy either as in transition to market capitalism or as having been taken over by powerful vested interests that have stifled any further opening of the economy to competition and free markets.[1] At times the transition versus takeover debate gets sidetracked by definitional disputes or is papered over by qualifying Russia as a "democracy with adjectives."[2] The real problem, however, is finding out how Russia's postcommunist institutions and processes actually work. Only by seeing how power is distributed and deployed can we begin to make meaningful comparisons between Russia and other postauthoritarian regimes. At some point, the analyst must descend from the airy world of terminological disputes and investigate how politics actually works.

This book accordingly has two goals: to describe how Russia's parliamentary institutions arose, and to assess how they operate in practice. The premise is that parliaments are the indispensable instrument of political representation in democracy; without elected representatives deliberating on the issues confronting the society and giving their assent to policy decisions through legislation, no country in the modern age can be considered democratic. But legislatures may work well or poorly, for reasons some of which are under their collective control, and others of which may lie embedded in the wider social environment of which they are a part. An essential part of our task in this book is to investigate how well Russia's parliamentary institutions have worked in the light of several criteria that may reasonably be applied.

Still, the debate between takeover and transition perspectives in Russia's case is only partly an empirical question. It echoes a long-standing difference in perspective among scholars of institutions, that between those who investigate the efficiency-enhancing properties of institutional arrangements, particularly those that enable social actors to capture the benefits of exchange or collective action, and those who emphasize the way in which institutions distribute advantage unequally. Russia's recent history offers ample instances of the latter. The process of privatization without the market, in which powerful bureaucrats and oligarchs wound up with control of formerly state assets, readily illustrates the ability of the powerful to design institutional arrangements to suit their private benefit rather than to enhance social welfare or efficiency. In the political sphere, the creation of representative institutions subject to manipulation by the powerful and wealthy serves a similar purpose. Rather than equalizing rights of participation in the political arena, such institutions redistribute political resources to those best able to seize the advantage from them. Democratic representative institutions are collectively beneficial to the country through their ability to confer procedural legitimacy on decisions and their ability to incorporate a wider range of interests and information into decision making than would have been taken into account in a closed system. In some cases, however, institutional innovations that are redistributive in purpose and result may have longer-term efficiency-increasing benefits, if only by stabilizing a decision-making environment and encouraging actors to take a longer view of their interests and goals. For that reason, institutional change may have consequences that are not anticipated by those who created the new arrangements. It is one of the arguments of this book that mechanisms adopted by Russian political leaders for short-term political gains turned out to have lasting results as they were modified and preserved in subsequent periods. Their persistence suggests that they solved collective dilemmas for ambitious politicians, who in turn adapted their own political strategies in light of them.

The argument thus consists of a series of logical steps. If we accept that democracy requires effective parliamentary institutions, which both convey demands and information to decision makers, and make policy decisions in the form of binding laws, then we must ask what it is that enables such institutions to work well or poorly. To the extent that some, at least, of the influences on their ability to work well have to do with the way in which elected representatives organize themselves to frame options and choose among them, then we should be interested in knowing how these organizational forms arise and how they work. Moreover, if we agree that such institutions may be created under one set of political circumstances, perhaps to lock in distributional advantage to a particular set of actors at a given moment in time, but have quite different longer-term results, then we need to ask how these arrangements have affected the political goals and strategies of politicians once they are accepted as part of the given rules of the game. In turn this perspective suggests that institutions created as part of a takeover at an early stage in a regime transition may conceivably impel the regime toward greater (or less) democracy over time. Institutional choices that are endogenous to a game among politicians at one point become exogenous conditions for the political game as time passes.

This book has been long in the making. It has benefited from the material support of several organizations and the intellectual support of numerous colleagues, both in the United States and in Russia. In many ways it began with a senior fellowship at the Harriman Institute of Columbia University in 1989. The generosity of the Harriman Institute and the wealth of its intellectual resources gave me the opportunity to follow at close hand the extraordinary proliferation of political expression and movements in the Soviet Union in that year, particularly the remarkable contested elections of deputies to the USSR Congress of People's Deputies held in March of that year, which launched the great experiment in parliamentarism. Support from the International Research and Exchanges Board (IREX) and the National Council for Soviet and East European Research (as it then was called) enabled me to spend four months in Moscow in spring 1991, interviewing members of the USSR parliament as well as the Russian Republic parliament, and of many other city and district soviets in the last period of the Soviet Union's existence. I was able to conduct around thirty interviews with USSR deputies, half of whom were chairs of committees or leaders in interest group or political factions. Intrigued by the enormity of the effort to give some institutional form to what had been a "socialist pluralism of opinions," I wanted to know whether these new, uncertain soviet bodies—whose deputies voiced profound frustration with their inability to reverse the country's disintegration—had any chance of becoming effective parliamentary structures. Amidst the bitterness expressed by many of the deputies that they were being used in other people's games, there were clear indications that parliament's creation had opened new avenues for ambitious young politicians to influence policy and make political careers. The outlines of a system of parliamentary parties were coming into view. Specialization and professionalism were developing. The organizational forms in which the new deputies were working were grotesquely unsuited to the tasks they were called upon to address: the USSR Congress comprised 2,250 deputies; Russia's republic-level Congress 1,068; Moscow's city soviet had 500 deputies. Such bodies were better suited for mass demonstrations than for legislative deliberation. They were easily, and frequently, paralyzed by mass walkouts, by procedural chaos and confusion, and by constant negative majorities formed against any but the blandest decisions.

The dissolution of the Soviet Union meant that the USSR-level parliamentary bodies vanished by the end of 1991. But Russia's own Congress and Supreme Soviet, and the regional and local soviets, remained, as did Russia's presidency. Russia now was a sovereign, independent state, which enacted its own program of radical market reform on the second day of 1992. Immediately politicians formed sides. Gradually the cleavage between supporters and opponents of radical economic reform came to coincide with the institutional line separating parliament from president. With the support of the National Council for Soviet and East European Research I returned to Moscow in spring 1992 and spring 1993 to study Russia's Supreme Soviet at firsthand and to survey its members. In spring 1993 the constitutional crisis was growing acute, but politicians were also preparing for new parliamentary elections, which it was widely assumed would be held sometime in the next several months. Politicians also accepted that the elections would feature some combination of the traditional single-member district plurality races and proportional representation through party list races, and they were already forming electoral coalitions in anticipation of the as-yet unscheduled elections.

In view of the terrible violence surrounding Yeltsin's dissolution of the Russian Congress and Supreme Soviet, it was remarkable that the new State Duma and Federation Council took form and began working relatively smoothly. One reason for this was that they were leavened with a number of experienced parliamentarians who had served as deputies in the USSR and Russian Supreme Soviets and were able rather quickly to establish new rules and procedures. In chapter 7 I detail this process closely. The striking thing is the degree of continuity between the two previous, dissolved parliamentary systems and the new bicameral parliament created under Yeltsin's constitution. The deputies discarded some institutional forms and modified others, as will be seen in this book; therefore an understanding of the development of the earlier, transition models was crucial to understanding how and why the new Federal Assembly was organized.

I returned to Moscow to study the new Duma and Federation Council in 1994 and each subsequent year, interviewing deputies, staffers, scholars, and political observers; gathering documents and records; and observing sessions, surveying the deputies, and gathering data on roll-call voting in the Duma and its predecessor bodies.

This decade-long project has been supported by a number of organizations. Several research trips were funded by the Ford Foundation through its grant to the Center on East-West Trade, Investment and Communications at Duke University; Emory's University Research Committee and Halle Institute; the National Council for Soviet and East European Research (subsequently National Council for Eurasian and East European Research); and the National Science Foundation. To these organizations I wish to express my appreciation for their support, and of course they must be absolved of any responsibility for the judgments offered here.

I also wish to acknowledge the advice and assistance provided by a variety of host institutions in Russia, particularly the Institute for State and Law of the Academy of Sciences, and the Center for Political Technologies. I am particularly indebted to Vladimir I. Lysenko of the Institute for State and Law, and to his colleagues Yuri Vedeneev, William Smirnov, Alexander Yakovlev, and Vladimir Kazimirchuk, and to the director of the institute, Boris Topornin. Igor Bunin and Boris Makarenko of the Center for Political Technologies have been valued partners in much of this research. I am grateful as well to Nikolai

Petrov and Mark Urnov for their insights on Russian politics. Let me also cite the unique role played by INDEM, its founder Georgii Satarov and programmer Mikhail Zakhvatkin to this research. The herculean work of INDEM in gathering and systematizing the voting records of the union and RSFSR Congresses and of the first years of the State Duma made it possible to construct data sets of individual voting records.

The late Alexander Sobyanin was unfailingly generous in sharing his unique knowledge and prolific reports about parliamentary politics. His passing is a great loss.

Many deputies, past and present, have given me the benefit of their knowledge and experience, among them Vladimir Isakov, Nikolai Medvedev, and Viktor Sheinis.

Through the East-West Parliamentary Practice Project I have had a remarkable opportunity to get to know a great many elected deputies from Russia and other countries and to learn firsthand about the problems Russian representatives confront both at the federal and regional levels. To its executive director, Jill Adler, and to Vladimir Podoprigora, member of its Steering Committee and organizer of the Russian programs, I wish to note my profound gratitude for the opportunity to work with them on the Russia workshops.

At earlier stages, the book manuscript benefited considerably from thoughtful and detailed comments made by Timothy Colton, Gerhard Loewenberg, and Steven Solnick.

I have also been fortunate in being able to call upon the work of a number of graduate research assistants at Emory, among them Greg Haley, Dawn Plumb Jamison, Laura Kennedy, Scott Langford, Kathleen Montgomery, Kami Rynish, and Dmitry Savransky; and I wish especially to single out the extraordinary contribution of Moshe Haspel.

Throughout, Steven Smith has been a close companion in the research for this book and a strong influence on its content. This book has a different purpose from our co-authored book, *The Politics of Institutional Choice,* but is intended to complement it. I am deeply indebted to Steve for his collaboration, encouragement, and friendship.

Finally, I would like to express my gratitude to my wife Nancy for her steady support throughout this project. I affectionately dedicate this book to her.

Chapter 1 Political Representation and Parliamentary Power

In this book I shall explore the emergence of Russia's parliament between 1989 and 1999. This period can be divided into three phases, the first two of which overlap. The first phase began in 1989 with the establishment of a new legislative structure designed by Gorbachev to replace the old Supreme Soviet. This stage ended with the August 1991 coup and the subsequent breakup of the Soviet Union. The short life of the legislature of the Russian Republic (Russian Soviet Federated Socialist Republic, or RSFSR) in the 1990–93 period is the second phase. This structure, formed one year after the new USSR legislature continued to function as the parliament of an independent Russia after the breakup of the union. Closely modeled on the USSR-level parliament in its organization, this RSFSR parliament followed a similar historical trajectory toward catastrophic demise in 1993. Then, following Yeltsin's forcible dissolution of parliament in September 1993, a new Federal Assembly was created in December 1993. The 1993 constitution and the Federal Assembly it established remain in force as of this writing. (See figure 1.1 for a timeline of these phases and table 1.1 for a list of the dates of the USSR and RSFSR Congress and Supreme Soviet sessions.)

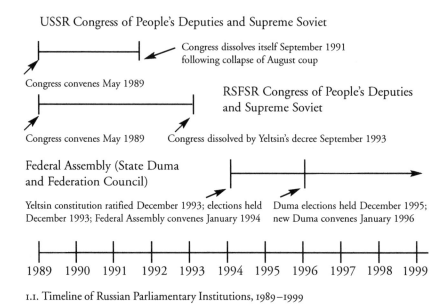

USSR Congress of People's Deputies and Supreme Soviet

Congress dissolves itself September 1991
following collapse of August coup

Congress convenes May 1989

RSFSR Congress of People's Deputies
and Supreme Soviet

Congress convenes May 1989   Congress dissolved by Yeltsin's decree September 1993

Federal Assembly (State Duma
and Federation Council)

Yeltsin constitution ratified December 1993; elections held   Duma elections held December 1995;
December 1993; Federal Assembly convenes January 1994   new Duma convenes January 1996

1989   1990   1991   1992   1993   1994   1995   1996   1997   1998   1999

1.1. Timeline of Russian Parliamentary Institutions, 1989–1999

The immediate purpose of this book is to trace the emergence of two crucial representative institutions over the decade from 1989 to 1999—parliamentary parties and bicameralism. In doing so I hope to shed light on the more general problem of explaining how these features of parliamentary organization have contributed to the stabilization of political conflict in Russia and to explain how new representative institutions are adopted by political actors who are engaged in an all-out contest for power. The rapid succession of legislative forms in Russia over this period offers us a valuable case study in the creation of democratic institutions because in the compressed time span of a decade, three different sets of legislative arrangements have been established.

Skeptics might object that Russia's parliamentary evolution is incomplete and that the institution itself is too much an instrument of presidential domination and the play of powerful and wealthy outside interests to justify a serious examination. If parliament does not constrain elite political behavior significantly, what theoretically interesting conclusions can be drawn from a study of its formation?

Certainly institutional choices in recent Russian politics have been driven by a fierce power struggle in which the very definition of the state is at stake.[1] By and large, Gorbachev and Yeltsin wrote constitutions that served their immediate power needs and imposed them on the country. When Gorbachev proposed

Table 1.1. Dates of the Sessions of the USSR and RSFSR Congresses of People's Deputies and Supreme Soviet, 1989-1993

Body	Session	Dates
USSR CPD	1	May 25, 1989–June 9, 1989
USSR CPD	2	Dec. 12 1989–Dec. 24, 1989
USSR CPD (Extraordinary)	3	Mar. 12, 1990–Mar. 15, 1990
USSR CPD	4	Dec. 17, 1990–Dec. 27, 1990
USSR CPD (Extraordinary)	5	Sept. 2, 1991–Sept. 5, 1991
USSR Supreme Soviet	1	June 3, 1989–Aug. 4, 1989
USSR Supreme Soviet	2	Sept. 25, 1989–Nov. 28, 1989
USSR Supreme Soviet	3	Feb. 14, 1990–June 14, 1990
USSR Supreme Soviet	4	Sept. 10, 1990-Jan. 16, 1991
USSR Supreme Soviet	5	Feb. 18, 1991–July 12, 1991
RSFSR CPD	1	May 16, 1990–June 22, 1990
RSFSR CPD (Extraordinary)	2	Nov. 27, 1990–Dec. 3, 1990
RSFSR CPD (Extraordinary)	3	Mar. 28, 1991–Apr. 5, 1991
RSFSR CPD (Extraordinary)	4	May 21, 1991–May 25, 1991
RSFSR CPD (Extraordinary)	5	July 10, 1991–July 16, 1991
RSFSR CPD (Extraordinary)	5	Oct. 28, 1991–Nov. 2, 1991
RSFSR CPD	6	Apr. 6, 1992–Apr. 21, 1992
RSFSR CPD	7	Dec. 1, 1992–Dec. 14, 1992
RSFSR CPD	8	Mar. 10, 1993–Mar. 13, 1993
RSFSR CPD	9	Mar. 26, 1993–Mar. 29, 1993
RSFSR Supreme Soviet	1	July 3, 1990–July 14, 1990
RSFSR Supreme Soviet	2	Sept. 3, 1990–Dec. 21, 1990
RSFSR Supreme Soviet	3	Jan. 21, 1991–July 6, 1991
RSFSR Supreme Soviet	4	Sept. 19, 1991–July 22, 1992
RSFSR Supreme Soviet	5	Sept. 22, 1992–Dec. 25, 1992
RSFSR Supreme Soviet	6	Jan. 13, 1993–July 23, 1993

a new two-tiered parliamentary system with competitive elections at the Nineteenth Party Conference in summer 1988, the erstwhile Soviet parliament, the USSR Supreme Soviet, dutifully went along and gave him the constitutional amendments that he sought. When Gorbachev wanted to establish a presidency for himself, he forced it through the new parliament and had himself elected to the post by the parliament. Yeltsin, for his part, introduced a Russian presidency to counter Gorbachev, pushed to weaken and dissolve the Soviet Union, finally disbanded the Russian parliament when he could no longer tolerate its opposition, and proposed a constitution creating a new parliament to the country in a nationwide yes-or-no vote: vote for my constitution, or face the consequences of chaos, he implied. The voters gave him the constitution he wanted. It is a constitution that gave him as president the power he demanded to enact policies over the opposition of all but the most concerted parliamentary opposition. In the pursuit of power, Yeltsin wound up the winner, president of an independent Russia, with a strong presidency facing a weak parliament. On the face of it, anyway, the period is hardly a story of the triumph of democratic institutions.

Because coercion and intimidation were used to force the pace of change, new representative bodies, such as the parliament, have made little apparent headway at taming power, the task that White, Rose, and McAllister regard as uppermost for Russia's development: "In the United States the very act of invoking the Constitution to justify actions implies recognition of the rule of law; it also accepts that presidential actions can be challenged and even nullified in the courts. In Russia, by contrast, the word for political power, *vlast,* refers to domination by the powers that be. Yet democracy is not a system of domination; it is about taming power. In Russia, there is a need to tame *vlast* on a continental scale."[2] If constitutional reform has been motivated by the struggle for *vlast',* and if the winners have always shaped institutional arrangements to strengthen their power positions, then once we have accounted for one contender's victory over another, what is left to explain?

If Russia's institutional development in this period were really so simple, there certainly would be no need to probe more deeply. But there are some problems with this account. For one, if winners always knew what they wanted, and always got their way, how can we explain the disastrous outcomes of their behavior? If Gorbachev could whistle up institutions to suit his interests, why did his reforms result in the collapse of the country and his humiliating exit from power? Why did Gorbachev first reject the idea of creating a presidential system, then embrace it? Why did Gorbachev's apparently tractable creature, the parliament, which was firmly controlled by his longtime ally Anatolii Luk'ianov turn against him and join with his enemies in the August 1991 coup? Why did Yeltsin reject the idea of dissolving parliament in fall 1991 when many of his advisers sought new elections, or a new constitution, or both, and accept it in September 1993, when his opposition was vastly more powerful? And who, in 1993, would have predicted that by decade's end, both the first and second State Dumas should have served out their full terms while President Yeltsin would have voluntarily resigned seeking his nation's forgiveness? It turns out that the history of constitutional forms in this period is one of improvisation, uncertainty, experimentation, and miscalculation. Evidently the game was more complicated than it seems because institutional choices had consequences that were neither desired nor expected by their authors.

There are more puzzles. Despite Yeltsin's use of force to disband parliament in 1993, and the heavy loss of life that followed from the shelling of the parliament building after his opponents rose up to seize power, all major sections of organized political opinion immediately agreed to participate in the new parliamentary arena he decreed into being. Moreover, his fiercest antagonists wound up playing by the rules of the parliamentary game. Even more surprising, so did Yeltsin. For instance, in August 1998, when the Duma credibly signaled that it would not accede to Yeltsin's pressure to confirm Chernomyrdin as prime minister—as it had done for Kirienko in April 1998 under the threat of dissolution and early elections—Yeltsin surprisingly backed down and nominated a figure far more to the Duma's liking.

The point is that institutional choices have unforeseeable consequences because of the way they guide subsequent interactions of the relevant political actors. The establishment of new arrangements for deciding the outcome of political competition changes the stakes or payoffs of the game. If institutions are instruments by which political actors achieve such ends as shaping policy for their community, or simply gaining power and status for themselves, they may devote resources to acquiring influence over the institutions. New institutions bring new participants into the political arena and alter the calculations of those already in the game. Moreover, new or changed rules of the game affect the players' expectations about what other players will do. Once actors revise their expectations about how others will behave, they may act differently themselves. Actors adjust their mutual expectations and adapt their behavior in order to achieve their goals. Some may prove successful at taking advantage of new opportunities presented to them. Rivals may collude to raise the hurdles to entering the game in order to shut out any further competition or loosen the barriers to entry to admit more potential allies. New contenders arise to challenge the previous majority by finding new issues and conflicts to exploit. They may press in turn for new institutional reforms that broaden their access to power. Because the groups are now organized, it becomes much costlier for the rulers to go back to the status quo ante. At moments when politically repressive regimes begin to liberalize representative institutions, the demands for still wider participatory rights can have explosive effects.[3] A good example is the effect of the opening of the electoral arena under Gorbachev. The opportunity to win parliamentary mandates motivated activists to use the election campaigns of 1989 and 1990 to mobilize followings around such popular causes as nationalism and democracy that had not been organized or represented before.

In this book I will argue that the accretion of institutional changes over this period resulted in a Federal Assembly that has been more stable and more effective than its two transitional predecessors. Not only has it survived far longer than either, it has also had some success in taming the naked struggle for power. Certainly it has had a greater capacity to exercise influence than anyone anticipated, Yeltsin included. But the increase in parliament's institutional capacity did not come about through a process of adaptive evolution to the greater demands of a new political environment. It came about because the design of the Federal Assembly incorporated new sets of representative rights that gave political actors a reason to abide by the new rules of the game. The adoption of these features was the outcome of a series of institutional choices made by politicians seeking to satisfy more immediate interests. The bargains they struck on sharing power turned out to have a significant cumulative impact on the way they interact in the parliament, and the way parliament interacts with the larger political system. The case illustrates the point that institutional choices can have consequences that differ from the objectives that the actors had in creating them.[4]

In the case of the parliament, if the new Federal Assembly is more effective than its predecessors, this fact would influence the behavior of the president, interest groups, courts, regional leaders, aspiring party leaders, opinion leaders, business, and other political actors. A more effective parliament would be a powerful impetus toward the consolidation of a democratic political system—toward taming *vlast'*. Since parliaments are a central feature of democratic political systems, the way they are formed and the way they make decisions has a significant impact on other elements of the political system.

PARLIAMENT AND DEMOCRATIZATION

The premise that the way a parliament is organized will affect how well it represents diverse interests and exercises influence over policy making needs to be elaborated. That parliaments are crucial, even defining, features of democracy is not disputed. William Mishler and Richard Rose cite John Stuart Mill's observation to the effect that the best type of government is that in which: "the whole people, or some numerous portion of them, exercise through deputies periodically elected by themselves the ultimate controlling power."[5] They observe that parliaments are virtually universal institutions and that "leaders of diverse persuasions certainly behave as if legislatures are conducive to the success of democratic governments." Wherever democratic government has struggled to replace authoritarianism, legislative institutions are established or reformed.

Why are parliaments central to modern democratic government? Two answers recur throughout the literature on parliamentary institutions: people want to have a voice in government decision making and consider parliaments an indispensable (if never entirely perfect) means for giving voice to their desires; and parliaments universally are institutions by which elected representatives confer legitimacy on legislative decisions.[6] Without legislative bodies to give their approval to policy decisions, power-holders rule without being held subject to deliberation, debate, and formal approval by a body of elected representatives. Without an effective legislature to check it, the executive aggregates demands and makes decisions alone, whether the wielder of executive power is a Politburo, a monarch, or a military junta. Over many ages and in many different societies people have designed legislatures for the purposes of representation and decision making.

A well-established axiom in political science holds that no one set of legislative arrangements can simultaneously maximize both the objectives of representativeness and effectiveness in decision making. A legislature that is perfectly representative of a populace would include every member of the society and deliberation and decision would be coterminous with the life of the society. Most basically, representative institutions economize on a community's scarce resources, such as time, but at the cost of narrowing and simplifying the range of options available.[7] Much as a mass meeting can readily be reduced to frustrating incoherence by the diversity of demands for issues to consider and the number of people who want their voices heard, a perfectly representative law-making body would be ineffective. Therefore, to be able to form a collective will, a representative body requires a means for reducing the complexity and diversity of demands to a smaller number of alternative decisions that can then be voted on. To represent the collective choice of the body, at least one of the options must be able to command the support of a majority. If more than one alternative is supported by the required minimum number of members, there must be an institutional means for choosing one over another, lest instability result through the inability of a majority to reach a decision.[8] At the opposite end of the spectrum, a legislature that always endorsed the legislative proposals of a dictator would be efficient at decision making, but representative only in the most trivial or negligible sense. In the communist era, soviet-type legislatures were "decisive but not autonomous," as John Carey, Frantisek Formanek, and Ewa Karpowicz write. "That is, these legislatures were ineffective not because of coordination failure or the inability to reach collective decisions; rather, they were ineffective because they were not repositories of policy expertise or arenas of deliberation independent from the Communist Party bureaucracies."[9] But as the diversity of the interests and goals represented in parliament increases with democratization, such a legislature must find a way to aggregate its members' preferences and pose alternatives for majority decision. It can do so more or less efficiently, but its decisions will generally divide winners from losers.

If it is to be effective at decision making, therefore, a legislature must be able to choose from among a range of alternatives one that can command a majority and to maintain that choice in the face of other options. The more that it excludes some alternatives from being considered, though, the less likely it is that groups which favor the discarded options will consider themselves committed to abiding voluntarily by its decisions. By the same token, a legislature without the means to aggregate preferences and form a collective will is unlikely to be effective in setting policy or to tame *vlast'*.[10] We can suppose that a legislature can increase its overall ability both to represent diverse interests and to make effective policy decisions by changing electoral rules and its own rules of procedure, as well as by gaining broader constitutional authority. Similarly, we can suppose that a legislature can fall well short of its maximum potential capacity for representation and decision making if its own internal arrangements keep it paralyzed to act except on uncontroversial matters. Such a body might have enormous constitutional prerogatives on paper but be prevented from realizing more than a fraction of them by its own inability to produce coherent decisions. Another legislature might have more limited constitutional powers but turn out to be a significant source of policy influence and a force the executive must reckon with.

Depending on the constitutional framework, legislative decisions may include the formation of the government as well as the nature of policy acts. In a parliamentary system, the most important policy decision may be approval of the composition of the government; once formed, the legislature's decisions on legislation may be little more than a confirmation of an existing balance between majority and minority camps. But even in many parliamentary systems, and in mixed parliamentary-presidential ones as well as in separation of powers systems, the legislature's assent to legislative acts requires extensive debate and bargaining.

The idea that there is a trade-off between decision-making effectiveness and representation has a long pedigree in the literature on legislative structure and covers both parliamentary systems, where parliament forms government and government makes policy, as well as legislatures in separation-of-power systems.[11] Depending on such factors as the party system and constitutional rules, as well as its own internal efficiency, a legislature may produce a united, cohesive executive commanding a secure majority—and able to carry out its policy—or it may expend a great deal of its members' time and resources to internal bargaining and mutual accommodation in policy making, at the expense of coherence and accountability. Matthew Shugart and John Carey pose the trade-off as one of efficiency—the ability of the institutions to give the voters the means to choose between alternative governing teams, so that the outcome of their votes determines the direction of policy—as against representativeness, the availability of voice for diverse interests in the legislature.[12] Kaare Strom defines electoral "decisiveness" as the degree to which the elections directly affect the composition and direction of government. Where nongovernment parties exercise considerable influence on policy through committees and legislative logrolls, and the composition of the government does not directly reflect electoral victory and defeat, electoral decisiveness is low and opposition influence high.[13] Giuseppe Di Palma's study of the Italian parliament paints a portrait of a legislature unable to make major policy decisions because of the high degree of opposition party influence over legislation, but which accommodates many patronage-oriented "little laws" that serve the electoral needs of multiple government and opposition parties.[14]

Logically, the problem of the trade-off between efficiency and representativeness can be applied to either problems of the formation of a cabinet or of reaching policy decisions, since both categories of decision depend on parliament's means to produce a stable majority choice. Both problems arise in mixed parliamentary-presidential systems, such as those of France and Russia. The constitutional model of the French Fifth Republic was intended by de Gaulle to solve a structural flaw in the French Third and Fourth Republics, where the constitutional powers of parliament coupled with the diversity of interests represented in it made negative majorities easy to assemble but stable majorities in support of a policy or cabinet difficult and fragile. To overcome cabinet instability and parliamentary fragmentation, therefore, de Gaulle's advisers designed a constitution that would establish single-member districts, plurality elections, a powerful presidency, and far-reaching rights of control by the government over legislative decision making.[15] These institutional arrangements have narrowed and simplified the range of choice available to legislators, yielding more efficient, decisive, and coherent policy making. With control of the agenda, the agenda setter can pose alternatives to guarantee a stable outcome—but at the expense of the freedom of the legislators to consider other alternatives. The constitution of the French Fifth Republic is a powerful example of the use of institutional design for explicit policy ends. It is one of the clearest modern examples of the use of constitutional engineering to alter the mixture of legislative effectiveness and representativeness in policy making. Yet, curiously, it produced results that were neither expected nor desired by its framers, de Gaulle and Michel Debre. By giving parliament a greater institutional capacity to aggregate preferences and form a collective will, de Gaulle's constitution paradoxically strengthened both parties and parliament: outcomes that have necessitated phases of "cohabitation" between presidents of one political family and parliamentary majorities and governments of another.[16]

The global wave of transitions to democracy in the last two decades has invigorated these older questions about the sources and consequences of different mixtures of institutional arrangements, both at the constitutional level and in reforming or creating legislative structures.[17] Much of the literature has focused on the ability of a legislature's structure and decision-making procedures to manage social conflict and has focused on the trade-offs between the accountability and decisiveness of policy making attributed to presidential systems and the inclusiveness and flexibility of parliamentary government. The concern is that groups that consistently lose out in decision making will opt out of the parliamentary game and seek redress through violence, secession, or other undesirable exit options. Alfred Stepan and Cindy Skach find that presidential systems are more prone to breakdown than parliamentary systems.[18] Arend Lijphart, Juan Linz, and Donald Horowitz have debated the use of parliamentary and electoral engineering to solve social problems by moderating the intensity of social divisions, encouraging leaders to negotiate with one another and settle differences peacefully, and getting them to abide by a common set of constitutional arrangements. In a very influential line of argument, Linz has emphasized the desirability of avoiding winner-take-all arrangements where the stakes of winning and losing office are so high that players are tempted to resort to unconstitutional means to win and preserve power.[19] Lijphart has examined empirically whether more consensual, representative arrangements yield better economic and political performance than institutions maximizing decisive and responsible government and finds that consensual arrangements—

those lying further on the curve toward representativeness—perform no worse than more efficient majoritarian ones.[20] Based on a comprehensive comparative analysis of policy making under a variety of constitutional forms, Kent Weaver and Bert Rockman conclude that effective policy making seems to be affected more by contextual factors than by simple institutional factors, such as whether the executive is formed separately from the legislative majority or whether a plurality or proportional system is used in distributing seats.[21] Shugart and Carey have advanced the discussion of presidentialism further by distinguishing among presidential systems. They find that the most unstable arrangements are those in which an executive must be simultaneously answerable to both a parliament and a separately elected president, and the president, moreover, has significant policy-making powers.[22]

The problem of guaranteeing commitment to the new arrangements by opposing sides in fact has two faces. One is the dilemma of overcoming the mistrust that the "outs" have toward the "ins" by persuading them that they have more to gain from playing by the rules than by staying outside the game. Such solutions as supermajorities, veto rights, and guaranteed reserve domains of policy have been identified.[23] The other side of the coin is the dilemma for a strong player, such as a sovereign ruler, who, recognizing that there is more to gain from establishing new institutions that lower the costs of transactions with competitors than from remaining in a prisoner's dilemma of mutual mistrust and mutual defection, agrees to limit his own power in a visible, credible, and enforceable way.[24] This is often called the problem of credible commitment. Whether the immediate problem is inducing the participation of outside challengers in a reorganized electoral and constitutional framework, or of credibly demonstrating commitment to it by the former rulers, the problem is one of coordinating the strategies of actors with divergent interests around a common set of institutional arrangements. As Schmitter and Karl observe, democracy requires that elected representatives simultaneously compete and cooperate in maintaining democratic institutions.[25] Over a range of social settings, representative institutions that overcome the mutual mistrust and uncertainty of political actors sufficiently so that they can make decisions and abide by their results provide a number of benefits for the larger society by reducing the level of costly conflict and increasing society's capacity for collective action.

Explaining Institutional Choice

So far I have noted that there is general agreement on two premises: that legislative bodies are indispensable elements of democratic government, and that as the diversity of interests represented in a legislature widens, the institution's ability to make and hold to decisions depends upon finding institutional solutions to the dilemmas of collective choice which allow them to aggregate and narrow the range of choices available. Whether greater representativeness or greater efficiency in decision making is preferred may be debated because they are linked to different understandings about the ordering of priorities for a political system, such as political stability and effective policy. The optimal prescription for any given system will depend on the social and political environment as well as on the preferences of the designers. There is a notional maximum level at which the legislature can serve representative and decision-making ends and this is set, at least to some degree, by such external constraints as the constitutional framework and the electoral system. In contrast, the degree to which the legislature achieves its maximum potential level of efficiency for this mixture of objectives is a product, at least to some degree, of its own arrangements, such as its rules and procedures for reaching decisions.

How do representative institutions arise? At the cost of some simplification, we can identify three major perspectives on institutional choice. The first weights environmental influences most heavily and explains institutional forms as adaptive responses to environmental pressures selected through a process of trial and error. This perspective stresses the "demand" side of institutional evolution. Over time, institutions are adopted that enable collectivities to cope with the demands of their environments. The mechanism for selection is trial and error, the adoption of conventions that are codified, then modified. Natural selection models need an account of innovation ("bids," in Hugh Heclo's term) and adoption (institutionalization, in the famous account by Nelson Polsby of the long-term growth in institutional capacity in the U.S. House of Representatives).[26] Over the long term, the theory posits a tendency for structures to reach an equilibrium relationship with their environment by meeting needs for successful behavior in it, and to the extent that the environment is changing, so too are the adaptive responses of the structures. Legislative organizations, like bureaucratic and other forms of government for which social development induces a long-run tendency to increase in institutional capacity, should manifest rising organizational complexity and adaptiveness.[27] These normally take the form of organizational responses that build capacity through specialization, division of labor, and increased command of information.

Institutional adaptation models are dynamic and grounded in history. Their predictions of a long-term equilibrium between the political system and its political institutions tend to work well over long stretches of time and for large-scale cross-sectional comparison of systems. But they work poorly over short runs. They do not yield predictions about some of the most important kinds of variation in legislatures and constitutions, such as the relation between parties and committees, and the nature of leadership, rules, and decisions. Choices over electoral systems and constitutional balance between president, government, and parliament seem to be better explained by accounts of the bargaining power and interests of competing groups, for instance, which may have long-lasting effects downstream. Significantly, such arrangements sometimes appear to lock in inefficiency for protracted historical periods.[28] Evolutionary adaptation cannot readily explain, except by ad hoc considerations, "market failures" of institutional choice, when a demand or need for an institutional solution was not met by a corresponding supply.

Therefore we need a different theory to explain the *supply* of new institutions, since we cannot count on historical pressures to match supply with demand. These weaknesses of adaptive approaches would be less troubling if we were confident that the same outcomes would have occurred regardless of the particular choices that were made at a point of historical change—that the outcome was independent of the path taken to reach it. In fact, a great deal of evidence tends to suggest the opposite: that the rules and constraints affecting choice and the strategies of the actors devising new institutions may have long-lasting influences on the outcomes. As much recent institutionalist literature demonstrates, a demand for efficient institutional solutions to collective action problems does not automatically lead to their supply; market failures are common enough to require invoking political explanations for the supply of new institutions. Suboptimal, that is, inefficient, institutional arrangements may be stable in the sense that they are equilibrium points in a game of institutional choice and may be self-perpetuating over time.

A second perspective explains the adoption of new institutions as the solution to a coordination problem: a group of actors with competing interests find an arrangement that allows them to coordinate their efforts in such a way as to allow all of them to benefit. Certainly some institutional arrangements do leave everyone better off in that they reduce the costs of transaction and help competing interests coordinate their actions such that the joint result of their efforts yields a greater benefit. The general problem is one of finding a way to enable self-interested actors, whose gains and losses are determined by the joint outcome of one another's actions, to find a way to coordinate their actions for mutual benefit. They need to solve the problems of the provision of efficient arrangements, enforcement of the rules in a cost-effective way, and guaranteeing the commitment of the participants to arrangements that pose a temptation for cheating.[29] This approach to institution building identifies the many problems that political actors face that resemble prisoner's dilemma problems. In such cases, a set of actors, anticipating that they will have to deal with one another over the long haul, seek institutions that maximize collective benefit. As theories of efficient institutions emphasize, time horizons are a critical factor in actors' willingness to accept institutions that limit their present or potential power. Efficient institutions enable participants to base their actions on the anticipated value of a stream of benefits over a longer period of time rather than simply the payoff from seizing what is available at a given moment.

Models of pacts as efficient solutions to coordination problems often work well in explaining the collective choice of an institution at any single point in time, but they tend to be static. The availability of an equilibrium solution to a social choice dilemma that is necessary and sufficient to bring about the appropriate institutional arrangement *explains* the choice. It also explains the persistence of the arrangement because no actor individually is strong enough to overturn the outcome and no coalition of actors can improve its situation by altering it. For the same reason, the actors seek collective benefits by improving the efficiency of the rules of the game and are willing to fo;ego particular and immediate benefits. If the strong are not interested in maximizing the value of a future stream of benefits from the interaction with competitors, they are unlikely to accept institutional reforms that limit their ability to claim short-run advantages.[30]

But, as the third school argues, contests for power among actors with unequal resources may yield institutions with unequal distributional consequences: winners use institutions to codify their power advantages. Not all institutions are chosen with a view to maximizing collective efficiency. Some are designed to codify a temporary advantage and make it more stable. This approach conceives of institutional choices as the expression of the relative bargaining power of self-interested actors and the information they possess.[31] Institutions are not mainly intended to enable actors to capture the gains from trade. Rather, they serve the interests of actors depending on the particular benefits they seek to gain from them. The strong devise institutions to make their advantage costlier to reverse. The intensely motivated or the cohesively organized, or the possessors of the means of coercion, set the rules, providing enough inducements for their rivals to participate peacefully. As the actors' power resources and goals change, and alliances shift, the rules are likely to be overturned or modified. We might suppose that the arrangements last so long as no coalition of losers can form that is stronger than the winners. An interesting question is whether arrangements made under these circumstances can provide external public goods—such as efficiency, legitimacy, stability, confidence, effectiveness—that are not captured by the dominant interests. For instance, side deals made to win a rival's acceptance of a particular institutional choice may alter the balance of interests and affect subsequent choices. Uncertainty about the likely distributional consequences of a set of new arrangements is likely to result in more equitable arrangements and more dispersed access and veto points than in cases where the stronger parties can foresee downstream outcomes more clearly.[32] Therefore, arrangements adopted as the outcome of a zero-sum distributional contest may have efficient properties by altering the balance of information and advantage over a period of time and allowing actors to find more efficient ways of coordinating their behavior.

THE RUSSIAN CASE

Let us apply these competing perspectives to the evolution of Russian parliamentary institutions over the last decade. This period has witnessed a series of discontinuous changes and deeper, though less visible, continuity and incrementalism. The Russian deputies who took office in the new Congress of People's Deputies that Gorbachev established in 1989 inherited an institutional framework that had originally been formed in 1936 in conjunction with the Stalin constitution. It was a faithful agent of the will of the party-state administrative apparatus, but the new deputies of 1989 sought to alter it in favor of a structure that would allow them to exercise greater control over the executive. Agreement over new institutional forms to replace the old ones was hard to achieve, however, in part because of the different consequences of alternative arrangements for different groups of deputies. The new electoral and constitutional arrangements that Gorbachev put into place did lead the deputies to agree on some modest reforms and innovations that helped them to articulate and resolve their differences over legislation. Among them were embryonic parties. The general crisis of Soviet state authority prevented them from developing further into full-fledged parties, and the weak instruments that the deputies possessed were insufficient in themselves to resolve the political crisis.

As we know, the August 1991 coup dealt this legislative structure a mortal blow. Shortly after the coup failed, the congress convened in emergency session and, at Gorbachev's suggestion, approved a resolution to dissolve itself. The USSR Supreme Soviet remained formally in session through the end of the year, although its activity was almost entirely dissociated from political life due to the rapid disintegration of the power of the central, union-level government. For all practical purposes, Gorbachev's transitional parliament of 1989– 91 did not survive the August coup.

Nonetheless, despite its ungainly organization and catastrophic demise, the short-lived transitional USSR parliament of 1989–91 had a major impact on subsequent legislative development in Russia. Its members established or refined most of the organizational instruments that became salient features of the subsequent parliaments: a division of labor over policy jurisdictions through a system of differentiated committees; legislative specialization by individual deputies; a procedure of successive readings for floor deliberation over legislation; regular constituency visits by members; separation of the policy interests of the two chambers of the parliament; and, perhaps most important, the beginnings of legislative factionalism. At the same time they shed several features of the traditional legislative arrangements that did not serve their interests, including the territorial delegations and "Council of Elders," which in the past had ceremonially ratified decisions about the Supreme Soviet's agenda and committee memberships.

In 1990, the Russian Republic formed a legislative system nearly identical to the one adopted for the Soviet Union. Its initial set of rules and procedures, though, were affected by the fact that the deputies who were elected in 1990 had observed the union parliament's first year and agreed on some changes in the way their legislature worked. The initial practices in the RSFSR parliament therefore incorporated judgments about the problems with the union system. Then it, too, evolved in structure and processes. The members' decisions about how to run the Russian parliament also strongly reflected the tremendous political battles in which the parliament was a critical player, the struggle by Yeltsin against Gorbachev, Russia against the power of the central union government; the battle over economic reform; the breakup of the union; and the high-handed use of presidential power by Yeltsin. These issues influenced the agenda of policy and institutional questions taken up by the deputies and the alignments among deputies in voting.

The cataclysmic end of the transitional Russian parliament in 1993 might well lead the observer to overlook the substantial continuities between the new post-1993 system and its immediate predecessor, the transitional congress-Supreme Soviet model of 1989–93. To a remarkable extent, the evolution of parliamentary structure and process was incremental. In particular, the following chapters will call attention to the way partisanship and bicameralism arose and gained formal recognition over these three phases of development: the USSR transitional structures of 1989–91, those of the RSFSR in 1990–93, and the new State Duma and Federation Council formed by the 1993 constitution. I consider the piecemeal and continuous modification of the operating rules and structures of parliament to reflect a series of bargains on rights of representation, which were enacted in constitutional changes, new electoral rules, and new Standing Orders in each chamber. Under the new governing arrangements after 1993, parliament was genuinely bicameral, and the lower chamber was governed by a council made up of each party faction. At the same time, I argue that it is this system of balances and counterweights between the chambers and within the lower chamber that has allowed the parliament to exercise a degree of influence in the face of a president whose constitutional powers are exceptionally strong and who was previously willing to ignore constitutional constraints. Parliamentary capacity, in short, enables members and parties to participate in power and check executive power—to tame *vlast'*, in short, by sharing it.

This capacity for reaching agreement, I shall suggest in this book, was the consequence of bargains made between executive leaders and parliamentary politicians, each acting in the pursuit of immediate political advantages, that fostered greater benefits for partisan groups as a reward for giving leaders greater autonomy. Separation of a lower, popular chamber from an upper, "federal" chamber, and granting rights to party factions in the lower chamber lowered some of the impediments deputies faced in generating options and deliberating on them, determining where support and opposition lay, and ultimately in aggregating preferences. As parties have gained greater institutional status in the Duma, they have helped deputies overcome the obstacles to realizing their collective power that have kept legislatures in most other former Soviet republics weak and marginal. No outside force created these governing arrangements: they were the outcomes of the competitive pursuit of political self-interest by politicians forced to accept one another's political existence. The argument is that the sequence of choices over governing arrangements of the Russian parliament, for all the surface turmoil and conflict, is surprisingly incremental because at each point, the choices made between parliament's leaders and the ambitious political figures who sought to use parliament to advance their policy and career goals made the next such choice a logical further step as it increased members' familiarity with new forms of parliamentary work. It is not only that individual members adapted their own behavior as they gained knowledge about how to achieve their goals under the system. They also codified rules and arrangements that lowered the barriers to a further expansion of collective party control over the lower house and to establish a separate chamber for representation of regions.

To be sure, Russia's postcommunist history makes a tough case for theories of institutional choice and change. Democratic institutions are weak and ineffective at best; public dissatisfaction with them is extremely high.[33] A decade after free electoral mobilization began, nearly all of Russia's political parties remain fluid, personalistic, and Moscow-centered. Some comparativists interested in explaining institutional choice in postcommunist societies, in fact, simply ignore Russia.[34] The weakness of its civil society and the depth of social conflict impede the formation of coherent political groups that can bargain successfully or link representative institutions with larger constituencies.[35] Many scholars believe that since the dominant tradition in Russia's political culture is autocracy, coupled with a patrimonial relationship between rulers and society, democratic structures have little likelihood of flourishing.[36] There is little useful organizational inheritance, such as experienced party politicians or autonomous interest associations.[37] Many observers would predict that any given set of constitutional arrangements will be largely irrelevant to the outcome of the transition because over the longer term, outcomes will revert to the central tendency of Russian political development. In view of the adverse environmental circumstances, therefore, it is fair to say that if democratic institutions are able to take hold in the face of centuries of autocracy and the dismal failure of the economic policies of the 1990s, the case will supply strong evidence that political institutions can exert an independent impact on the flow of history.

This book covers three phases of development of Russian parliamentary institutions since 1989—those of the new USSR transitional legislature of 1989–91, the equivalent structure at the level of the Russian Republic in the 1990–93 period, and the new legislature created under Yeltsin's constitutional reform of 1993. Chapters 2, 4, and 6 provide broad historical overviews of the constitutional struggles that led to reforms of parliament's organization and powers in each of the three phases, whereas chapters 3, 5, and 7 detail the way members organized themselves for legislative decision making in each phase. The focus is on the ways that political actors deployed institutional reform to serve their political goals in their dealings with one another. I shall identify points where competing political leaders were frustrated by mutual deadlock, points where they created institutional solutions to their problems. In these settings, the language of games is employed in order to explain equilibria and disequilibria in outcomes. But in other settings, the relevant vehicle for institutional choice was a parliament operating under majority rule, and then outcomes are explained according to whether actors were able to reach stable majority-supported decisions. The three stages form a sequence of development such that the last step represents a largely incremental change over the preceding one, but after several such incremental steps, we end up with a Federal Assembly that bears only a limited family resemblance to its evolutionary ancestor, the Stalinist Supreme Soviet.

The book is based on materials from a variety of sources, including such official documents as stenographic reports and electronically tallied votes; hundreds of interviews and conversations over a period of years (1991 to 1999) with members of each of these parliaments, staffers, and experts; and newspaper and scholarly literature. One purpose is purely descriptive. The development of parliament is a story that has not been told before and needs to be historically documented. But I believe that the case also speaks to an enduring problem of democracy: how can self-interested political actors create stable and effective representative institutions that bind *vlast'* and expand freedom?

Chapter 2 Gorbachev's
Constitutional Reforms

The end of communist rule in the Soviet Union had profound consequences, for Soviet citizens as for the rest of the world. One of its
most extraordinary results was the breakup of the union state itself.
The sudden disappearance of one of the world's mightiest political
structures has been as difficult to explain as it was to foresee; although
neither Gorbachev nor Yeltsin wanted to bring about the complete
collapse of the union, their struggle brought about an outcome neither desired or intended.[1] The result of their inability to coordinate
on a strategy for preserving the union may be compared to the outcome of the "defect, defect" strategy pair in a prisoner's dilemma
game: neither Gorbachev nor Yeltsin wanted to lose the union, but by
seeking an all-out victory rather than a power-sharing solution, neither was willing to pay the price to save it.

In this chapter I characterize Gorbachev's reforms of legislative and
executive institutions as a series of moves in a political game involving
his conservative flank, the radical democratic camp, and, above all,
Boris Yeltsin in the Russian Republic. Gorbachev wanted to shift
power away from the party and into a new set of democratized state

structures and a new state presidency; Yeltsin and other republic leaders wanted to increase the autonomy of their republics at the expense of the center; democrats wanted to scrap the old system of central planning and party dictatorship in favor of a liberal, democratic system; and conservatives wanted to return to the certainties of the pre-perestroika system with its seeming stability.[2] Gorbachev adeptly formed and switched tactical alliances as he schemed to win the party's consent to *creating* the new institutions. His plans were ultimately frustrated, however, by his own and his rivals' unwillingness to *commit* themselves to abide by the new rules.

For most of the time he was the country's leader (from March 1985 until he resigned as USSR president in December 1991), Gorbachev possessed the initiative in reforming policies and institutions. Following time-honored Bolshevik tactics, he vigorously took advantage of this right to force his rivals to respond to his moves. And there was an endless succession of moves to which they had to respond. Gorbachev was an inveterate tinkerer, constantly devising new policies and institutions to mobilize support for his objectives and to weaken his opposition. His institutional fixes characteristically served two purposes: on one hand, to free himself of dependence on his fellow party leaders and, on the other, to reform the Soviet political system along democratic lines. Evidently he believed that some form of socialism could be retained and the union preserved as new liberal democratic institutions were incorporated into the system. But he believed that he needed time to prepare public opinion and gradually disarm his conservative opposition. Therefore he had to be able to control ultimate decision-making authority in order to keep the reform process on course. He intended the establishment of the new quasi-democratic parliament to be a halfway measure that would buy him time for later maneuvers.[3]

Gorbachev's innovations generally had very short life spans. Either they sank forgotten into the morass of bureaucratic inaction, or they had serious unintended consequences, so that Gorbachev had to devise ad hoc solutions to problems that earlier reforms had created. Ultimately both his improvised reforms as well as the foundation of Soviet institutions they reformed came crashing down in 1991.

Typically Gorbachev had enough power to obtain formal enactment of his desired reforms, but not enough to make the new institutions effective instruments for achieving his policy goals. In part this was because he had surrendered some of the most important levers of power that the communist party and its leaders traditionally exercised, including the ability to control the mobilization of public support for policy and the recruitment of elites. Moreover, to the extent that his institutional engineering was intended to strengthen his own personal power, rival leaders had every reason to sabotage them. Many pursued entirely different policy aims. Conservatives grew increasingly alarmed as they watched Gorbachev systematically undermine the entire edifice of Soviet power, while nationalists in the republics and liberal democrats had no use for the Soviet state or the communist regime in the first place. Gorbachev undoubtedly expected that by expanding the arena of participation in a reformed, democratic parliament, all sides would have reason to resolve their differences peacefully under the new rules. In the end, though, much as in the case of the fall of the provisional government in 1917, almost no one cared to defend Gorbachev's system. Soon after the failure of the August 1991 coup attempt, the USSR Congress of People's Deputies met in emergency session and dissolved itself. The deputies of the Russian Republic's Supreme Soviet, although bitterly divided on most other issues, then voted unanimously to endorse that decision.

That Supreme Soviet in turn was dissolved two years later. The Russian Republic had dutifully replicated the USSR's parliamentary reform by establishing its own congress and Supreme Soviet structure in 1990, but President Yeltsin's September 1993 decree disbanding it—followed by the forcible suppression of an uprising against Yeltsin led by parliament's leadership—brought that period to an abrupt end. Thus both the USSR Congress-Supreme Soviet institutional system and the equivalent structure for the RSFSR ended in catastrophic failure. The constitution of 1993, proposed by Yeltsin and approved in a nationwide referendum in December 1993, then established a new bicameral parliamentary structure called the Federal Assembly. It has remained in place to the present. The question that arises from this sequence of events is whether the institutional modifications embodied in the post-1993 parliament can help to explain the relative stability of the Federal Assembly as opposed to the instability of the previous arrangements. The answer I propose in this book is that they can; the system of parliamentary parties governing the State Duma and the separation of an upper, federal chamber from a lower, popular chamber have helped to stabilize the political contest in Russia under more generally accepted rules of competition. Our more immediate task, however, is to identify the origins of these institutional innovations.

To do so, we need to make two basic assumptions. First, institutional reform is the product of political struggle. I will treat the creation of new political structures as outcomes of interacting strategic choices by politicians. This means that leaders did not have an entirely free hand to reconfigure constitutional arrangements, although they may have a dominant position over their rivals. Just as Gorbachev never had complete freedom to alter the structure of the Soviet party-state but was constantly contending with rivals in the party leadership and political forces aligned around him, so Yeltsin also had to take account of the interests and resources of his opponents. Here the theory of strategic choice developed in game theory will help to explain why some institutional outcomes have been stable while others were unstable.

Second, I will argue that there have been two major lines of conflict in Russian contests over power and policy and that these tended to cut directly across one another. Accounts featuring only one or the other will therefore fail to grasp why the new system was so hard to put in place but has been relatively stable once established. First is the fight over reform where the polar positions are defined by market liberals and statist conservatives. Second is the struggle between center and the regions. In the late Soviet period this was a conflict between those wanting to preserve a strong central government for the union, and those wanting to devolve power to the republics or even grant them independence. In the post-1991 period, an equivalent tension has defined relations between regional leaders and the central government in Moscow. Understanding the alignments of political actors along these two intersecting cleavages will go far toward explaining their strategies in the struggle over new institutions. For this purpose, a spatial model will clarify why some policy solutions have failed and how changes in the institutional environment have affected Russia's ability to make policy.

Let us turn now to an examination of Gorbachev's objectives in reforming Soviet state structures. What was he seeking to accomplish and why did he embark on this radical and risky course? Specifically, what were Gorbachev's purposes in creating the new congress-Supreme Soviet and later the presidency?

GORBACHEV AND THE DEMOCRATIZATION OF PARLIAMENT

Gorbachev is often compared unfavorably to the Chinese leadership for having liberalized the country's political system before liberalizing its economy, but in fact, Gorbachev turned to radical political reform only after failing to generate satisfactory progress in his program of economic reform (*perestroika,* or restructuring).[4] Nonetheless, his institutional schemes were often improvised solutions to problems created by previous reforms. In fact, the most plausible explanation for Gorbachev's move to democratize Soviet structures of participation and representation—especially the use of contested elections and democratized soviets—is that they served a strategy of channeling the ideological pluralism stimulated by *glasnost'* into institutional arenas where it could be safely contained.[5]

To see this, we must recognize the importance of ideological control for the communist party's power.[6] When *glasnost'* loosened party ideological controls, it posed a threat to the most fundamental features of the Soviet regime, including the principle of the leading role of the Communist Party of the Soviet Union (CPSU) in all political and social processes. The party's monopoly on political expression and aggregation preserved integration of the multi-ethnic Soviet state and prevented any opposing political movements from challenging it. Relaxation of party controls on political expression therefore signaled to political activists that they could risk mobilizing followings around alternative ideologies. *Glasnost'* therefore allowed a variety of political movements at the center and throughout the national republics to arise, among them drives for workers' rights, liberal democracy, republic nationalism, religious revivals, monarchism, and hard-line Stalinism.

Loosening party ideological controls, therefore, was not a matter of changing rhetoric: ideology was a set of commitments to Soviet domestic and international arrangements that Soviet leaders were loathe to alter for fear of risking calamitous consequences. Conservatives were particularly aware of the vulnerability of the system to ideological pluralism. They often cited Lenin as saying that "any weakening of socialist ideology must necessarily lead to a strengthening of bourgeois ideology." The behavior of Soviet leaders until Gorbachev was consistent with Lenin's maxim because after the New Economic Policy (NEP) and until Gorbachev, Soviet leaders avoided taking any steps that would give capitalism and liberal democracy an opportunity to take root in Russia. Even after it had retracted some of its controls over expression and association, the party clung to the principle of its leading role. Only in early 1990 did Gorbachev authorize the amendment of the symbolically important Article 6 of the constitution, which declared the CPSU to be "the leading and guiding force of Soviet society, of all state organs and public organizations." Thereafter multiple parties were constitutionally permitted. Still, for some months afterward, the CPSU continued to harass and repress the small independent parties that challenged it and to lavish official attention on certain quasi-parties that enjoyed close ties to the authorities, such as Zhirinovsky's Liberal Democratic Party.[7]

In launching *glasnost'*, Gorbachev certainly recognized the danger that ideological pluralism would stimulate demands for open party competition. Accordingly, at first he called for "a socialist pluralism of opinions" as if the sphere of ideology and communication could be kept separate from its organizational consequences.[8] Through 1987 and early 1988, his position was that debate and criticism were acceptable, but not challenges to the communist party's monopoly on power. But in mid-1988 he proposed a more radical institutional reform. At a specially convened party conference in June 1988, he outlined his plan.[9] He called for significantly increasing the political power of soviets at all levels, outlined his scheme for a democratized union legislature, and proposed a quasi-constitutional court to decide on the constitutionality of legislative and executive acts. He called for free elections to the new USSR parliament in 1989, followed by elections in 1990 to reform soviets and Supreme Soviets in the republics and localities. Gorbachev described the new framework of state power that he was proposing as a "socialist system of checks and balances." His proposals were adopted almost unanimously and almost without change by the outgoing Supreme Soviet at the end of 1988 after a scarcely a month of public discussion.

Gorbachev's model for a new Soviet legislature left many elements of the old Supreme Soviet intact. In place of the old Supreme Soviet, however, he outlined a two-tiered structure, with a larger Congress of People's Deputies electing a smaller full-time Supreme Soviet from among its members. The old Supreme Soviet had 1,500 deputies, 750 elected in ordinary territorial districts based on equal population, and 750 elected in national-territorial districts that corresponded to the different ethnic territorial subdivisions of the country. Gorbachev envisioned adding another 750 deputies for a total of 2,250. The 750 new deputies were to be selected directly from such existing recognized "public organizations" as the CPSU, the trade unions, the Komsomol, the Academy of Sciences, and others. The name, "Congress of People's Deputies," given to the new and expanded body suggested its role as a representative and deliberative body, whereas the smaller, inner parliament that it elected would act as if it were a democratic parliament.

Gorbachev's proposals were drawn up in two draft documents, a set of constitutional amendments and a law on the electoral system. The commission that drafted the constitutional amendments embodying Gorbachev's plans was chaired by Anatolii Luk'ianov, a close associate of Gorbachev with long experience in CPSU and Supreme Soviet staff work; it was Luk'ianov who proposed the two-tier system of congress and Supreme Soviet.[10] The plan was subjected to a brief media campaign and debate. In several union republics, opposition was aired because some leaders feared that the organizational representation for all-union public associations would over-represent the interests of the central union bureaucracy at the expense of republican interests. In keeping with the old practice of ceremonial voting, however, the outgoing Supreme Soviet dutifully approved Gorbachev's proposals by the margin of 1,344 to 5 opposing, with 27 abstaining.[11]

The new system of parliamentary representation proposed by Gorbachev served several ends. The use of reserved seats for the communist party and other established public organizations, together with the call for open and contested elections in territorial seats, suggest that the new parliament was intended to coopt the rising forces of popular opposition manifested in the explosive rise of informal associations and in the massive turnouts for protest demonstrations. He sought both to encourage and to contain the new political forces that had mobilized under the impact of the *glasnost'* policy.

At the same time, Gorbachev hoped to provide reassurances for the forces of the party-state bureaucracy that were opposed to political liberalization; their representation would serve to give the new parliament ballast, neutralize the radicals, and thus give him greater room to maneuver between camps. Undoubtedly the use of three categories of seats—territorial, national-territorial, and organizational—was intended to prevent either the old elite or the rising new popular elites from going outside the system. By guaranteeing political representation for a variety of old and new elites, Gorbachev must have expected to give them all a stake in the new institutions.

But the new system would also serve the purpose of reducing Gorbachev's dependence on the communist party, or any single power base. Gorbachev was shifting power from the party to the state but doing so in such a way as to prevent the new democratic and nationalist movements from capturing control of the executive. He wanted to use the elections, as he had used *glasnost'*, to activate mass-level participation as a way to pressure the party-state bureaucracy into complying with his policy reforms.[12] But he wanted to be able to channel and harness that popular pressure into the directions that would serve his purposes.

At this point, Gorbachev was not advocating a presidency; 1988–90 was the high point of the political elite's call for a return to the classical Leninist principle of soviet power. This meant a reversion to the older Bolshevik idea of concentrating state power in soviets and not dividing power into distinct and equal branches. Executive power was to be fused with the soviets, and Gorbachev would straddle his party and state posts.

A number of hedges were built into the design of the new parliamentary structure to limit the new system's potential to escape his control. Among these were its matrëshka doll-like organization in which successively smaller inner bodies were nested within larger, outer ones; the preservation of the Presidium to coordinate and control the whole system; and the wholesale transfer of the staff structure (*apparat*) of the old Supreme Soviet to the new one. So too the elaborate rules governing the nomination of candidates for the elections created many filters that adept officials could use to control the outcomes of the election.

Yet despite these checks, the reforms had profound repercussions that far exceeded Gorbachev's intentions or expectations. This is so despite the fact that the new parliament dissolved along with the country in 1991. The 1989 elections proved to be a turning point in the unfolding of reform, and some innovations in parliamentary organization adopted by the new congress-Supreme Soviet outlived their origins and were taken over and modified in the RSFSR parliament and the Federal Assembly after 1993.

Open political mobilization in 1989 meant that regional and local party and government elites could no longer count on Moscow's support for their power: now they had to face the electorate.[13] Therefore one important effect of the elections was to loosen Moscow's ties with political leadership at the periphery, reinforcing the need for local political accommodation by regional elites and stimulating nationalist and other centrifugal forces. And they stimulated the coalescence of a counterelite of liberal-democratic deputies, organized and self-aware, from Moscow and other important industrial cities.[14] The new corps of deputies was neither a cross section of the former "nomenklatura" elite nor predominantly composed of opposition counterelites, but it was a mixture of both, mainly comprising such social elites as managers, specialists, and professionals.

The elections also set up a duality between the power of the old and new institutions, not because the new elected soviets were able to challenge the party for control over government power, but because of the impetus they gave to the formation of alternative political organizations and, in particular, to the rise of national coalitions in the republics.[15] At the center, Gorbachev used the elective state organizations to counterbalance the communist party. Following the 1989 elections, he engineered the resignations of seventy-four voting members of the Central Committee.[16] But although he was weakening the Communist Party of the Soviet Union by striking a blow at the chain of vertical accountability of lower to higher leaders that was its organizational core, he was at the same time weakening his own position within it. Bosses who found themselves in the unpalatable position of having to satisfy the demands of voters in order to stay in power were hardly likely to thank Gorbachev, still less if the economy's growing disorganization left them even less equipped to meet popular demands than before.

Yet Gorbachev's base of popular support was weak. Gorbachev evidently anticipated that newly active political movements would back him in his struggle for reform. Instead, many wanted to scrap the Soviet system entirely. Certainly, as most commentators have argued, the success of nationalist movements in the elections of 1989 and 1990 surprised Gorbachev and weakened his power and that of the central government more generally. Gorbachev failed to develop an electoral following of his own to counter that of Yeltsin and other politicians. He could dominate the congress through his control of the party and parliamentary staff, but he had no independent political resources in the new arena of open electoral politics. As he found out, control of the parliament proved to be useless in controlling the party-state bureaucracy.[17] Nor could he count on the communist party to serve him as a significant organizational resource because the effect of his democratization program had been to loosen the party's cohesion and antagonize its conservative wing. Thus neither state nor party provided him with a secure base of power.

In contrast to the regime transitions in Poland, Hungary, East Germany, and Czechoslovakia, then, the Soviet leadership did not bargain over the shape of the new electoral and parliamentary system with an organized opposition. No pact governed the formation of a new constitution or electoral law. Rather, Gorbachev crafted new institutional arrangements to coopt his opposition. Rising popular movements gained representation alongside the trusted members of the establishment through the system of reserved seats in the Congress of People's Deputies. But the reforms failed to give newly elected soviet deputies real leverage over the state bureaucracy. As a result, democratic challengers who won seats in the USSR, Russian, and local soviet bodies found it nearly impossible to convert electoral success into policy influence. In contrast, the electoral movements of 1989 created popular followings for radicals and nationalists who had little incentive to ally with Gorbachev in behalf of the *perestroika* program. Many who might have been potential allies for Gorbachev in his struggle against the conservative party-state bureaucracy were instead fighting him for sovereignty in newly democratized republican institutions.

This point is most vividly represented by the meteoric comeback of Boris Yeltsin, whom Gorbachev had removed from the position of Moscow city party leader in October 1987 and soon afterward from the Politburo.[18] Yeltsin came to champion the democratic cause, leading populist opposition to the power and privileges of the party apparatus and successfully positioning himself as its victim. Yeltsin rode the electoral wave to a remarkable series of political victories in 1989–91. First he won in a landslide in the 1989 elections of USSR deputies, receiving 90 percent of the popular vote in the race for Moscow's at-large seat in the congress. The following year Yeltsin won a seat as well in the Russian congress, running from his home base in Sverdlovsk and winning with 80 percent of the vote against six candidates. Yeltsin then was narrowly elected chairman of the Russian Supreme Soviet, a position from which he was able to oppose Gorbachev's temporizing policies by counterposing Russia's national power to union authority. Finally, having succeeded in winning the congress's approval for creation of a directly elected state presidency in Russia, Yeltsin ran again as president of Russia against a field of five other candidates, and won with 58 percent of the vote. Yeltsin's power base in the Russian Republic, combining his official position in parliament and later the presidency with his personal popularity, enabled him to block nearly any move Gorbachev made in the power game.

THE FIRST CONGRESS OF PEOPLE'S DEPUTIES

The First Congress convened on May 25, 1989, and lasted until June 9. The congress was a sensational event for the political drama it produced.[19] Covered live by radio and television, Soviet citizens watched and listened attentively to its theatrics. Many celebrities from all spheres of society had been elected as deputies and eagerly sought to make their voices heard. From the beginning, an organized caucus of radical democrats denounced Gorbachev's efforts to manipulate the proceedings and demanded deeper political and economic reform. They and other deputy groups had their origins in the the 1989 election campaign, when candidates in some regions coalesced around far-reaching political platforms. In the Baltic states, races for USSR deputy had been swept by national independence movements. Deputies affiliated with these movements had little interest in democratizing the USSR but aimed to use their influence at the center to attain national independence for their republics. Soviet citizens were treated to the extraordinary spectacle of vigorous political debate conducted by elected representatives representing a variety of political tendencies.

The congress reflected a significant step toward democratization of the Soviet system. But opening the national legislature to vastly expanded participation widened representation without also making any complementary institutional reforms that would have given the congress a capacity to act on its own. Therefore it could not and did not resolve any of the great crises tearing at the system: as we have seen, Gorbachev designed it primarily to coopt and neutralize opposing political camps, not to decide contentious policy issues. Nor did he submit to it any major policy questions, using it rather to ratify policy choices he had already made. The congress and Supreme Soviet did pass some important legislation, however, and, more significantly for our purpose here, established some precedents in parliamentary organization and procedure that were carried over and modified in the RSFSR congress and Supreme Soviet. The USSR Supreme Soviet proved to be unexpectedly resistant to manipulation and took unexpectedly seriously the duty it had to confirm candidates for the government nominated by the chairman of the Council of Ministers, Nikolai Ryzhkov. The Supreme Soviet subjected the candidates to intense questioning in committee and on the floor and, in the end, rejected about one-third of Ryzhkov's original nominees.[20]

As many politicians came to agree, the congress as event, and as form, was more a rally than a parliament. Simply to maintain order frequently strained Gorbachev's powers as chairman, and he resorted to turning off the microphone of a speaker who had exceeded his time limit. Voting had to be performed by counting hands—this in a body of more than two thousand deputies—because there was no electronic voting system.[21] Any decision therefore needed to be carefully prepared beforehand by consultation with representatives of select groups. The wild inefficiency of the free-for-all on the floor became a convenient argument used by the leadership for maintaining tight control in the hands of the apparat and the chairman.

Whoever chaired the sessions of the congress possessed overwhelming agenda power. Motions put to the floor by the chair typically passed with overwhelming margins. Given the absence of any other institutional means for aggregating opinion among 2,250 deputies, the chair's proposal on an important organizational matter frequently implied a Hobson's choice: support the alternative proposed by the leadership or face the consequences of chaos. Many deputies, accustomed to the ceremonial routines of Soviet public life, undoubtedly reasoned that the new congress was simply a modified version of the rubber-stamp soviets of the past. Therefore opposition to the chair's proposals was tantamount to disloyalty to the regime and implicitly threatened to bring down the entire system. Rules of procedure were spotty: there was no rule on calling the previous question, no rules governing germaneness, no rules on the order in which amendments were to be considered, no rules on the order in which speakers were to be recognized. The chair arbitrarily refused to put some motions to a vote or substituted others for them. The chair sometimes arbitrarily cut off debate. The distinction between the congress's powers and those of the Supreme Soviet was vague and encouraged deputies on the floor of the congress to propose a wide variety of issues.

In the end, the chairman's control over the agenda and the proceedings enabled him largely to control the outcomes of the congress's decisions. Nearly all of the First Congress's decisions were consistent with Gorbachev's wishes: Gorbachev was elected chairman; the congress approved the makeup of the two chambers of the Supreme Soviet proposed to it; and the leadership was able to fend off all challenges to Gorbachev's constitutional scheme. Yuri Afanas'ev, a prominent figure of the radical democratic camp, early on complained that the congress was dominated by an "aggressively obedient majority." For many democrats, the memory of Gorbachev turning off Andrei Sakharov's microphone at the end of the congress was emblematic of Gorbachev's dictatorial treatment of the new structure. The same centralized organizational structure that enabled the chairman to dictate decisions in the congresses, however, also rendered the new legislative institutions a weak resource for Gorbachev in the larger power game outside.

PRESERVING THE UNION

Thus the problem for Gorbachev was that the more he reinforced his ability to control the outcomes of the new processes of democratic representation that he created, the more irrelevant they became in the face of the deepening crisis of the Soviet system. Over the course of 1989, events were spinning out of control. Characteristically, Gorbachev responded with new institutional improvisations, further marginalizing existing structures without infusing new ones with effective power. By the time the Second Congress of People's Deputies convened, on December 12, 1989, the Soviet "outer empire" of Eastern Europe had entirely slipped out of the Soviet Union's grasp. One by one, every Soviet bloc country had undergone a fundamental regime change and had held open elections or was planning to do so in spring 1990. Communist rule in Poland, Hungary, East Germany, Czechoslovakia, Bulgaria, and parts of Yugoslavia had collapsed. Gorbachev had done nothing to preserve the "fraternal communist regimes."

Within the Soviet Union, both labor and nationality-based unrest had reached extraordinary levels as well. In summer 1989, localized protest strikes by coal miners in the Kuznetsk basin spread quickly to most of the other great coal-mining regions of the country until 300 to 400,000 workers were out on strike in July. Even more impressive were the numbers of people mobilized in nationalist protest. In August 1989, a human chain of a million people connected Vilnius in Lithuania to Tallin in Estonia to commemorate the fiftieth anniversary of the Soviet-German nonaggression treaty, whose secret protocols had effectively ceded the Baltic states to Stalin. In May and August, respectively, the popular fronts in Latvia and Lithuania published demands for full independence for their republics. Ethnic rioting, communal violence, and civil war erupted in the Transcaucasus and Central Asia.

Observing Moscow's tolerance for the breakdown of communist rule in Eastern Europe, communist leaders in the union republics of the USSR must have reasoned that they, too, needed to find some new formula of rule if they were to keep their power. In a few, the communist leadership allied itself with radical democratic and nationalist movements. In most, they turned to more traditional means of keeping power. The dissolution of communist party rule, which was bringing about the breakup of the Soviet state itself, posed an insuperable challenge to Gorbachev's new parliamentary institutions.

By late 1989, preparations were underway in each union republic for elections of deputies to the republic-level Supreme Soviets. Nationalist movements were beginning their election campaigns in several republics. In most cases, such movements took the form of a popular front, an umbrella organization uniting a number of cultural and political organizations around the goal of greater rights for the national republic. Although the details of the formation of the popular fronts in each republic differed, the processes were broadly similar in form. In each, scholars and creative intellectuals helped to organize local territorial units of the nascent popular front movements, unify the diverse currents of national sentiment around a common platform, and planned constituent congresses for October. Given the massive size of demonstrations that occurred in the Baltic republics in 1987 and 1988 on anniversaries of the signing of the Hitler-Stalin pact, Stalin's deportation of the indigenous nationality, and the declaration of national independence after the First World War, and the acute sense of environmental crisis that had arisen in each republic, the leaders of the popular fronts sought to channel popular energies into forms of activity that were likely to be tolerated by Moscow. But, notwithstanding the pains taken by both party and intelligentsia to keep the programs for republican sovereignty as reasonable in Moscow's eyes as possible, the programs were radical in that they would be satisfied only by full independence.

Estonia, Latvia, and Lithuania were unusual among Soviet republics in the massive support the indigenous populations gave to independence movements. Nowhere else did popular movements assume so wide a scale. The party leaderships found it preferable to ally with them rather than to seek Moscow's assistance in crushing them. In several other republics, however, nationalist movements led by the intelligentsia rallied widespread popular support around national causes as well. And in nearly all republics, the same menu of issues—ecological crisis; promotion of national cultural interests, particularly language; commemoration of historical injustices; and the desire for national sovereignty—prompted the founding of broad umbrella organizations on the Baltic model. Popular fronts with similar goals formed in Ukraine, Georgia, Azerbaijan, Belorussia, Moldavia, Kazakhstan, and Uzbekistan.

By December 1989, therefore, nationalist movements had organized throughout the country and protest was growing more radical. These movements were preparing to contest the coming republican elections. Party and state officials could not be sure that Gorbachev and the central party leadership would act to preserve the regime. Having observed Moscow's nonresponse to the complete breakdown of communist party rule in Eastern Europe, having been forced to compete in elections in 1989 and in some highly visible cases to lose, now facing a second round of elections for republic-level Supreme Soviets in 1990, republican and regional officials had to choose their own strategies for holding on to power.

While the Second Congress was still in progress, in fact, the Lithuanian Communist Party declared its independence from the Communist Party of the Soviet Union. Forced to choose between throwing its lot in with the national independence movement, which entailed enormous risk, and continuing loyalty to the central party leadership, the Lithuanian Communist leadership had decided to support independence and maintain its electoral viability in the coming republic-level elections.

The Second Congress was helpless to preserve the union in the face of the national mobilization in the republics. It made minor modifications to the constitution to allow republic legislatures greater autonomy in writing their election laws and structuring their Supreme Soviets. It made no major modifications to the constitution to accommodate the wave of nationalist pressure. The First Congress had approved a decision to form a commission to draft a new constitution for the country, but Gorbachev decided in early 1990 to use a completely extraparliamentary mechanism to solve the problem of finding a new formula for a federal union.[22]

ADDRESSING THE ECONOMIC CRISIS

The congress was no more successful in dealing with the breakdown of the economic system. Output was slowing: in fact, 1989 was the last year when economic growth was positive. Ties among regions were breaking down and spot shortages of basic consumer goods were widening. Most economists agreed that the economy was reaching the point where radical reform that would introduce such market principles as price liberalization and private property was required. They disagreed, however, on the pace and sequencing of such reforms. Some believed that the central government's administrative controls were stifling economic activity and that central planning should give way to decentralization in which each republic and region showed a positive economic surplus, thus eliminating inequities in the terms of trade across regions. Others believed that such decentralization would merely allow regional leaders to substitute their own administrative controls for those of Moscow and that the liberalization of the economy overall would be set back. Still others agreed that although the center must allow prices to rise so supply would eventually meet demand, it must do so in small and slow stages, so that no catastrophic social shock occurred.

Gorbachev attempted to find common ground among reformers and conservatives, convening a huge conference in October 1989 of 1,400 economists, managers, and party officials to forge a consensus economic program. The program was a contradictory mixture of elements, which called for a cautious movement to a "regulated market economy" over a five to six year "transition period."[23] The program left the status quo intact and was grossly inadequate to reverse the deepening crisis.

Substantively, the economic and nationalities policy issues were closely related. The decentralization of political control that nationalists demanded would have deprived the center of the financial levers it needed to launch liberalization. But both the reformist and conservative camps were divided. Among the reformers, one wing believed that the USSR needed to adopt fundamental, radical, democratic, and market-oriented reform throughout the country and thus it was crucial to preserve the union. Another wing of democrats, however, regarded the political independence of the national republics as highest priority and demanded the deconcentration of administrative control over resources to the republics in order that the republics could carry out their own reforms. The danger in the latter course was that republic leaders would replace Moscow's bureaucratic power with their own, retarding liberalization in their own republic and collecting rents from exchange with other republics. Conservative administrative elites at the union level, of course, opposed *both* market liberalization *and* radical deconcentration of administrative control to the republics, but many republic-level officials were eager to gain greater administrative control at the expense of the union center.

These two axes cut cleanly across one another: both democrats and conservatives were divided between centralizers and decentralizers.[24] The result was that no meaningful policy change could attract a majority. Gorbachev attempted to find a zone of agreement between prounion reformers and prounion conservatives, but the policy program that resulted was an incoherent amalgam of mutually contradictory elements.

With the leadership divided over economic policy, it was impossible for the congress to devise any policy decision that was any more coherent or practical because its own decision-making capacity depended entirely on the executive. Lacking the means to generate policy solutions that enjoyed substantial political support from large sections of the congress, to compare their backing and to examine their merits, the congress was irrelevant in the face of the country's constitutional crisis. Since Gorbachev effectively made it impossible for the congress to act autonomously, the Second Congress made no significant legislative or constitutional decisions. The compromise plan on economic policy that Gorbachev presented to the congress and which it debated and eventually approved avoided making any serious policy choices, postponing decisions on all the difficult issues on how to replace central planning with market instruments.[25]

Similarly, the congress took no significant action in the political arena. Radical democrats wanted to debate the issue of eliminating Article 6 from the constitution, and Andrei Sakharov proposed instituting a directly elected Soviet presidency. The conservative majority was able to defeat motions to put both subjects on the agenda. Although he knew well that Article 6 would have to be eliminated sooner or later,[26] Gorbachev opposed the democrats on this point at the congress, even refusing to allow Academician Sakharov to present a petition on the subject. His stance at the congress was probably motivated by the fact that he did not have sufficient support among the party leadership for so serious a step, and he believed that he needed to win CPSU approval for it before putting it to the congress. The democrats' pressure on him and the growing sense of crisis among the political elite were useful instruments for him in persuading the party Central Committee that an independent center of executive power was needed to cope with the country's problems, but at the Second

Congress he evidently calculated that the time was premature. He therefore let the congress proceed in vigorous but idle debate.[27]

ESTABLISHMENT OF THE PRESIDENCY

That Gorbachev had intended well before this to shift his power base from the party to a powerful state presidency, but needed to time to prepare support for the changes, is suggested by the rapidity of his change of positions. Soon after the Second Congress, Gorbachev visited Lithuania, where he offered assurances that the new parliament would soon adopt a law providing a legal procedure for a republic to secede. Upon his return to Moscow, he addressed a party Central Committee meeting in early February and proposed a twofold constitutional change: Article 6 of the constitution would be altered so as to eliminate the provision on the communist party's "leading role" and a presidency would be created that would have strong executive powers.

These proposals were logically related.[28] The party's power in society to make policy decisions and oversee their execution by the state bureaucracy made the party, in effect, the source of political initiative and direction. An American-style executive presidency would therefore replace the policy-making responsibilities of the party general secretary and Politburo, either weakening the party or antagonizing it. An executive president would govern alone; a party general secretary was always part of a collective leadership. Gorbachev had been consistently careful to avoid steps that would prompt party conservatives to organize a conspiracy to remove him as party leader. Therefore Gorbachev preferred to weaken the party in steps and to prevent it from removing him. Article 6 had become a symbolic focal point for the debate on the communist party's monopoly on power. Removing it was understood by party leaders and opposition alike as a signal that open party competition was constitutionally and politically legitimate. Gorbachev, aiming to weaken the communist party's power and to reduce his own dependence on it, therefore coupled the proposal on the elimination of Article 6 with a proposal to create a post that would be filled independently of the party and give him control of the executive.

Having won the Central Committee's approval for both steps in February 1990, Gorbachev then had them enacted by the Extraordinary Third Congress of People's Deputies in March 1990. Gorbachev's strategy at the congress was to unite conservatives alarmed at the acceleration of the country's breakdown with democrats who wanted to move more quickly toward radical reforms in support of his plan; he wanted a presidency, he wanted to occupy it but at the same time to keep control of the levers of party power as well; and he wanted to occupy it immediately by the expedient of having the congress elect him to the presidency. He won on every issue. The strategic significance of Gorbachev's plan becomes clearer in the debate over the question of whether the president should be required to give up his party post. CPSU conservatives understandably opposed allowing Gorbachev to occupy both the party general secretary position and the new Soviet presidency since he could play party off against state more effectively that way. They therefore supported an amendment that prohibited the president from holding any other political or state office. In this they were supported by radical democrats, for whom the presidency was a means of weakening communist party domination of society and who therefore wanted the new president to be free of any party accountability or responsibility. The coalition of conservatives and democrats yielded 1,303 votes in favor of the separation of presidency from communist party leadership, but a constitutional amendment required a two-thirds majority, or 1,497 votes.[29] The challenge therefore failed.

Similarly, Gorbachev persuaded democrats and conservatives, both of whom were divided on the issue, that in view of the severity of the national crisis, it was imperative that he be elected president at the congress, rather than waiting for the outcome of a divisive and uncertain popular election.[30] That outcome, too, was relatively close (1,542 yea, 368 nay, 76 abstaining), but Gorbachev carried many democrats and many conservatives. Then the congress elected Gorbachev as president, in a secret ballot with no other candidates, by a vote of 1,329 to 495.[31]

The congress endowed the presidency with wide but not unlimited powers. The president was named head of state and "guarantor of the observance of the rights and freedoms of Soviet citizens, the Constitution and laws of the USSR." He was to report once a year to the congress on the situation in the country. He appointed the chairman of the Council of Ministers and several other senior state officers and was to present their candidacies to the Congress of People's Deputies for confirmation and to obtain the congress's and Supreme Soviet's consent for their removal. He could submit a motion on the government's resignation to the Supreme Soviet and, with the consent of the chairman of the Council of Ministers, remove members of the government. He could veto a law passed by the Supreme Soviet, which by a two-thirds vote in each chamber could override the veto. He could suspend orders of the government. He could declare martial law following procedures that remained to be determined by legislation. He could declare a state of emergency, with the consent of the Supreme Soviet, and institute temporary presidential rule. States of emergency and presidential rule were also to be further defined by law. If the two chambers of the Supreme Soviet deadlocked over an issue, the president could propose to the congress the dissolution and reelection of the Supreme Soviet. The president was also to head a "Council of the Federation" with a broad but consultative mandate to be made up of the ranking state officials from each union republic. This body, representing equally the leaders of the constituent units of the federation, was an institutional precursor of the Council of the Federation in the post-1993 Russian constitution. Likewise the president was to head a "Presidential Council" to advise him on policy questions.

The president had the right to issue edicts (*ukazy*) with the force of law "on the basis of and for the execution of the Constitution of the USSR and the laws of the USSR." By a two-thirds vote of the congress, the president could be removed from office. The amendments did not call the president chief executive, but the right of decree gave him executive powers in fact, and he had ample authority as guarantor of the constitution and by virtue of appointing the prime minister to direct government. The new language did not provide for any veto or confirmation of presidential decrees by congress or Supreme Soviet, but the wording that such decrees were "on the basis of and for the execution of" laws and constitution appears to suggest that the president could not use a decree to alter current legislation. In effect, the new office inherited some of the legal rights traditionally vested in the Presidium of the Supreme Soviet as a collective state presidency, which included some quasi-executive powers, as well as the powers to direct and supervise the government (Council of Ministers) that the CPSU's central organs had possessed. The powers of the government itself were untouched, but now the president rather than the CPSU would control it.[32]

Since the constitutional amendments the congress had adopted prohibited the president of the USSR from serving as a people's deputy and thus from holding the position of chairman of the Supreme Soviet, a new chairman had to be elected. Anatolii Luk'ianov, who had been Gorbachev's immediate deputy and the architect of Gorbachev's parliamentary strategy from the beginning, and who was supported by the conservatives, won election to the position by a wide majority of 1,202 votes in a field of eight candidates.

The constitutional reform creating the presidency had two immediate implications for the evolution of parliament. It separated the state presidency from the parliament, and it ended seven decades of the communist party's legal monopoly on political power. It represented the first of a series of institutional reforms in Russia in which a chief executive traded off expanded rights to parties to organize and compete for parliamentary office for an increase in powers for himself. As president, Gorbachev was not accountable to the congress or to the communist party. The constitutional amendments gave him extraparliamentary deliberative and consultative bodies, which he was free to use or ignore as he saw fit; and he turned to the Federation Council as the vehicle for finding a new basis for preserving the federal union.

As Gorbachev came to acknowledge, once again he had failed fully to anticipate the strategic implications of a constitutional reform. Much as the formation of the congress-Supreme Soviet structure and his own post of chairman in it had failed to provide him with the power he needed to carry out his policy reforms, so also the creation of the presidency backfired. As president, Gorbachev wrote, he found himself in the position of a commander surrounded by staff officers but completely lacking in army units, or the infrastructure needed to carry out his commands. Moreover, he had to give away too much power to win a majority for his new scheme. To Gorbachev's chagrin, leaders of the union republics supported Gorbachev's presidency on the condition that they establish their own presidencies. This immediately "cut in half the gains we had expected from improving the authority of the central power."[33]

THE 500 DAYS AND GORBACHEV'S
STRATEGIC DILEMMA

Economic reform and preservation of the union were Gorbachev's most urgent priorities in 1990. Rival teams of economists from the government and academic institutes proposed plans differing over the pace of reform. The immobilism of the USSR Congress of People's Deputies and the bureaucracy's conservatism collided with demands for a radical transition coming from many economists and international lenders. Gorbachev equivocated until Yeltsin's victory in gaining election as chairman of the RSFSR's Supreme Soviet forced his hand. Finally he agreed in July 1990 to work with Yeltsin jointly on carrying out radical reform according to a plan that was known as the "500 Days program."[34] But Gorbachev's power position was weak and the policy distance between reformers and conservatives was widening. Yeltsin was the champion of the democratic camp while Gorbachev's standing in the party leadership was rapidly declining. Gorbachev could no longer play one side off against another: if he allied with his colleagues in the party leadership, he had to back down from support for radical economic reform. If, in order to win acceptance of the

500 Days reform plan, however, he allied himself with Yeltsin and the ascendant democratic majority in the Russian parliament, he would have had few independent resources with which to influence policy and preserve his own power and preserve the union. He chose to throw his lot in with the old guard in the party; in retrospect, this choice was probably a fatal error.

The 500 Days program marked the high point of centrally initiated policy development. If adopted, it would have broken with the Soviet system, as we have defined it here, in two crucial respects. It would have recognized the fundamental precedence of republican property rights over those of the union government in disposing of state assets, and it would have introduced private property in the major means of production. Clearly this was too much for Gorbachev's colleagues in the central leadership: they forced him to renounce his previous acceptance of it. His rejection of the 500 Days at the end of summer 1990, coinciding with the resurgence of the disaffected conservative forces in the party, military, and economic bureaucracy, marked the beginning of the final crisis of the country.

Similarly, his effort to negotiate a new treaty of union ran afoul of the election results in the republics in 1990. In particular, the March elections in the Russian Republic enabled Boris Yeltsin to attain a position of leadership in the new Russian transitional parliament that then allowed him to counter virtually every move Gorbachev made: the simple fact of Soviet politics was that there could be no union without Russia's participation. Given Russia's vast size and central location, Yeltsin's electoral mandate and election to the post of chairman of the Supreme Soviet of the RSFSR (see chapter 4) meant that Yeltsin could effectively set the conditions for any voluntary new association of republics. Yeltsin's condition was Gorbachev's assent to radical market and democratic reform. When Gorbachev rejected cooperation with Yeltsin in carrying out the radical economic program, he initiated a power contest with Yeltsin that he could not win. Once the Russian congress passed the "Declaration on Sovereignty" in June 1990, the remaining months of 1990 were occupied with a bitter struggle for supremacy between the central union government, headed with increasing tenuousness by Gorbachev, and the government of the Russian Republic. No expansion of Gorbachev's constitutional powers as president of the USSR, short of brute coercion, could have given him the means to defeat Yeltsin since Yeltsin had proven electoral support, and the heads of the union bureaucracies on whom Gorbachev depended to carry out his policies had turned against him.

EMERGENCY POWERS

Characteristically, faced with a deteriorating political situation, Gorbachev demanded still greater *formal* prerogatives as president. In September the Supreme Soviet passed a law granting the president "the right to issue timely normative decrees in correspondence with the Constitution of the USSR" for a six-month period for the purpose of "stabilizing the situation in the country." These powers were to be used to make decisions on economic policy, including property relations, as well as to create new state agencies that would hasten the formation of a unionwide market economy.[35] The Fourth Congress of People's Deputies in December 1990 reinforced Gorbachev's legal powers further with a new set of constitutional amendments. Under these, Gorbachev now headed "the system of organs of state government and ensures their cooperation with supreme organs of state power of the USSR," named and dismissed the government (now renamed "cabinet of ministers") with the consent of the Supreme Soviet, could suspend government acts of the union republics, and headed the newly created Security Council. The Federation Council was given new responsibilities, of coordinating state policy in the republics, and its decisions were to be enacted in the form of presidential decrees.[36] The president, in short, had many ways of bypassing parliament to make policy decisions, but none of them gave Gorbachev any more actual power than he had previously, and the changes only weakened parliament further. There was less and less reason for any significant political group to work *within* parliament to build a majority for a policy decision, and more and more reason to go *outside* parliament, using force, or taking to the streets, or declaring national independence. Gorbachev's victories therefore further reduced what little capacity parliament had to induce opposing political groups to cooperate in preserving democratic representative bodies at the union level.

The Fourth Congress also approved Gorbachev's proposal to conduct a USSR-wide referendum in March 1991 on preserving the union. This step, too, neither contributed to strengthening the authority of parliament nor to solving the crisis of the state. The wording of the question that was put to the voters ("do you consider it necessary to preserve the Union of Soviet Socialist Republics as a renewed federation of equal sovereign republics in which the rights and freedoms of people of all nationalities will be fully guaranteed?") had little substantive bearing on any actual policy decisions faced by leaders in the center or the republics, and, still worse from Gorbachev's standpoint, its political significance was neutralized by the counter-referendum that Yeltsin held on establishing a state presidency in the Russian Republic. The rapid pace of institutional innovations adopted by Gorbachev in this period strongly suggests that Gorbachev was desperate to find organizational expedients that would solve crushing substantive problems.

Gorbachev now faced an open revolt on his conservative flank. Conservative and nationalist officials in the communist party formed a breakaway Russian Communist Party in June 1990. At the Twenty-eighth Party Congress in July, conservatives fearlessly attacked Gorbachev for conceding political power to antisocialist forces. Gorbachev could not get the congress to agree on the long-awaited new party program, and Yeltsin dramatically walked out of the congress declaring that he was quitting the party. His gesture, which was quickly followed by other prominent democratic reformers, triggered a massive exit of members from the CPSU.[37] Gorbachev became severely isolated. He was met with open hostility and scorn when he addressed the Supreme Soviet on November 16, and again, later the same day, when he met the party Politburo, and three days earlier when he addressed a gathering of top military commanders.[38]

Gorbachev evidently calculated that, given a choice of allying with democrats and Yeltsin or with union-level conservatives, he had more to gain from the latter course. No doubt he hoped to play on the conservative anxiety over the general breakdown of regime authority in order to win more power for himself. In a speech in November Gorbachev complained of a "paralysis" and "vacuum" of power. Presidential acts were not being carried out, he complained, but were debated and challenged. Union republics were passing laws contradicting federal legislation. Decisive measures had to be taken immediately to reverse the crisis of state authority.

In November Gorbachev granted the military the right to fire on civilians in case of attack; in December he appointed two highly conservative figures, a KGB major general and a prominent army general who had commanded Soviet forces in Afghanistan, to run the Ministry of Internal Affairs.[39] The KGB chairman declared in December that "extremist" groups in the USSR were receiving help from abroad, while Gorbachev's prime minister, Valentin Pavlov, claimed that Western financial circles were conspiring to bring down the Soviet economy. Gorbachev's close ally and foreign minister, Eduard Shevardnadze, resigned in protest at the antidemocratic trend. In January, military and paramilitary forces aligned with the party and KGB attempted to carry out a coup d'état in Lithuania and another in Latvia, but popular resistance, mounting protests in Russia on the part of workers and democratic intellectuals, Yeltsin's strong defense of Baltic autonomy, and immediate international protest at the violent repression seem to have sufficed to prevent further action. Many believe that the shadowy forces that acted in the name of the "national salvation committees" of Lithuania and Latvia were actually elements of the party, KGB, and military that were rehearsing for a coup d'état in Moscow as well. The events of August 1991 make it impossible to rule this out. Moreover, nearly all of the individuals whom Gorbachev appointed in this period to senior positions later conspired to form the State Committee on the State of Emergency the following August.

ENDGAME: TOWARD A NEW UNION TREATY

Gorbachev shifted positions radically in spring and summer of 1991 and sought an agreement with Yeltsin and the other leaders of the union republics on yet another, more drastic reconfiguration of the Soviet constitution. This turn was prompted, in part, by another dramatic manifestation of Yeltsin's political power. In March, with miners' strikes spreading and popular dissatisfaction with Gorbachev at a new high,[40] conservatives in the Russian Congress of Deputies attempted to remove Yeltsin. Instead, the congress reconfirmed Yeltsin's power and approved Yeltsin's plans to hold an election for a popularly elected president of the RSFSR. The strong approval he received for this institution in the March referendum had strengthened Yeltsin's hand, as did Gorbachev's failed effort to force Yeltsin's removal.

Faced with undeniable evidence of Yeltsin's sturdy base of popular support, Gorbachev shifted alliances and agreed to seek an agreement with Yeltsin and the other union leaders on a new union treaty that gave the republics most of what they demanded. The results of the negotiations took the form of an agreement known as the "9 + 1" or "Novo-Ogarevo" agreement reached on April 23, 1991. ("9+1" referred to the fact that nine republican chief executives plus Gorbachev representing the union were signatories; Novo-Ogarevo was the name of the dacha outside Moscow where the negotiations were held.) The agreement created a framework for a new union treaty, one that would fundamentally alter the distribution of power between center and republics. Under the agreement, Gorbachev relinquished all claims of union government sovereignty and renounced any right of interference by the union in the affairs of the republics.[41] On July 24, Gorbachev announced that the republics had agreed on the text of the treaty itself; the treaty would create a new union called the Union of Soviet Sovereign Republics in which the central government would coordinate security, energy, communications, and transportation policy with the republics and leave all other powers to the republics themselves.[42]

By summer 1991, Gorbachev was left with almost no winning cards. In Russia, the presidential election June 12 had produced a resounding victory for Yeltsin, while among his own cabinet, Gorbachev's senior ministers were plotting against him. The policy distance between Gorbachev, advocating a much looser union, and the conservative opposition had grown extremely wide. Gorbachev had no major allies on his democratic flank; nearly all had defected to Yeltsin and the cause of Russian sovereignty. Yeltsin was fighting Gorbachev over issues of radical economic reform and Russian sovereignty. Isolated and increasingly powerless, Gorbachev could not remove his opponents before they sought to remove him. Parliament remained largely on the sidelines. None of the parliamentary structures played any part at all in the negotiations leading to the new union treaty. Indeed, on the day when agreement of the republic leaders with Gorbachev on the final draft of the 9 + 1 accord was announced, Gorbachev's prime minister spoke on the floor of the Supreme Soviet to urge the deputies to grant him emergency powers to restore economic order. But if parliament was irrelevant to major policy decisions, so was the central party leadership. What was left were the forces of coercion, which had demonstrated their power in the Vilnius and Riga adventures and which were becoming sympathetic to the demands for a military coup voiced with growing urgency by the hard-line conservatives.

COUP AND COLLAPSE, AUGUST-DECEMBER 1991

The final chapter in the history of Gorbachev's reforms was the August coup and its aftermath. Some details remain obscure, but the outline of events is familiar. Even before the plotters struck, their intentions were patently clear—so much so, in fact, that the extent of Gorbachev's complicity in the coup remains a question. In June, his prime minister once again appealed to the USSR Supreme Soviet for emergency powers and demanded that it declare a state of emergency in certain branches of the economy. The Supreme Soviet called Gorbachev to declare whether this demand had his approval. When an embarrassed Gorbachev declared that the request had not been cleared with him, the demand was tabled. One prominent deputy called the move an attempt at a velvet coup. In late July, a group of hard-line conservatives, including senior officials from the government who later led the coup, issued a public appeal to save the country. Gorbachev, meantime was being urged to declare a state of emergency and given misleading information designed to prompt him to do so.[43] For whatever reason, Gorbachev neither complied with the demands of the right wing nor removed its representatives from power.

The union treaty was to have been signed on August 20. On August 19, a group of senior officials, who included the vice-president, the prime minister, the defense minister, the KGB chairman, the interior minister, and the heads of three other bodies, placed Gorbachev under house arrest at his vacation home in the Crimea and declared a state of emergency in the country. On the third day the coup faltered and collapsed. On August 22, Gorbachev returned to Moscow and over the next several days the leaders of the coup were arrested and charged with state treason.

Immediately after the failure of the coup, the chairman of the Supreme Soviet, Anatolii Luk'ianov, convened an emergency session of the congress. The Fifth Congress of People's Deputies of the USSR was also its last: the congress adopted a resolution suspending itself and transferring executive power to a new State Council, which was to govern until a new constitution could be adopted. A vestigial USSR Supreme Soviet continued to function, but it was in a dubious twilight zone of constitutional and political legitimacy since neither Russia nor the other republics recognized its decisions as having legal force. Anatolii Luk'ianov was arrested and convicted as a co-conspirator with the eight individuals who had attempted to seize power. Although he protested his innocence, it is clear that he had indeed aided the coup. Luk'ianov had met and discussed the conspirators' plans with them on the eve of the coup, he had attacked the union treaty just as they acted to prevent its being signed, and he had refused to convene the congress or Supreme Soviet to protest the coup. From being one of Gorbachev's oldest and most loyal associates—Gorbachev and he had been two years apart as students at the Law Faculty of Moscow State University in the early 1950s—he had thrown his lot in with Gorbachev's fiercest opponents and led the parliament to a calamitous end.[44] Thus, rather like Khasbulatov in the transitional Russian parliament two years later, Luk'ianov was a first deputy chairman and a faithful supporter of the top leader, who moved into the chairman's post when his patron moved into the presidency, then allied himself with the forces of reaction against the president, before ultimately helping to organize an unsuccessful conspiracy to seize state power.

The events of August altered the balance of power irretrievably. Not only Gorbachev's power, but that of the union state as well, was fatally weakened. Yeltsin issued decrees suspending the operation of the CPSU and freezing its assets. Over the next four months, all the republics except Russia adopted declarations of independence. Russia assumed formal control over the union's economy in November and had the de facto support of the armed forces command and the KGB. Although Gorbachev labored to revive some form of economic union (winning agreement, for example, of seven republican leaders on November 14 to create a Union of Sovereign States), the ministries of the union government were being merged into RSFSR ministries or interrepublican coordinating committees. On December 1, Ukraine's population voted for independence in a referendum by a 90-percent margin. One week later, Yeltsin, the Ukrainian president, and the chief of state of Belorussia met, declared the USSR dissolved, and formed a new Commonwealth of Independent States in its stead. Subsequently the Muslim republics (Azerbaijan, Kazakhstan, Turkmenia, Kirgizia, Tajikistan, and Uzbekistan), Moldova, and Armenia joined the new commonwealth as well. Because the commonwealth had no government (although it maintained nominal control of the Soviet armed forces), the governments of the separate republics inherited the sovereign powers of the former union. On December 25, 1991, Gorbachev resigned as president and turned control of the Kremlin over to Yeltsin.

Gorbachev later observed of this process: "If there is no Union without Russia, so it will be hard for Russia without the Union. I said all this to Boris Nikolaevich [Yeltsin] face-to-face. My meetings with him were always very open, very free. Nonetheless the Russians went that way: in order to free itself of the center, Russia sacrificed the Union."[45]

Chapter 3 Organizing the New
USSR Parliament

In chapter 2 the decisions over parliament's structure and powers were treated as the products of Gorbachev's political strategies. It was argued that although he had the power to create the congress and Supreme Soviet, and later the presidency, he could not use these new institutions to solve the country's crises because he could not build a coalition of political elites in support of a policy position that would simultaneously advance market reform and hold the union together. Both his new parliament and the new presidency were marginalized, unable to reverse the polarization of political camps at the center or the loss of the center's power over the republics.

In this chapter I shift the focus to the parliamentary arena itself, asking how the politicians elected to Gorbachev's parliament in 1989 used the limited powers they had to devise new ways of influencing policy through legislation. Although Gorbachev's constitutional changes set the outer bounds of the parliament's powers, its leaders and members were able to decide the rules and procedures under which it would run. In this chapter, I will therefore examine those arrangements in closer detail, focusing on four sets of issues in particular: the relation between deputies' electoral mandates and their participation in the Supreme Soviet, its two chambers, and the parent congress; the standing committees and legislative procedure; the Presidium's governance of the entire system; and the formation of deputy groups. These arrangements, which shaped parliament's capacity to use the constitutional powers that Gorbachev gave it, represented modifications of the old Supreme Soviet and its internal organization. Our task is to understand how the leaders and members of the parliament adapted the structures and processes of this odd hybrid creature to their political ends.

CONGRESS, SUPREME SOVIET, CHAMBERS: MANDATES AND MEMBERSHIP

The Three Classes of Electoral Mandates

Gorbachev's plan called for a two-tiered legislature: a larger Congress of People's Deputies comprising 2,250 deputies, and a smaller Supreme Soviet elected by the congress from among its membership. The 2,250 USSR People's Deputies were divided into three equal categories of members according to category of mandate.

1. Public organizations: 750 deputies were chosen from a set of approved public organizations, such as the Communist Party of the Soviet Union (CPSU), the Komsomol (Communist Youth League), the trade union federation, and the Academy of Sciences, as shown in table 3.1;
2. 750 deputies were elected in single-member territorial districts of equal population (*territorial'nye izbiratel'nye okruga* [territorial electoral districts], or TIOs); and
3. 750 deputies were elected in single-member national-territorial districts (NTIO) using a formula similar to that used in old USSR Supreme Soviet for elections of deputies to the Council of Nationalities (see table 3.2).

This tripartite electoral system had significant consequences for the representation of the electorate. The distribution of deputies varied considerably across the three mandate types both demographically and ideologically. For example, women's participation was substantially boosted by the use of organizational seats. Women made up 15 percent of all deputies. Half of them came from public organizations; 30 percent were from national-territorial districts, 20 percent from territorial districts. The public organization members were

Table 3.1. Distribution of 750 USSR Deputy Mandates Reserved for Public Associations, 1989

Organization	Number of Mandates Allocated
CPSU	100
Trade unions	100
Cooperatives, including collective farms and state consumer cooperatives	100
Komsomol (Communist Youth League)	75
Soviet Women's Committee	75
Veterans of Labor and War	75
Academy of Sciences	75
Creative unions (writers, cinematographers, composers, journalists, etc.)	75
Other	75

also significantly older, on average, than the territorial and national-territorial deputies: the average age of the organizational deputies was 62, whereas it was just 57 and 58 for the territorial and national-territorial deputies, respectively.

Because more of the territorial district races were open contests where radical democrats could challenge establishment candidates than were NTIO races, the deputies from territorial districts tended to be more reform-oriented in their policy positions, on average, than other deputies. Deputies from public organizations tended to be the most conservative.[1] Deputies from big cities were more likely to be liberal, while delegations from the most tightly controlled regions and republics reflected the conservative, bureaucratically dominated political establishments in their home regions. Overall, the social composition of the new corps of deputies revealed the mixture of old and new elites arising from the uneven distribution of opportunities for open electoral competition in different regions and sectors of the country.[2]

Two Tiers of Parliament

The constitutional amendments creating the new congress and Supreme Soviet system left a good deal of overlap between the powers of the congress and those of the Supreme Soviet. The congress delegated some of its powers to the Supreme Soviet for the purpose of making laws and overseeing government, but it retained the right to preempt or override any actions the Supreme Soviet might take. It also elected the members of the Supreme Soviet from its own membership.

Table 3.2. Election of USSR Deputies, National-Territorial District
Apportionment, 1989

Type of Unit	Number of Units	Single-Member Districts per Unit	Total
Union republic	15	32	480
Autonomous republic	20	11	220
Autonomous oblast	8	5	40
Autonomous okrug	10	1	10
Total			750

The constitution described the congress as "the highest organ of state power of the USSR" with the right "to consider and decide any question assigned to the jurisdiction of the USSR." It was given a number of exclusive powers, among them the right to adopt and amend the constitution; define the borders of the country; determine the basic direction of the country's foreign and domestic policy; elect the Supreme Soviet and its chairman; confirm the chairman of the Council of Ministers (that is, the head of government, or prime minister); nullify acts adopted by the Supreme Soviet; pass laws and decrees (*postanovleniia*); and decide to conduct a popular referendum.[3]

The Supreme Soviet, in turn, was assigned powers derived from those of the congress. In addition to enacting legislation, it could call parliamentary elections, name the chairman of the Council of Ministers and confirm his candidates for government positions; annul decrees and orders of the Presidium of the Supreme Soviet and orders and regulations of the government; ratify treaties; and oversee the government's fulfillment of the national economic plan and budget.[4] It could decide any question in its sphere of authority, but its decisions could not contradict those of the congress or resolve matters assigned exclusively to the congress.

The Supreme Soviet was to be made up of two chambers of 271 seats each, the Council of the Union and the Council of Nationalities. The profiles of the two chambers differed slightly, corresponding to their different norms of composition. The Council of the Union was to be made up of deputies elected in TIOs, plus deputies elected from public organizations, according to the number of voters per district. The Council of Nationalities was to be elected from among deputies elected in national-territorial electoral districts and deputies from public organizations, ensuring structured representation from each eth-

Table 3.3. Norms of Election of USSR Deputies to Supreme Soviet Council of Nationalities

Type of Unit	Number of Units	Deputies per Unit	Total
Union republic	15	11	165
Autonomous republic	20	4	80
Autonomous oblast	8	2	16
Autonomous okrug	10	1	10
Total			271

nic-national territorial unit according to the formula outlined in table 3.3. Each chamber was entitled to take up any matter in the jurisdiction of the Supreme Soviet as a whole, but each was assigned a particular profile of responsibilities that followed from its electoral composition. The Council of the Union was to concentrate particularly on matters affecting economic policy for the country as a whole, foreign and defense policy, and individual rights. The Council of Nationalities would handle questions pertaining to ethnic-national relations and the status of ethnic groups in the country. Each chamber could pass its own decrees, and the consent of both was required for laws to pass.

The rules on the formation of the chambers were carried over almost identically from the old, Stalin-era constitution into the Gorbachev transitional parliament. The fact that there were now 750 additional deputies who had to be accommodated in the new Supreme Soviet added a new wrinkle, however, to the symmetry of the old scheme.[5]

Full-Time vs. Amateur Deputies

A significant change from the old system was the expectation that the new Supreme Soviet was to work on a full-time basis, staying in session roughly six to eight months per year, divided into spring and fall terms. This point, a crucial part of Gorbachev's vision that the new Supreme Soviet would exert some real legislative power, required an entirely new form of participation for deputies.

In the past, a soviet deputy's service had been largely honorific. It was typically taken on by prominent citizens as part of their expected public activity. The time demands were slight since no deputy was a full-time legislator. Staff officials did all the work of preparing the agenda for soviet sessions and managing the processes of sign-offs and clearances and language-polishing needed to prepare bills for the sessions. The deputy's job at a session was to vote ceremonially in favor of the motions that the Presidium brought to the floor. Off the floor, deputies were often active in constituency service, intervening with the bureaucracy on behalf of constituents.[6] Lawmaking was not a job for deputies, however. Laws were written by specialists, including officials of state agencies affected by a particular law and by legal scholars from state institutes and universities. State officials had served as deputies and therefore used the soviets as a specialized arm of the bureaucracy to formulate policy decisions as law.

The amateur ideal of the old system did not affect legislative effectiveness, in part because not many laws were needed, nor were laws a particularly important form of policy decision. Decrees and resolutions of the Presidium of the Supreme Soviet, the Council of Ministers and the Central Committee of the Communist Party of the Soviet Union, and sometimes the trade union association were the main forms of legislation. Relatively few measures were handled as statutes. The volume was not only low, but it was also subject to detailed planning, so that output was extremely steady over time, usually running between ten and fifteen laws per year (see table 7.17 on output of Soviet and Russian parliaments).

Now that parliament was to become a site for serious lawmaking, workload of its members would expand considerably. As a result, the issue of whether to require deputies elected to the Supreme Soviet to serve on a full-time basis became a point of contention. Many newly elected deputies, particularly the radical democrats, fully expected to become full-time legislators. They had clear goals for legislative action, were not beholden to the state bureaucracy, and wanted to use the legislative powers of the new parliament to strike a blow for the democratization of the Soviet system. Their very appearance in the parliamentary arena threatened the power of those who had entered parliament facing little or no electoral competition and wanted to prevent any meaningful liberalization of the political system. A rule that deputies had to give up their outside jobs as a condition of service in the Supreme Soviet would seriously undermine the political power of the old nomenklatura, officials employed in the state bureaucracy, economic enterprises, and public organizations.

The drafting commission agreed on compromise language in the rules over this controversial point. The old rules had *required* deputies to serve *without* giving up outside employment. This provision was dropped from the rules. At the First Congress, reformers attempted to *require* Supreme Soviet members to work on a full-time basis, but this proposal was defeated. Instead the new rules provided that "as a rule" deputies were to give up outside employment for the period they served in the Supreme Soviet. However, even this watered-down rule was not enforced. As of December 1990, 306 members (57 percent) of the union Supreme Soviet combined work in parliament with outside employment.[7]

The rigidity of the constitutional rules on the formation of the Supreme Soviet made it difficult to find Supreme Soviet seats for all deputies wishing to work in parliament on a full-time basis. Under the constitution, one-fifth of the members of the Supreme Soviet were to be rotated out every year and replaced with new deputies. (It came as a surprise to many deputies to realize that despite this rule, very few of them would ever have a chance to serve.) So many deputies wanted to leave the Supreme Soviet, or were so inactive that the leadership wanted to replace them, that the December 1990 rotation released some 35 percent of the members. The problems arising from the need to accommodate members who wanted to work full time in the Supreme Soviet while maintaining the strict quotas for nationalities and other categories of deputies were among the reasons deputies generally concurred that the future parliament should return to a one-tiered parliamentary system. Supreme Soviet deputies who were serious about legislative work were frustrated that the system created so many barriers to legislative effectiveness.

THE COMMITTEE SYSTEM
AND THE LEGISLATIVE PROCESS:
NEW COMMITTEES FOR OLD

New Committees for Old

A system of standing legislative committees has been a standard feature of each Russian legislature since well before Gorbachev's reforms. The pre-reform Supreme Soviet used a structure of parallel committees for each chamber that were identical in name, jurisdiction, number, and size.[8] This structure bespoke a bureaucratic concern with symmetry but did not reflect any difference in profiles of the chambers' interests.

Gorbachev delegated to Anatolii Luk'ianov, a longtime associate of Gorbachev with extensive staff experience in parliament, the task of designing the new parliament. Luk'ianov smoothly drafted a plan for the committee system of the new parliament and won approval for it. Under his direction, the staff drew up a proposal for a committee system and conducted a survey among the elected USSR deputies asking them whether they had any suggestions regarding the proposal and inviting them to indicate which if any committees or commissions they would like to serve on.[9] According to Luk'ianov, the overwhelming majority of responses approved of the proposed committee structure. Luk'ianov's conception was that each chamber should have four unique commissions while the two chambers jointly should have committees. The commissions would reflect the policy profile of the two chambers; the Council on the Union would handle policy issues that were common to the entire union, while the Council on Nationalities would deal with questions concerning the relations of the republics and other territorial units with the union. The joint bodies would be called committees and would serve the Supreme Soviet's collective needs. The proposal served the conception Gorbachev and Luk'ianov were elaborating for moderate democratization and decentralization, where greater autonomy over economic and cultural issues would be granted to the union republics while allowing the Gorbachev leadership to preserve its strategic control over major areas of policy.[10] Luk'ianov consulted with the "Council of Elders" (which comprised the heads of territorial delegations of deputies) on the structure and makeup of the committees, then presented it to the Supreme Soviet itself.

The proposed commissions and committees, their names, structure, jurisdictions, possible subcommittees, and responsibilities were actively debated in the chambers and by the Supreme Soviet. Luk'ianov responded and parried, usually inviting deputies themselves to propose amendments. But the basic scheme was drafted by the Presidium, the staff, and Luk'ianov as first deputy chairman.

In effect, the Presidium chose the committee and commission chairs. After the chairs and deputy chairs of the chambers had been selected (through votes in the Council of Elders, then approval in the full chambers), these chamber chairs met and discussed their recommendations for chairs of committees. Their nominees were then presented to the floor, debated, voted on, and approved. Then followed, in similar fashion, the proposals for selection of membership. Here the principle was that 400 Supreme Soviet members would serve in the commissions and committees, or about 80 percent of Supreme Soviet members, as would a like number of deputies who were *not* members of the Supreme Soviet. Undoubtedly the apparat and leadership took both professional and political considerations into account because they proposed two well-known democratic radicals as well: Boris Yeltsin for chairman of the construction and architecture committee, and Yuri Ryzhov as chairman of the science and education committee. Then lists of proposed members, which were drawn up taking into account deputies' wishes as expressed in the survey conducted by the apparat, were presented.[11]

Gorbachev and Luk'ianov got their way in structuring the new parliamentary bodies and choosing their leaders and members. To do so, they adapted well-established procedures from the old Supreme Soviet to structure the leadership and agenda of the new Supreme Soviet. As a result, by careful sequencing of decisions, the leadership could control the outcome of the nominally open decision-making process. Gorbachev and Luk'ianov were skillful at accommodating others' interests, including the pressure from the radicals, who wanted to turn parliament into an instrument of social change, just enough to ensure that their proposals would defeat all alternatives.

The Presidium's control over committees was demonstrated in late 1990 and early 1991 in a fight over the chairmanship of the science and education committee. The committee's chairman was Yuri Ryzhov. Ryzhov was an outspoken, politically independent scientist who commanded respect from both conservatives and liberals. He was rector of the prestigious Moscow Aviation Institute (and later Russian ambassador to France). As committee chairman, he provided a political refuge for members of the Inter-Regional Group of Deputies (IRGD) who used their committee assignments, according to opponents, more for advancing the political interests of their group than for making laws. The committee aroused rising hostility from the nationalist-communist camp as it became one of the last shelters for the democratic radicals in the union parliament. Ryzhov also irritated the conservatives by joining a team of advisers to Boris Yeltsin in his capacity as chairman of the Russian Supreme Soviet. In spring 1991, the conservatives sought to purge his committee of its radical members and to remove him as chairman.[12]

Luk'ianov handled the challenge to Ryzhov and his committee with his customary dexterity. Claiming, disingenuously, that the question of how many members of the Inter-Regional Group happen to belong to the committee "does not play any role whatever for me," he proposed a compromise solution. He suggested voting for the membership of the committee separately from the chairman. The slate he offered then omitted two of the more outspoken pro-democratic members of the committee. The motion passed. He then held votes on the candidacies of those two members, and each failed. Several days later, when a deputy protested that several committees had been purged of their radical democratic members and demanded that the question of the composition of committees be reconsidered on the floor, Luk'ianov disavowed any involvement: the leadership of the Presidium, he claimed, had nothing to do with the changes in committee membership. Rather, the changes had been the natural result of the rotation of members from the Supreme Soviet and the wishes of the committee chairs. This was quite false; Ryzhov had argued forcefully against the purge of his committee.

Presumably Luk'ianov had sized up the political balance and concluded that conservative strength in the Supreme Soviet was more than sufficient to remove the outspoken figures of the Inter-Regional Group but that the cost of removing Ryzhov would be too high. The significant consequence of this episode, however, is that it contributed to the establishment of the rule of factional balance in parliamentary government. During the debate over purging the science committee, conservatives could cite relatively few grounds in the rules for getting rid of a committee's members against the wishes of its chairman. Doing so, in fact, was a serious and almost unheard of violation of the institutional norm that chairmen could control their committees' membership. Consequently, apart from charges that the democrats spent all their time playing politics and were not working conscientiously on the committee's business, the critics invoked a new norm—proportional representation of political groups on committees. In floor debate and interviews, deputies then often cited this principle, holding it as self-evident that no one committee should be dominated by a particular group but that groups should be more or less evenly represented across committees. Here the politically conservative origin of the campaign against Ryzhov tended to strengthen the growing tendency for policy making to become organized along partisan lines as in a parliamentary system. Thus although it was the Inter-Regionals who had introduced the concept of legitimate partisan opposition, and it was they who, ironically, fell victim to its manipulation by the conservatives, the informal rule of representation by political group was itself reinforced in the process.

The Legislative Process

In bill procedure, even more than in other ways, the new parliament carried over the old rules with little change. The passage of bills and decrees (*postanovleniia*) required a majority of the votes of the total number of deputies, and this was true both of the congress and of the Supreme Soviet. In the Supreme Soviet, each chamber had to give its approval by a majority of the total number of deputies. As before, in case of disagreement between the two chambers, a conciliation commission was to be formed on a parity basis, after which the bill was to be considered again by each chamber in joint session. If agreement was still not found, the matter was to be taken up by the congress.

A bill could be considered separately in each chamber or in joint session. Here Presidium discretion was implied to determine where a bill would be given its first reading. With time the practice developed of letting the two chambers consider legislation separately and approve it in first reading. Then, after committee work was finished, the Supreme Soviet would discuss it in second reading in joint session.

The Presidium referred bills to the appropriate standing committees, but the legislation committee (now named the Committee for Legislation, Legality, and Legal Order) retained its position as an additional review mechanism for all legislation. A lead committee was named for each bill. The chairman and presidium also determined whether a matter was to be presented to the congress or could be handled entirely by the Supreme Soviet. The congress or Supreme Soviet had the right to decide when a bill would come up for consideration and could instruct a committee to prepare a bill by a certain deadline for its first reading. Although the Presidium and chairman were not specifically mentioned in this connection, they had the actual power to make decisions on bill referral and scheduling.

Committees were authorized to form "joint preparation commissions" when multiple committees managed a bill. They convened "working groups" and "editorial groups" that could include specialists and officials and deputies from other committees. Committees could also consider alternative drafts of a bill, deciding which draft to recommend as the basis for further work. In case of disagreements among committees, an issue was to be referred to the floor of the Supreme Soviet.

All draft laws were to be given two readings, regardless of whether they were handled by the congress or the Supreme Soviet or both. But the rules specified that matters affecting the interests of the union republics were to be considered by the congress, usually after Supreme Soviet consideration. If more than one draft bill were proposed on a particular topic, the first reading determined which draft to be taken as basis for further consideration. Failure at first reading sent the bill back to committee or to its sponsors for reworking. Deputies generally understood passage in first reading to be approval of the general conception of a bill, and the chair generally ruled amendments in second reading that would fundamentally alter its conception as out of order. Some deputies complained that Luk'ianov was able to manipulate the outcome of legislative processes by using this rule. For a measure whose passage he wanted to ensure, he would urge deputies to pass it in first reading so that parliament would have an opportunity to work on it further, but he then prevented parliament from modifying its original intent too greatly on the grounds that parliament had already approved its conception in first reading.

As in the pre-Gorbachev Supreme Soviet, the division of parliament into two chambers remained purely nominal because the chambers were so closely managed by the Presidium. With time, to be sure, the two chambers did come to acquire somewhat different political personalities corresponding to their different electoral origins. The differences were not major, however. Although the chambers held some separate sessions, close supervision by the Presidium ensured that the agendas were nearly identical. The same committee and government representatives typically presented a bill to both chambers, and usually the outcome was the same. Occasionally one chamber did not pass a bill that the other passed or modified its wording. The most conspicuous difference was that the Council of Nationalities suffered from chronic quorum problems. This was partly a consequence of the fact that the Baltic delegations stopped taking part in its work, and of the fact that its membership, which came from national-territorial electoral districts, tended to include a number of ranking officials in ethnic territorial units who frequently missed sessions. The quorum threshold was high: two-thirds of the members of each chamber had to be present. In April 1990, the Supreme Soviet lowered the quorum threshold slightly (to 177 deputies in the Council of the Union, and 171 in the Council of Nationalities) in view of the boycott by the Baltic delegations and the regular nonattendance by members who held full-time positions elsewhere. Vitiated by the centralization of agenda power through the Presidium, committees, and staff, the inherited bicameral division of chambers brought no more than the faintest echoes of the great struggle between center and republics into parliamentary deliberations.

Staff Support and Deputy Resources

Deputies' ability to participate meaningfully in lawmaking and oversight of government was severely limited. The expertise that the legislature possessed largely resided in its staff organization—the secretariat and its apparat—which for the most part was directly controlled by the chairman. As many as a thousand employees served in the secretariat, which was the old secretariat of the Presidium of the Supreme Soviet, and these were supplemented with several hundred additional employees who transferred from the party's Central Committee secretariat. The secretariat had its own departments, corresponding to the committees in structure, and to some extent these departments served the committees.

The relation between the apparat and the members of the Supreme Soviet was ambiguous but evolved gradually in the direction of greater control by committee chairs over the personnel assigned to their committees by the secretariat. Still, many deputies expressed frustration that they did not have direct access to staff assistance. Access to the resources of the secretariat was stratified, with chairs and other trusted insiders able to call upon the staff, while rank-and-file deputies lacked the most rudimentary facilities for research, administration, and simple clerical tasks. Those deputies who were not leaders of committees but had significant legislative ambitions were the most frustrated at the absence of staff support and criticized Luk'ianov and the existing structure of the Supreme Soviet for keeping them weak and dependent.

This impression of a deputy corps dissatisfied over its inability to exert much influence on decision making is corroborated by evidence from a survey of USSR Supreme Soviet members conducted by Timothy Colton in May 1991. Colton found that only around one-third believed that they always or most of the time could exercise any influence over lawmaking.[13] This figure was considerably lower than the comparable figures for their counterparts in the RSFSR parliament at the time, or the Ukrainian parliament, and was roughly equal to the rate reported by Kazakhstan's deputies. Moreover, only 3.8 percent of USSR Supreme Soviet deputies expressed an intention of running again.[14]

Legislative Initiative and the Agenda

Committees, not deputy groups or individual deputies, were the most important source of legislative initiative. The Presidium regularly consulted with committees to assess the priority and readiness of bills in order to determine which bills to introduce into a given session or during a session. Committee chairs thus had a good deal of power to argue for "their" bills, depending on their sense of the urgency of a particular piece of legislation; individual members of the Supreme Soviet exerted their greatest influence on the legislative process through their committee chairs, and only secondarily through their deputy groups. The cabinet of ministers and various government agencies (and, in the earlier points of the Supreme Soviet's existence, the party Central Committee as well) also introduced bills. Often, especially in the first period of the parliament's existence, government ministries were the principal sponsors of legislation. Regardless of the source of the initiative, however, all bills passed through committees before reaching the floor. In later sessions, committees grew more active in drafting their own legislation. Committees then took it upon themselves to generate majority support for their products, bill by bill.

A committee chair who sponsored the law on local self-government and the local economy—the law that for the first time established independent budget and political powers for local jurisdictions—recounted in an interview the legislative drama involved in passing that law. Our committee, he explained, had many members with work experience in local soviets and government at every level, from villages to republics. Before our committee took charge of the bill, a government commission had worked on it for around two years. When we looked closely, we saw that much in the draft had been taken from a decree that had been adopted some years ago, but which was not working properly. The problem was that that decree, and the bill then circulating, took the traditional approach to local autonomy: the center delegates rights and duties. So the committee had to develop, in effect, an alternative bill: "We were the first committee to junk a government draft and present an alternative. For me as chairman it was a thrill (*'nu i drozh' byla'*) to present the bill for its first reading to the Supreme Soviet and see it passed by such a wide margin. I felt like saying 'hurrah'—that was real satisfaction in my work and an affirmation that we were on the right track since the Supreme Soviet supported our approach. This was in the period when many bills presented by the government were not passing. That was real satisfaction." To be sure, he continued, in the second reading:

> everyone wanted to flesh out the ideas—to add this, that or the other thing to the bill. For example, some wanted to revise the provisions on the budget, what goes into the budget, budget structure, and so on. Then opposition formed to the bill. The republics and oblast soviets had serious reservations because the law gives a number of rights to lower levels (cities and rural districts, as well as village soviets). We gave them rights; after all, people live there. But the higher levels, the republics and oblasts, didn't accept that. Moreover, we specified six sources of revenues for city and district levels, bypassing the republics. Republics didn't like that either. We had to fight with the ministries of finance of republics. The country's budget is formed from three sources: income tax, turnover tax, and deductions from profits (*otchisleniia ot pribyli*). We gave the income tax directly to the lower soviets; we gave part of the taxes from profits to all levels of soviets, including republican. But a number of republics opposed us.
>
> Moreover, some committees did not fully support us. Neither did the Ministry of Finance. On the second reading we did not get it through but we refused to budge. There had to be a third reading.[15] We had to prove that we were not adding new taxes. But finally the bill was adopted, and with only two, if I am not mistaken, opposing votes. So there was struggle and tension, and then victory. That was satisfaction.

Committees did have some ability to develop legislation and to win passage for it on the floor. Success required that they persuade the Presidium to support their bills and schedule them for floor consideration. This agenda-setting process, which in effect predetermined the outcome of the legislative process since virtually every bill introduced onto the floor eventually passed, took the form of consultations between the Presidium and the committees. The Presidium set the agenda through the discussion and agreement of the committee chairs, with the chairman of the Supreme Soviet helping it to reach its decisions. Interviewed committee chairs who attended the Presidium meetings reported that meetings were lively and open, and sometimes heated; and most claimed that that there was ample opportunity for a committee chair to argue for the importance of his committee's bills. The criteria for selection of bills for inclusion in the agenda seemed to be twofold: the urgency of a bill from the standpoint of the country's needs, and the degree of "readiness" of a bill, with "readiness" reflecting a vague understanding about the degree to which the responsible committee had built sufficient support for it on the floor.

Committee chairs were expected to represent their committees' interests at the Presidium, and the stronger and more independent chairs did so, while others were content to allow Luk'ianov and the consensus of the Presidium to determine the order of priority of their bills. Occasionally a deputy might introduce a bill on his or her own initiative; a deputy might decide to publish an "author's draft" of a piece of legislation, generally more to stimulate discussion and influence public opinion than to influence the movement of a bill, because, as in the Congress of the United States, a bill lacking a broad base of support had no chance of surviving the legislative mill. Deputies could and did propose bills for consideration in floor debate, when the agenda was discussed. It was unheard of for an individually sponsored bill to be approved for consideration on the floor, but some bills that a group of deputies were vitally concerned about might be moved onto the agenda by this method. As the calendar of items accepted for consideration continuously increased faster than the capacity of the parliament to process them, deputies reported that the backlog of legislation kept growing despite the increase in legislative output.

Individual deputies' goals influenced their choice of legislative tactics. A deputy who wanted to be effective in passing laws played "inside" politics, seeking influence within the committee so that the committee could achieve its legislative goals via Presidium agreement to push the bill onto the agenda. Members who chose to play to the public worked from outside the legislative process, trading influence for visibility. Generally deputies, when asked which members of the Supreme Soviet they respected most, tended to agree both on the particular individuals and on the reasons—they admired those who were quietly effective in forging compromises, mastering the issues, and working hard; they tended to disdain those whom they regarded as grandstanders. In such respects, the USSR Supreme Soviet resembled legislatures in the west. Committees, likewise, were slowly becoming centers of specialization and influence as deputies began to use them to develop and build support for legislation. Yet while the Supreme Soviet grew more effective at passing laws, the laws it passed were increasingly irrelevant to the greater drama unfolding outside its walls—the breakdown of the union.

THE PRESIDIUM AND PARLIAMENTARY GOVERNANCE

Until the 1993 constitution finally did away with the Presidium once and for all, the governing body for every Soviet and RSFSR parliament since 1937 was its Presidium. Although it changed over time in composition and formal powers, it was always an instrument for centralized political control over all aspects of legislative structure and process.

The Supreme Soviet Presidium as Collective Head of State

The old Presidium had remarkably wide nominal powers, not only to govern the Supreme Soviet but to act in its name. The Presidium even had the right of enacting legislative decrees (*ukazy*, or edicts) on its own authority, subject to confirmation by the Supreme Soviet. Thus when Gorbachev gained the power to issue decrees with the force of law under a September 1990 Supreme Soviet law, he was assuming an expanded version of the powers that the Presidium had long possessed and that the tsars had exercised before the revolution. In Russian legal theory, an *ukaz* is a legal act nearly equivalent to a statute (*zakon*).[16] An *ukaz* is generally considered to be a binding, policy-making act, which differs from a statute in that it regulates a specific case rather than an entire class of instances. An *ukaz* may be normative (policy making) or nonnormative (an implementing act), but an *ukaz* ranks higher in the hierarchy of rule making than other types of binding acts, such as *postanovleniia* (decrees or resolutions that can be issued by the parliament or government), *polozheniia* (ordinances), *rasporiazheniia* (orders), instructions, and other "sublegal acts." *Ukazy* have traditionally been a prerogative of the head of the Russian state and not of its government or prime minister. Even during the Soviet period, the CPSU did not have the power to issue *ukazy*.

Stalin's constitutional model distinguished between the collective state presidency—the Presidium—and the government (Council of Ministers). This distinction is formally equivalent to the difference between president and government in parliamentary systems.[17] However, the collective state presidency represented by the old Soviet Presidium differed from most Western presidencies in two respects: it was collective, and, collectively, it had decree power. Its chairman was not so much the equivalent of a state president as the representative of a collegial body that collectively exercised the powers of a chief of state. Although a minor formality in the old regime, given the overwhelming influence of the communist party in policy making, these institutional features of the Soviet system became valuable assets once the Supreme Soviet itself began to acquire real weight in the political system. If the Supreme Soviet mattered, then the power to govern it and the power to issue edicts in its name became important powers. This institutional inheritance, therefore, helps explain the tenacity with which Luk'ianov and Ruslan Khasbulatov, his counterpart in the RSFSR parliament, clung to the older model in which the legislative branch held supreme state power, and within it the Presidium could act in the name of the legislature.

Decree power passed to the president when Gorbachev demanded and received emergency powers to rule by decree in September 1990, then again in the RSFSR transitional period when Yeltsin demanded and gained emergency decree powers in November 1991. But these were delegated decree powers.[18] Constitutionally settled decree powers were only granted the president once Yeltsin codified his conception of a presidential republic in the 1993 Russian constitution. But it should always be borne in mind that decree power became a significant legal resource only at the point that the executive had some independent power to regulate and allocate: so long as the communist party ruled the country, the Presidium's decree power served as no more than a formality. At the same time, the Presidium's power to govern the parliament's own proceedings enabled the staff officials of the communist party to determine how particular policy decisions would be formalized into decrees or laws. Until 1989, the Presidium did not serve as a deliberative body but as an institution for transmitting policy direction from the Central Committee of the CPSU to the Supreme Soviet staff. Since the person who served as chairman of the Presidium held that post on an honorific basis, the secretary of the Presidium managed the processes of bill assignment, drafting of decrees, and supervision of the staff. The chairman and the secretary signed the laws passed by the Supreme Soviet and the decrees and other decisions adopted by the Presidium and were given no authority to withhold or delay their signature.[19]

The Standing Rules (*Reglament*) of the pre-1989 USSR Supreme Soviet described the Presidium as a "permanently operating body of the Supreme Soviet of the USSR, accountable to it in all its activity and carrying out, within the limits envisioned by the Constitution, the functions of a supreme organ of state power of the USSR in the period between its sessions."[20] The Presidium managed and coordinated the Supreme Soviet's role in this process: staff specialists under its direction did the legislative drafting, and the Presidium decided when and how to enact the decisions, preparing and presenting the sessions' legislative calendars.[21]

The evolution of the Presidium's formal composition from the Stalin model to the new Gorbachev model is shown in table 3.4. For each period it summarizes the rules on membership for both the USSR and RSFSR levels. Note that the major change made in the 1989 rules (and the equivalent 1990 rules for the Russian parliament) was to add the chairmen of the standing committees and commissions to the Presidium as voting members and to drop the ordinary deputies and other token representatives, such as the heads of the Supreme Soviets of the constituent territories. This provision greatly increased the Presidium's capacity to coordinate the far more extensive legislative workload of the new parliament.

In contrast, the 1989 rules deprived the Presidium of some of its nominal powers. The Presidium could no longer amend laws provisionally pending approval by the Supreme Soviet, as it did under the old union and Russian constitutions, remove and appoint government ministers, declare a mobilization of the country, interpret laws, and so on. Similarly, in the 1989 Constitutional amendments of the RSFSR, these powers were explicitly assigned to the Supreme Soviet rather than the Presidium.

Likewise the old Standing Rules of the union and of Russia specifically gave the Presidium the power to organize the staff and the budget of the Supreme Soviet. The new union Supreme Soviet rules gave the same power to the Presidium but stipulated that the views of committees and commissions must be taken into account. These changes demonstrated the designers' intent to reduce the ability of the Presidium to usurp the legislature's authority in making policy decisions as well as managing the legislature itself.

Table 3.4. Membership of the Supreme Soviet Presidium, 1937–1993

USSR Supreme Soviet Presidium, 1937–89:
• chairman
• 15 deputy chairs/chairs of Supreme Soviets of union republics
• secretary, to direct the apparat
• 20 rank-and-file deputies

RSFSR Supreme Soviet Presidium, 1937–89:
• chairman
• 17 deputy chairs, including the chairs of Supreme Soviets in the 8 autonomous republics
• secretary, to direct the apparat
• 20 rank-and-file deputies

USSR Supreme Soviet Presidium, 1989–91:
• chairman
• first deputy chair
• 15 deputy chairs/chairs of Supreme Soviets of union republics
• chairs of joint standing committees of Supreme Soviet and of commissions of chambers
• chairs of chambers
• chair of committee of People's Control

RSFSR Supreme Soviet Presidium, 1990–93:
• chairman
• first deputy chair
• deputy chairs
• chairs of chambers (Council of the Republic, Council of Nationalities)
• chairs of joint standing committees of Supreme Soviet and of commissions of chambers

The Presidium's Powers in Practice

A general characteristic of the lawmaking process before Gorbachev's reforms was its combination of strong centralized direction with time-consuming procedures for bureaucratic consensus building. Lawmaking was subject to the same planning and administrative control as economic production. The executive drew up an agenda of legislation that the Supreme Soviet was charged with passing in a given session.[22] It fell to the Presidium to coordinate the necessary meetings between Supreme Soviet committee staff officials and staff officials from the ministries, public organizations, and research institutes to draft the legislation and to ensure that all affected organizations were satisfied with it. Their approval was signified in the form of "sign-offs" or "clearances" in a procedure known as *soglasovaniie.* The cycle of meetings, consultations, and sign-offs to obtain the agreement of interested parties was highly time-consuming. But, because the legislative workload of the Supreme Soviet was very light, and most policy acts took the form of decrees by other bodies, the inefficiency of such procedures was not in itself particularly costly to the political system.

The design of the new congress-Supreme Soviet system in 1989 preserved most of the structures and procedures of this inherited system of lawmaking. It was a system that enabled the Presidium—especially its staff—to serve as an agent of the executive in the legislature. The Presidium transmitted policy direction and coordinated the lengthy process of consultation through which laws were drafted. Both the centralization and the use of multiple filters and sign-offs were brought into the new parliamentary system under Gorbachev. So, too, were rules enabling the chairman to control floor proceedings so as to prevent any one deputy or group from paralyzing and hijacking the institution: they gave the chairman the authority to maintain order on the floor and prohibit deputies from speaking too often and from straying from the subject at hand.

Gorbachev clearly intended to take advantage of the Presidium institution when he created the new congress-Supreme Soviet model. Because the new system was so complex, the Presidium was an invaluable way to control the overlapping structures that the new constitutional amendments established, ensuring the coordination of their activity and the political content of their decisions. To be sure, Gorbachev and his associates made some adjustments to the rules. They stripped the Presidium of its former power to issue edicts. Such archaic institutions as the Council of Elders were dropped. The territorial delegations and ad hoc commissions were given slightly stronger rights. These modifications were crafted by an ad hoc body called the "editorial commission," created by the parliamentary leadership, which gathered and sifted through numerous proposals on modifications of the rules. The commission reported its recommendations to the Second Congress on December 20, 1989. After discussion and votes on several particular motions, the commission's draft passed by an overwhelming margin: 1,729 in favor, 66 opposed, and 32 abstaining.[23]

The new rules retained much of the old language about the powers and obligations of the Presidium. The great difference was that now the Supreme Soviet was conceived as a permanently operating body, so that the powers the Presidium had enjoyed in the past by virtue of its status as a standing body, including decree power, were no longer seemly. Now, on such matters as cases of citizenship, amnesty and pardon, and state awards, the Presidium was to make recommendations for decision to the Supreme Soviet.

Yet, if anything, the new rules made the Presidium still stronger by removing some of its more purely honorific features and turning it into a site for actual decision making in a parliament whose responsibilities and workload had expanded substantially. The new rules dropped, for instance, the provision that twenty ordinary, rank-and-file deputies would serve as members. Instead, it formalized a practice that had long since become established informally: the membership of the chairs of the standing commissions. Previously, they had participated in Presidium meetings but without formal rights of membership.[24] Now, however, the Presidium would be a "committee of committees." In this case, the formalization of an informal procedure was not simply an automatic adjustment of institutional structure to the environment's needs. Through quiet, behind-the-scenes engineering, Gorbachev, Luk'ianov, and a team of experienced experts modified the institutional features of the old Presidium model, giving it greater capacity to respond to legislative initiatives arising from a more activist corps of deputies but retaining for the chairman the ability to dominate its agenda-setting and consensus-forming processes.[25]

With the benefit of hindsight, it is not difficult to reconstruct their thinking. If deputies were now to be elected in contested races, it was to be expected that they would enter the new congress-Supreme Soviet with independent political reputations and followings, defined political stances, and an agenda of policy demands that might differ from Gorbachev's. Indeed, widening the participatory arena to admit such new forces was precisely Gorbachev's goal. Therefore it was expedient for Gorbachev to build in mechanisms that would allow him to channel and direct the potential for serious political change generated by these constitutional reforms. These mechanisms included the complex, multitiered structure of the new parliament, the continuing monopoly on final political decision by the communist party, and Gorbachev's retention of the highest posts in both parliament and party.

The new rules drafted by the editorial commission reflected Gorbachev and Luk'ianov's institutional strategy of making the Presidium more powerful while granting the individual chairs of standing commissions greater opportunities to shape the agenda and to influence particular pieces of legislation. To act collectively, without any other mechanism for aggregating preferences over the agenda and the content of decisions, the committee chairs would rely on the chairman of the Presidium to shape the consensus for decisions. Observers all agreed that Luk'ianov understood this power well and employed it with great skill. So long as he accommodated intense or widely shared interests, an astute chairman could ensure almost any outcome he preferred: the chair could set the agenda of Presidium meetings; "call" the meeting and define the content of its consensual decisions; arbitrate disputes that arose among committee chairs and other participants; invite guests to the meetings; establish and allocate carrots and sticks for chairs and ordinary members, such as the use of cars and drivers, apartments, participation in delegations for overseas travel, and the like; and, perhaps most important, control the deployment of staff resources to commissions and other working bodies. The chairman, therefore, was indispensable to reaching collective decisions of the Presidium, which in turn were essential to coherent decision making in each chamber of the Supreme Soviet, the Supreme Soviet as a body, and the congresses.

The use of the Presidium for centralized control over legislative processes of course aroused opposition from democrats intent on combating the party-state bureaucracy. They argued that the Presidium's sweeping powers were inconsistent with the democratic principle that elected deputies, not state officials, should set policy. Committee chairs sought greater control over the staff assigned to support their committees. Democrats argued that the control over drafting, record keeping, finance, and other legislative functions by the staff, secretariat, and chairman usurped the rightful powers of elected deputies. But deputies disagreed over an alternative model of governance, and Luk'ianov skillfully manipulated the formulation of procedural alternatives in such a way that no proposals except for those he favored passed. He did this by a variety of means: deciding which forum afforded the best opportunity for him to achieve a desired outcome—congress, Supreme Soviet, individual chambers, or Presidium. He could formulate his major objective as part of a draft document adopted "as a basis" for further work, then rule significant amendments changing it as out of order during floor debate. He could shape a consensus in a smaller, inner body such as the editorial commission or the Presidium, then present a package to the floor knowing that no alternative commanding majority support would have a chance of passing. Aggregative and deliberative processes for formulating winning alternatives therefore all passed through him. So skillful was Luk'ianov at manipulating the rules to run the legislative process and attain his desired goal that one deputy called him a *naperstochnik*—master of the shell game.

The character of the Presidium did change over the 1989–91 period: as a collective actor its decisions reflected the joint preferences of a group of individuals among whom committee chairs predominated. For this reason a number of legislative proposals that committees backed became law. The chairman and staff of the Presidium had to accommodate the committees' desires. Yet the chairman of the Supreme Soviet, as head of the Presidium and manager of its staff and material resources, retained important prerogatives, and these allowed him to influence what the committees sought and obtained. Moreover, through the Presidium, the chairman decided which committee would be assigned a bill, controlled the technical work of printing and distributing the text of the bill, had the major say on the formation and staffing of an agreement commission as an alternative site for formulating legislation, and decided when a bill would come up for a vote on the floor. It was through the adept use of the broad, vague coordinating powers of the Presidium that the union-level and Russian-level Supreme Soviet chairs in the transition period almost always got their way. Committee chairs depended more on the the speaker than the speaker did on the committee chairs. Therefore if a speaker picked his fights carefully, as Luk'ianov did but Khasbulatov did not, he rarely suffered a defeat. Interviewed deputies could not recall more than one or two instances when Luk'ianov ever failed to achieve a desired result on the floor.

Because the Presidium was set up as an instrument of CPSU control over lawmaking, an arrangement that survived into the Gorbachev period, it is fascinating to speculate about who the Presidium was serving in the 1989–91 period. As the split between reformers and conservatives within the party leadership deepened, Luk'ianov seems to have become an independent political agent. A good deal of circumstantial evidence, in fact, suggests that the Presidium of the USSR Supreme Soviet became less the instrument for the political and policy goals of Gorbachev as time passed, and more a base of power for Anatolii Luk'ianov to counter Gorbachev by allying with Gorbachev's opposition. While Luk'ianov's own goals remain obscure, it is evident that he employed the Presidium as a means of steering the congress-Supreme Soviet system for the achievement of his ends. Originally Luk'ianov acted in tandem with Gorbachev when they designed and created a legislature to serve Gorbachev's policy and power goals. In 1990 and 1991, however, Luk'ianov began to play his own game. He widened his room for maneuver by exploiting a complex three-way competition among the legislature, the president, and the government.[26] In this triangle, Luk'ianov played prime minister off against president. Prime Minister Pavlov in spring 1991 was urgently requesting a grant of emergency power from parliament; parliament temporized. However, both Pavlov—who probably spoke for a tacit coalition of the future ringleaders of the August coup—and the majority of deputies in parliament were acutely opposed to Gorbachev's negotiations with Yeltsin and the union republic leaders over a new union treaty. Probably Luk'ianov and Pavlov arrived at an informal understanding about the need for emergency measures to prevent the new union treaty from coming into force. The impressive capacity of the chairman to control parliamentary decision making, however, had little significance outside parliament because the great political crises of the day were no longer parliament's to settle. Representation of the major organized political forces by 1991 had shifted to other arenas: to Russia's parliament; to the streets; to the forces of coercion. Luk'ianov's shell game was marginal to the struggles tearing apart the USSR.

DEPUTY GROUPS

New Players in the Game

Most of the features of Gorbachev's parliament were adopted with relatively modest adjustment from the pre-reform Supreme Soviet. The one modification that had lasting impact on Russian politics was the establishment of open partisan competition among groups of lawmakers through a system of factions. Like other changes, this resulted from the adaptation of previous institutions.

Until Gorbachev's reforms, the CPSU permitted no other parties to organize. Similarly, the only type of deputy group that could exist in the pre-Gorbachev Supreme Soviet was a territorial delegation. A territorial delegation was simply the set of all deputies from a particular region. At the start of each session, each territorial delegation met to elect its "elders" according to a formula under which the size of a delegation determined the number of elders it elected. Then the Council of Elders met with the Presidium and chairman of the Supreme Soviet to review the agenda for the coming session. These elders were the ranking officials from the regions. Probably they played a consultative role for the officials drawing up the agenda, conveying the temper of a region to the leadership and informing the members of a particular regional delegation of the issues scheduled to come up on the floor. Enforcement of a group voting position would not have been needed, of course, because it was understood that any motion put before the deputies should be supported. The use of representatives of territorial delegations as conduits of information and consultation before the opening of a session of the Soviet parliament must have been a regular practice, because it carried over into 1989.

Political guidance in the pre-1989 Supreme Soviet, however, was provided by the CPSU group, a body not recognized in the constitution or the rules. This was the caucus composed of all the CPSU members in the Supreme Soviet and was analogous to the "primary party organizations" made up of all the party members employed in any USSR firm or organization. The "party group," according to official descriptions of the old Supreme Soviet, presented proposals on such key matters as nominations of members to the Presidium.

These institutions, the territorial delegations and the CPSU group, were then modified to fit the democratized environment of 1989. They helped to solve the "supply" problem—how could deputies associate autonomously along political lines? These organizational forms gave deputies a model that could be easily adapted to the conditions of open political competition.

Generalizing, we can see a sequence of cumulative incremental changes in the institution of deputy groups from 1989 to 1993. Beginning with the system of elders and territorial delegations and communist party group taken over from the old Supreme Soviet model into the Gorbachev parliament, Russia gradually developed a system of collective party faction control over parliament. We can see this series of steps as an evolutionary sequence over the three periods of parliamentary organization:

1. First, in 1989, interest-oriented and political groups were given the right to register as groups and to act collectively to seek recognition in floor debate, to hold meetings using parliamentary facilities, to circulate their documents and so on;
2. Second, in 1991, the RSFSR parliament granted political factions a distinct and higher status than ordinary groups;
3. Third, in both the USSR and RSFSR parliaments, over 1990–91 and 1992–93, political factions acquired informal rights to represent their members and to advise the leadership on the views of their members, to negotiate agreements over legislation, and eventually to form a collective body of the leaders of the factions;
4. Finally, following the adoption of the new 1993 constitution, a council of faction leaders collectively replaced the Presidium as the governing organ of the new State Duma.

Superficially, this series of developments looks like the progressive adaptation of parliamentary organization to a pluralized political environment, driven by the need for adequate parliamentary representation of the diversity of political interests in society. But such an account squares poorly with the evidence of parliament's maladaptation in other respects and the catastrophic break-downs of 1991 and 1993. Closer examination indicates that each expansion of factions' rights in this process was the outcome of a tacit or explicit political bargain among actors with competing interests—usually the executive leader and a group of would-be party leaders—in which each side gained certain advantages in return for giving up some rights. *Each such choice in turn made the next expansion of rights for groups likelier.*

In exploring this process more closely, I will first track the changes to the Standing Rules of the USSR congress and Supreme Soviet with respect to the nature and rights of deputy groups. Then I will review the formation of the first independent deputy groups, trace their development over the short life span of this interim parliament, assess the role they came to play, and conclude by pointing to the emergence of an informal norm of the representation of political factions in parliamentary governance.

The Formation of Political Groups in the Congress of People's Deputies and Supreme Soviet, 1989–91

The opportunity to organize independent electoral campaigns in 1989 stimulated antiestablishment political groups to create electoral movements centering on democratic and national causes. These movements tended to be concentrated in particular regions, especially Moscow, St. Petersburg, and the Baltic Republics. The territorial base of such independent movements enabled them to convert the traditional institution of territorial delegations into a vehicle for the articulation of political programs in the new parliament. For a time, CPSU-dominated territorial delegations of the traditional type coexisted with a small number of radicalized democratic and nationalist delegations from more politically mobilized territories who wanted to reform parliament in order to democratize the state. The leadership continued to use the territorial group representatives when the newly elected Supreme Soviet met for the first time. Yet while Gorbachev and Luk'ianov were employing these traditional mechanisms of party control to ensure themselves a controllable parliament, independent political groups had already begun to operate. The leadership then looked for low-risk ways to accommodate them in the rules.

A large Presidium-appointed commission met through the fall of 1989 to draft a new set of Standing Orders (*Reglament*) for the USSR congress and Supreme Soviet to make them consistent with its new features, including the two-tiered structure and the political diversity of its members. The commission reported out its proposal to the congress in December 1989, and after a day of debate on the floor, the new rules were adopted with almost no dissenting votes. As we have seen, in most respects the the new rules adopted made only minor changes over the old system. The retention of the old system of elders and territorial groups is a case in point. But the new rules did add a new element: the right to form nonterritorial groups (Article 39). Luk'ianov evidently considered it less trouble to accommodate the new politically based and interest-based groups in the rules than to resist them. Nonterritorial groups were not further described; the rules were silent as to what kinds of groups might qualify for recognition and how they were to be composed.

As is so often the case in Russia, groups' rights were ordered hierarchically. If at least twenty deputies chose to form a group, they could seek official recognition for it. A group of twenty members had minimum rights: they could demand that the Presidium disseminate such documents as position papers to the congress as official documents. A group of one hundred members had wider rights. Such a group was made equal in status to territorial delegations. That is, they could demand the right to voice their group's position in floor debate and to draw up lists of candidates for election to the Supreme Soviet from among deputies at the congress. The rules granted these groups the right to recognition, so long as they notified the Presidium of their formation, composition, goals, and tasks and named the individuals authorized to speak on their behalf; they could also publish their programs in *Izvestiia* so long as these did not contradict the constitution. Deputies were to be notified of the formation of such groups.

The rules did not distinguish between ordinary deputy groups and those that had an explicitly political orientation. Nonetheless, in practice deputies recognized the difference, and political groups came to play a significant role in defining the lines of conflict over legislation.

Factions and Political Groups

Stimulated by the opening to independent political activity of the 1989 campaign, newly elected deputies had begun forming unofficial groups even before the First Congress opened. The first explicitly political, independent group, the Inter-Regional Group of Deputies, formed officially during the First Congress of People's Deputies of the USSR as an outgrowth of a series of meetings held before the congress among deputies oriented to radical democratic reform. During the congress, other groups formed as well, most with occupational or sectoral interests, focused primarily on distributive benefits. Among these were

Komsomol (Communist Youth League) activists, teachers, and environmentalists. The first interest group to form officially was the "agrarian group," which was dominated by officials from the state and collective farm sector.

The Inter-Regional Group of Deputies differed from the interest-based caucuses by virtue of its broader and more ideological goals. The group's interests were not primarily distributive. It did not focus its efforts on winning material benefits for a particular constituency. It had radical ideological objectives that its members understood very well and generally supported. Surveys of the members of the group consistently revealed that the two issues on which the members were fully united were support for a multiparty system in the Soviet Union and the demand for radical, market-oriented economic reform.[27] In March 1990, when the Lithuanian parliament passed a declaration of independence from the Soviet Union, the Inter-Regionals split over whether to support secession, although eventually they were able to find a compromise position that the whole group could accept. The issue whether to preserve the union or to break it up in favor of the independence of its constituent republics split the democrats down the middle. This supports the premise that the center-republics division cut evenly across the axis of left-right conflict.

From the IRGD's cohesive support for radical democratic and market reform, a number of closely related issue positions followed. One was the demand to eliminate communist party domination from Soviet politics through constitutional and electoral reform. Specifically, the group voiced a demand to revise or drop Article 6 of the USSR constitution, which assigned the CPSU the responsibility for leading the country. The group also demanded that an investigative commission be formed to determine who was responsible for the massacre of unarmed demonstrators in Tbilisi in April 1988; to study charges of corruption among the Central Asian party and government leadership; to assess the legality of the protocols to the Soviet-German Nonaggression Pact of 1939 in which Stalin had ceded Eastern Europe to Hitler in return for unopposed Soviet domination in the Baltic States; and to investigate the practices by which the political elite of the country enjoyed unpublicized material privileges. Its legislative agenda included judicial reform, freedom of the press, and reform of the electoral system to drop reserved seats for public organizations and to eliminate "electoral district meetings" from the nomination process.

The heavy concentration of its members in Moscow helped the Inter-Regionals overcome the difficulty of organizing for collective action but left it with a territorially unbalanced membership structure. Because of the intensely centralized nature of Soviet society, Moscow accounted for a substantial share of the country's professional, scientific, and media intelligentsia, and many of its members were well acquainted with one another from working in the same institutes or forming part of the same social circles. Moscow saw a sweep by radical democrats in the 1989 elections, seen most dramatically in Boris Yeltsin's landslide victory in Moscow's one at-large NTIO. But all through the city's twenty-six TIOs, underdogs, radicals, and liberal intellectuals had won seats.[28] Nearly all of the liberal and radical democrats elected as USSR deputies from public organizations were also based in Moscow and were scholars from research institutes in the Academy of Sciences system or prominent figures from the arts and the professions.

The radical democrats were therefore in a position to take advantage of the traditional institution of territorial delegations for explicitly political ends. In May 1989, after the elections but before the congress convened, the newspaper *Izvestiia* convened several of the newly elected deputies for a roundtable discussion of their plans. Although the article itself was never published, the deputies who participated decided to invite other democratically inclined deputies to meet and prepare a series of position papers. These could be used as the basis for their own set of procedural and agenda proposals for the coming congress. These activists then invited the other Moscow democrats, together with democrats from other cities and from public organizations, to a series of meetings in May. Gavriil Popov, later the mayor of Moscow, became their informal leader, although Andrei Sakharov and Boris Yeltsin were their most visible representatives. They were well aware that the very existence of an opposition caucus was a radical departure from Soviet tradition.

When the congress convened, the Moscow group was ready with its proposals as to procedure (hold the debate over the chairmanship first, then vote to elect a chairman) and substance (motions to demand gavel-to-gavel live television and radio coverage of the entire proceedings; form a commission to investigate the Tbilisi massacre; democratize the election law; and so on). They lost on nearly every point, although their demand for real-time broadcasting of the congress was accepted, but they immediately claimed the right to exist as a distinct political group and to pose collective demands. What had been a Moscow-centered deputy club became the Inter-Regional Group of Deputies when on the third day of the proceedings Popov proposed on the floor of the congress that all deputies who wished to join a cross-regional group of democratically oriented deputies were invited to enter the "Inter-Regional Group of Deputies." The group held its first meeting under that heading immediately after the congress, and attracted 256 members. It was an ingenious maneuver. It transformed the "territorial" delegation form into a cross-territorial, but explicitly ideological, body.

The Inter-Regionals represent a major step in the institutional evolution of the Russian legislative branch. They were the first explicitly political opposition since the first years of the revolution. It fell to Academician Sakharov, in fact, to remind his fellow democrats that they had to act not only as an opposition, but as a kind of "loyal" or "responsible" opposition, if they were to spur the formation of a multiparty parliamentary democracy. Indeed, it was Sakharov's idea that a democratic "opposition" be formed among the USSR deputies. At the time of the Second Congress, in December 1989, in remarks to the Inter-Regional Group made a few hours before his death the same evening, he formulated his conception of a political opposition in a way that was well ahead of its time by the standards of Soviet political thinking:

> I want to define "opposition." What is an opposition? We cannot take on ourselves the full responsibility for what the leadership is doing now. It is leading the country to a catastrophe, stretching out the process of perestroika by many years. It is leaving the country for these years in such a state that everything will collapse, collapse intensively. All the plans for a transition to an intensive, market economy will turn out to be unrealizable, and disillusionment in the country is already rising. And this disillusionment is making impossible an evolutionary path of development in our country. The only path, the only possibility of an evolutionary path is the radicalization of perestroika.
>
> At the same time that we declare ourselves an opposition, we take on ourselves responsibility for the solutions we propose. That is the second part of the term. And it is also extremely important.[29]

Other partylike groups followed the example of the Inter-Regionals, among them the Group of Communists, which was joined by around a third of the deputies, and a militantly conservative group, strongly hostile to nationalism in the republics, called "Soiuz" ("union").

Although the radical democrats could not seriously threaten the leadership's control over voting outcomes in the congresses, they could sometimes force votes on motions that sharply divided liberal democrats from the conservative majority. These votes can be used as an index to judge the strength of the different political camps among the deputies, as well as to measure the relative liberalism or conservatism of particular groups of deputies. Such a measure allows us to draw two clear conclusions: factional groups in the USSR congresses divided along an axis defined by the struggle for democratic reform; and the more a group defined itself ideologically, the more cohesive was the voting behavior

Table 3.5. Distribution of USSR Deputies on the Liberal-Conservative Dimension

Ideology Score (1 = most conservative, 5 = most liberal)	Number of Deputies	Percentage
1	239	10.6
2	686	30.3
3	604	26.7
4	454	20.1
5	280	12.4
Total	2,263	100.0

Note: The total is greater than 2,250 because the data set includes deputies elected after 1989.

of its members (see tables 3.5 and 3.6 and the appendix to this chapter). On a scale where the mean score for all deputies is 2.934, with a standard deviation of 1.191, the Inter-Regionals had a mean score of 4.256 and standard deviation of only 1.0, while their ideological opposites, the Group of Communists, averaged 2.392 with a standard deviation of only .971.

By the time of the Second Congress in December 1989, several types of deputy groups had formed, including regional, occupational, and political ones. No distinction was made among these different types of group, and their status was not defined in the rules. Members had a great deal of freedom to choose how to affiliate, and many belonged to two or three groups. By early 1991, about half of all deputies were members of at least one political group and about two-thirds were in one or more of the interest groups (of course, these are overlapping categories). Around a quarter of the deputies belonged to a political group but not an interest group. Leaders of ideologically oriented groups bemoaned the absence of differentiation between political and ordinary interest groups. A leader of the communist group observed: "Groups are given a kind of official recognition now, but this is both for political and occupational groups. What should be done with peasant or military groups? These interest groups lack a personality. They are little different from hobby groups, e.g., the dog breeders. They become a kind of trade union. Take the military group. All they have in common is epaulets: politically they are diverse. They don't have a direct relationship to the Supreme Soviet. Some day the lines will be drawn along political differences, but today it is a hodgepodge." Another moderate communist had proposed a rules change that would prevent members from belonging to more than one group but so far had been unsuccessful. He be-

Table 3.6. Mean Scores of USSR Deputy Groups on Liberal-Conservative
Dimension

Group	Mean Ideology Score	Standard Deviation	Number of Members
Inter-Regional Group	4.256	1.002	230
Radical Military Reform	4.078	1.077	128
Workers	2.828	1.109	297
Constructive Cooperation	2.816	1.193	152
Agrarians	2.579	1.031	411
Life	2.405	1.076	215
Soiuz	2.461	.996	542
Group of Communists	2.392	.971	732

Note: "Life" served as a women's interest group. Of its 217 members, 169 were women, or 78 percent.

lieved that this rule would create a more politically structured decision-making process and was likely to be adopted in the future. These rules changes, raising the status of political groups and forcing deputies to choose one group for membership, would have increased the leverage of group leaders over members in return for giving the groups more influence over parliamentary deliberations. Precisely such a rules change was adopted in October 1991 in the Russian Supreme Soviet.

The Role of Groups in the USSR Congress and Supreme Soviet

By December 26, 1990, twenty-two groups were registered with the Secretariat (see table 3.7). There is some evidence that Luk'ianov's strategy was to accommodate the formation of groups in such a way as to reduce ideological polarization and the power of political groups to influence the agenda. Luk'ianov never explicitly prevented deputy groups from forming (that would have been against the rules in any case, once nonterritorial groups were allowed to exist). Rather, he encouraged groups to proliferate and members to enter multiple groups; he tacitly encouraged the use of a norm of proportional representation in the makeup and leadership of committees, and he later invited group representatives to attend presidium meetings. By winter 1990–91, the Presidium was regularly inviting representatives of the political groups to its meetings to report on their groups' positions on the major issues of the day. Tolerance of multiple groups widened Luk'ianov's base of support by making each organized

Table 3.7. All Registered USSR Deputy Groups, December 1990

Group	Number of Members
Znanie	56
Siberia and the Far East	176
For the Protection of the People's Health	82
Radical Military Reform	52
Fatherland	120
Academic group	87
Scientific-Industrial group	89
Group on Questions of Development of Culture	112
Toward a Civil Society	38
Life	216
Agrarians	415
Workers	306
Group for Assisting Scientific-Technical Progress	90
Justice	40
Warrior-Internationalists (veterans of the Afghanistan war)	54
Group of Young Deputies	124
Ecological Group	220
Constructive Cooperation	155
Social Democrats	16
Soiuz	562
Inter-Regional Group	229
Group of Communists	742

group dependent on his goodwill and the resources of the apparat, which he controlled. Deputies' groups came to play a significant part in the work of the parliament. But we should not overstate their importance. First, although twenty-some different groups were formally recognized, only two or three played an important part as sources of opposing political perspectives on legislative business. These were the Inter-Regional Group and Soiuz, staunch guardian of the old system. Most of the registered groups existed only on paper.

Second, even those groups that met regularly and discussed their positions lacked any means of imposing or enforcing a group decision about a collective stance. The level of group activity and cohesiveness in voting was influenced by more than simply ideological affinity: it was also shaped by the incentives for cohesion embodied in the parliament's institutional arrangements. Because groups had few rights apart from articulating common positions on issues of the day, leaders had few carrots and sticks for maintaining discipline. There were few advantages to members, electoral or otherwise, from adhering to a group position when they had no policy preference for doing so. Although it is conventional to think of party development as a process of maturation, akin to natural processes, we will understand the development of partisanship in the Russian parliaments of this period better if we consider how leaders and members adapted their patterns of behavior to the incentives provided by the institutional setting of the parliament.

The existence of political groups provided information about the distribution of policy views among deputies that was useful for the parliamentary leadership, committee chairs, and individual members. This was so even though groups tended to keep their political activity separate from their lawmaking. To be sure, some laws and resolutions directly reflected the political agenda of particular groups, as when the communists proposed resolutions to commemorate Lenin's birthday. Rather, members adhered to a working norm according to which the "professional" work of lawmaking was kept separate from "political" activity. The fact that this rule of behavior was very widely shared across deputies of many different persuasions helped to preserve a working division of labor between committee chairs and faction leaders. Committee chairs accommodated partisan differences but kept factional differences in check, while factional leaders concentrated their efforts on information, coordination, and position-taking on political issues. Factional positions also guided members in floor debate. As one leading deputy put it, deputies took their cues on how to vote by observing the position of a known member of the Inter-Regionals or of Soiuz and deciding accordingly how to cast their vote. Groups were particularly helpful to deputies when the congresses convened. Then the groups helped link those deputies who were not regular members of the Supreme Soviet system with those who were. In the intervening periods, these links were sporadic at most.

The radical democrats initiated the process by which deputies grouped themselves politically, and they pressured the leadership to accept political factionalism as a regular part of parliamentary organization. The leadership responded by revising the rules and giving political factions certain recognized rights and privileges in fact. The radical democrats pushed for a system of political factions because they intended to use parliament for explicitly political ends: building a multiparty political system and establishing the rule of law. Their goals as legislators directly followed from their larger political agenda. They were far likelier than other USSR deputies to want to seek reelection, and they regarded legislative factionalism as vital to their policy and electoral objectives.[30] Their success in creating a recognized independent structure for coordinating their members' parliamentary activity stimulated other deputies to form their own interest groups and political caucuses. But the cumbersome, hierarchical structure of the parliament frustrated most deputies—democrats and others alike—who wanted to be effective parliamentarians. Mere recognition of the existence of groups did very little to offset the heavily centralized structure of this interim parliament.

The development of political groups in the union parliament was interrupted by the August 1991 coup, which brought about the self-dissolution of the union congress immediately afterward. Nonetheless, the political calculations and choices affecting the status of groups at the union parliament provided their counterparts in the Russian Republic congress and Supreme Soviet with an immediately usable body of experience. Convening one year after the new union parliament, the Russian Republic's parliament gave political groups recognized rights from the start.

Factionalism, therefore, had become a regular feature of the USSR parliament by the end of the Gorbachev period. Factional groups served deputies who were not Supreme Soviet members by linking them with those who were and providing them with political information on current legislative business. They enabled committee chairmen to ascertain the strength of support for and opposition to pending legislation and to work with group leaders to forge satisfactory compromises that would ensure passage of legislation. They even served the chairman of the parliament as a source of information about the distribution of political outlooks among deputies and, not incidentally, seem to have strengthened his hand inside and outside parliament. Deputies agreed that in a future parliament, while many of the structures and processes of the peculiar congress-Supreme Soviet system would be scrapped, parliamentary factions were likely to become much more important.

APPENDIX. CONSTRUCTING THE IDEOLOGY INDEX FOR USSR DEPUTIES

Unfortunately, the methods that we can use to study deputy alignments in the Russian congresses and in the State Duma since 1994, where large volumes of electronically recorded votes are available, cannot be applied to the union congresses because very few votes were tallied electronically. Indeed, there was no electronic tallying at all at the First Congress. In later congresses, most of the votes that used the new electronic voting system tended to produce overwhelming consensus around a valence position, so they cannot be used to sort out divisions among deputies on important issues. Therefore we must choose a set of test votes where there was substantial opposition to the motion and where the reformers took a clear stand and use these as measures of an individual deputy's support for the reform or anti-reform camp.

At the Second Congress several such roll calls were regarded as tests of strength for the democrats against the party-state establishment and had relatively close outcomes. The single closest vote was the first recorded vote at the congress, on whether to add to the agenda a debate over Article 6 of the Soviet constitution: Article 6 gave constitutional sanction to the Communist Party's "leading role" in government and society and was considered the principal legal barrier to a multiparty system. Such reformers as Academician Sakharov accordingly demanded its removal from the constitution. The vote on the motion to debate the issue was 860 in favor, 1,190 opposed, 53 abstaining, with 160 not voting. The other bellwether votes were more lopsided: a vote on whether to support the economic program submitted by the government (reformers considered Prime Minister Ryzhkov's plans a step backward from real reform) passed with 1,531 votes. A proposal from the Supreme Soviet that would have eliminated the constitutional provision (Article 95) providing for reserved seats in the union parliament for deputies from public organizations (democrats opposed providing privileged representation for party-controlled associations) failed to receive the required two-thirds majority for constitutional votes, but it still received 1,349 votes (60 percent). Approval of the motion to accept the report on evaluating the Molotov-Ribbentrop treaty of 1939—a demand of the Baltic delegations and the radical democrats—passed with 1,435 votes. A straightforward way of separating out radical democrats and conservatives is therefore to use these four votes.

A voting record in favor of the first, third, and fourth motions and against the second may be considered to indicate a radical democratic political stance. The opposite voting pattern indicates a conservative position. Using this scale, any aggregate of deputies, such as deputy groups, can be assessed ideologically by its mean score. A mean score closer to the radical democratic position indicates that the group contains a larger number of radical democrats. By the same token, a group with a larger number of conservatives will have a correspondingly lower score.

In constructing this index, the array of voting choices available to deputies was simplified to a dichotomy of "yes" and "no" positions. Any action other than a yes vote is treated as a no, including abstentions and absenteeism. A yes vote on each of the Article 6, Article 95, and Molotov-Ribbentrop pact measures is scored a 1 and summed. A nay or other vote (abstain, nonvoting) is scored a zero. A yes vote on the government program approval measure is scored 1 and nay, abstain, or not voting is scored zero. The government program vote, because it was a measure with a conservative vector, is subtracted from the sum of the votes on the liberal measures. Thus a radical democratic deputy who voted yes on the Article 6, Article 95, and Molotov-Ribbentrop pact votes and "nay" on the government economic program would be scored 3. A deputy who voted "yea" on all four measures would be scored 2. A very conservative deputy who voted against the Article 6 and Article 95 agenda items and the Molotov-Ribbentrop treaty issue but voted in favor of the government economic program would be scored −1 because he receives three zeroes on the first three measures, or 0; and his yea vote on the last measure is subtracted from that sum to yield a score of −1. Thus this scale produces five possible values: -1, 0, 1, 2, and 3. To make the scale easier to interpret, scores were rescaled by adding 2, so that 1 is the lowest and 5 the highest score. The higher the score, the more liberal the deputy. Although this is a somewhat arbitrary way of treating voting alternatives, the bias it introduces is conservative in that it reduces the number of yes votes that might otherwise have artificially exaggerated support for radical democratic and conservative positions, pushing a larger number of members into the middle than might have emerged had they been present and voted yes or no. Still, like other interest group rating techniques, this method tends to identify polar opposites more effectively than shades of opinion in between.

Chapter 4 The Power Game
in Russia, 1990–1993

In chapter 2, I argued that Gorbachev's innovations in the organization of legislative and executive power were undertaken for strategic
purposes, but that they failed to solve the policy and political problems he faced and instead led to some unexpected and unwanted outcomes. Within the parliament, as shown in chapter 3, power was
highly centralized. Central control was wielded through the chairmanship, Presidium, and apparat, which enabled parliament's leadership to frame alternatives that could command majority support. The
leadership adjusted parliamentary rules and practices to satisfy the demands of organized groups of deputies for participatory rights, and
ideological and interest groups became a regular feature of the legislative process. In a few cases, organized groups won significant legislative victories. For the most part, however, the arrangement of the legislature fostered elaborate consensus-building procedures that
produced majorities for proposals favored by the leadership but
avoided grappling with the deepest, most intractable problems of the
Soviet system—economic reform and reconstructing the federal
union. As a result, although the new parliamentary structure devel-

oped some lasting institutional innovations, these did little to resolve the general crisis of the system. Not only were deputies dependent on the chairman and Presidium to form majorities, they also had few means to link their electoral and policy interests with lawmaking or executive oversight. Once the presidency was created, the same institutional weaknesses compounded the problem of exerting their collective power vis-à-vis the presidency. Without an institutional capacity for articulating and resolving policy differences, deputies either deadlocked or let the leadership make decisions in their name.

Russia's interim parliament of 1990–93 closely followed the USSR example. In October 1989 the RSFSR republic-level Supreme Soviet passed constitutional amendments on a new structure of parliament and a new electoral system for the Russian Republic, which nearly replicated the union model. Russia retained the two-tiered structure of congress and Supreme Soviet but altered Gorbachev's scheme to the extent of eliminating mandates for representatives of public organizations. The size of the congress and Supreme Soviet differed from that at the union level because the system of allocating seats to territorial and national-territorial districts differed. The next chapter will review these details more closely. For now, suffice it to say that the structural features that Russia's legislature shared with its union predecessor were as follows:

1. The "matrëshka" doll structure:
   a. A large Congress of People's Deputies (2,250 seats in the union congress, 1,068 in the Russian) with the power to amend the constitution, pass laws, elect a chairman, and approve the head of government as well as other state officials;
   b. A smaller, full-time, bicameral Supreme Soviet (542 seats in the union version, 252 in the Russian), where one chamber was elected from among deputies from territorial districts of equal popular size, the other from a category of deputies elected in "national-territorial districts;" with a requirement of an annual rotation of a fixed proportion of members;
   c. Standing legislative commissions for each of the two chambers; plus a larger set of joint committees of the Supreme Soviet;
   d. A Presidium with wide powers to coordinate and manage the legislative process and set the agenda for both congress and Supreme Soviet sessions; the Presidium comprised the chair and deputy chairs of the Supreme Soviet itself, the chairs of its two chambers, and the chairs of committees of the Supreme Soviet and the commissions of its individual chambers;
   e. A chairman enjoying extensive procedural rights and patronage powers.

2. A system of recognized deputy groups and factions;

3. A strong staff organization administered by the chairman of the Supreme Soviet. Deputies had almost no staff resources of their own and depended almost entirely on committee staff for clerical and administrative assistance.

4. Constitutional incompatibility between the principle of "soviet power"—under which all state power, that is, both lawmaking and executive, was said to reside in the elected soviets—and the new principle of "separation of powers." Alongside these were elements of a "parliamentary" system in which the government had to enjoy the approval of a majority in parliament.

In addition to the structural parallels, the two legislative structures shared a strikingly similar history. Both at the RSFSR and the union levels, once executive power moved out of parliament and into a new presidency, the balance of political forces in parliament shifted away from support of the president. The reason was similar for the USSR constitutional system in 1989–91 and the RSFSR constitutional system in the 1990–93 period. In both cases, when the chairmen of the Supreme Soviet—Gorbachev and Yeltsin, respectively—became president of the country, they relinquished much of their will and their capacity to maintain majority support within parliament. In both cases the chairman's post was filled by the first deputy chairman. Like Luk'ianov, Ruslan Khasbulatov then had to form and maintain his own base of support. He did so by using the patronage devices available to the chairman and through selective tactical alliances. Like Luk'ianov, Khasbulatov traded procedural and material rights to political factions in return for their support. Both chairmen, however, found that they lost the political initiative to hard-line opposition forces intent on provoking an armed uprising against the state.

Both interim parliaments failed to overcome the polarization of their political environments. One might well argue that this failure should not be ascribed to their internal arrangements, as cumbersome as these were. Even the best of models, arguably, would have failed to allow either parliament to overcome the country's dilemmas and divisions. Against this, though, we must remember that the institutional arrangements used for the new USSR and RSFSR parliaments were chosen by Gorbachev and a small group of intimate advisers, rather than being the outcome of a grand constitutional pact reflecting the actual alignments of power and interest in the country. As a result, there were few incentives for other organized political interests to invest any effort in participating in these parliaments. To overcome the commitment problem, therefore, a parliament would have needed to find ways to represent opposing political camps meaningfully without sacrificing its ability to reach collective decisions over policy.

In this chapter I will outline the battles fought by Yeltsin and the other leaders of the RSFSR over the organization of legislative and executive power in the Russian Republic, battles fought between Russia and the union, and then between president and parliament within Russia itself, focusing on the 1990–93 period. From June 1990 to June 1991, Yeltsin was the chairman of the Supreme Soviet. Like Gorbachev at the union level, therefore, Yeltsin was thus the highest-ranking official of the Russian Republic. After June 1991, Yeltsin occupied the new office of president of the RSFSR. This meant that he vacated his old office of chairman, transferring his office and staff from the White House to the Kremlin. As had happened at the union level, the formation of the presidency created a duality of power in which the president and the parliamentary chair each claimed constitutional supremacy. For our purposes it is important to point out that control over the executive mainly belonged to the president once the presidency was created. The government, meaning the Council of Ministers and the ministries and state agencies that it directed, then answered to the new presidency.

In this chapter I will retrace the evolution of constitutional arrangements in this period using the congresses as landmarks. The Supreme Soviet, meeting in the intervals between congresses, passed hundreds of laws and also prepared texts of some of the constitutional amendments to be considered by the congress. But only the congress could adopt a constitutional amendment. Since much of this period was taken up with intense conflict over basic constitutional principles, examination of the action of the congresses will shed light on the chairman's ability to win victories on constitutional matters, and on the unfolding struggle between president and congress for supreme power in the state.

SOVIET FEDERALISM AND THE RSFSR

To understand the conflict between the Russian Republic and the central, union-level government, it is important to recognize the anomalous position Russia occupied within the Soviet Union. This will clarify Gorbachev's observation that in order to be free of the center, Russia sacrificed the union. The Soviet state was federal in form. Soviet federalism was based on representation for territories in which large ethnic nationalities were concentrated. Historically, Soviet federalism originated with the Bolsheviks' concern to grant symbolic jurisdictional rights to territorially compact ethnic minorities in return for their support. The actual power relations between the central, union-level government and the governments of the union republics, however, varied depending on the general policy of the leadership in power. In the post-Stalin period, with the generally lower level of reliance on fear and central control, federal structures facilitated maintenance of and even increases in ethnic national self-awareness on the part of many Soviet peoples.[1] So, too, of course, did the centralizing reform movement begun under Andropov and resumed under Gorbachev, which aroused the antagonism of entrenched elites in the national republics.[2]

The organization of state power adopted for the federal, or union, level of government was largely replicated in the fifteen union republics. Each republic provided formal representation to a major national group, which was provided with some opportunities to preserve national identity within certain changing limits. The model was not quite symmetrical in that some important structures were not replicated in the Russian Republic itself. Here the most striking anomaly was the absence of any communist party branch organization corresponding to the republic itself. Nor were there separate RSFSR-level branches of the KGB, Interior Ministry, the trade unions, Komsomol, or many other state structures. The reason is not hard to fathom. Apart from the needless redundancy that such agencies would have represented, they would inevitably have been separate power centers capable of opposing union-level structures. Union-level party and state organs thus doubled as Russian ones.

At the same time, by the institutional segmentation or compartmentalization of national republics, the regime limited their ability to influence federal policy. The center's domination of the republics was facilitated by the cultural segmentation of the republics as well as by the penetration of unionwide control structures. Yet republics possessed a certain limited autonomy, which enabled the cultures of the dominant, titular nation to be preserved, often at the expense of indigenous ethnic-national minorities residing within their borders. The federal model affected different groups differently. For some populations, it facilitated the spread of national self-awareness, while others preserved the memory of lost national statehood.[3]

The Soviet federal system also tended to preserve traces of the patrimonial style of rule characteristic of Tsarism.[4] In patrimonialism, the ruler treats the realm as an extension of his own household. Subordinate officials' territories are granted only conditional autonomy because the sovereign considers them part of his property. In Soviet federalism, while the union center controlled major productive resources throughout the country, including land, natural resources, industry, and human capital, the constituent republics were given lesser spheres of power over economic assets. Strategic decisions about economic development in the republics were determined by the center. The pattern resembled colonial imperialism in that a dominant metropolitan state developed the economies of peripheral territorial possessions for its benefit. Yet the Russian heartland did not unequivocally benefit from this quasi-imperial arrangement. The balance of trade among republics was not particularly favorable to the core republic. In many respects, because of the policy of cheap prices for energy and other industrial inputs, the Russian Republic ended up subsidizing the development of other republics. Centralized control and controlled prices made it impossible to judge who was exploiting whom, and the conviction was widespread within each republic that it was uniquely disadvantaged by the interrepublican terms of trade that Moscow had imposed.[5] This sentiment was widespread within Russia as well at the end of the 1980s, odd as that may seem today.

The Russian Republic was by far the largest component of the union, representing 51 percent of the Soviet population and 76 percent of its territory and dominating it culturally and linguistically. But many Russians considered themselves disadvantaged by their status within the union. They cited the fact that Russia lacked many of the structural features of statehood that the other republics possessed and expressed resentment that it subsidized the other republics with energy, raw materials, and industrial products at below-market prices. Many began to think that the price of empire was too high and argued that if Russia regained state sovereignty, it would no longer have to subsidize its fellow-republics (sometimes characterized as ungrateful younger brothers and sisters). For example, a deputy chairman of the RSFSR Council of Ministers complained that although 60 percent of the USSR's total economic output was produced on RSFSR territory, along with 80 percent of the country's hard currency earnings, the republic was in only eleventh place in per capita consumption.[6]

This outlook helps to explain why the demand to devolve economic sovereignty from the central government to the RSFSR was not necessarily linked to support for a market economy. Many conservative officials in Russia, as in other republics, simply wanted to replace Moscow's administrative control rights over economic resources with their own and advanced the rhetoric of national victimhood to justify their claims. In turn, liberals who demanded wider political and economic freedom and wanted to dismantle the old structures of central planning and political control could join with the old guard elites positioned in the party and state bureaucracies to demand greater autonomy for the Russian Republic against the union center.[7]

Thus the struggle for power between the union and Russian republican levels of the Soviet system, which at the time was often interpreted unidimensionally as a struggle between old-style hard-liners and insurgent democrats (or, still more simply, as a fight between Gorbachev and Yeltsin), was actually a contest pitting a tacit alliance of democrats and bureaucratic nationalists in the republic against the union center. In many ways it was a contest for control over state resources between elites whose institutional position was at the union level and the political forces stationed at the next hierarchical level down. In Russia, as Gorbachev aptly noted, this meant winning control over the Russian core by relinquishing rights of control over the outer empire.

POLITICAL MOBILIZATION
IN THE 1990 ELECTIONS

Rising popular support for greater autonomy for Russia within the union, coupled with radical democratic sentiments and the political mobilization of the electorate stimulated by the 1989 election campaign, shaped the 1990 elections in Russia. USSR deputies, especially the Inter-Regional Group, worked to build a coalition of democratic candidates to compete in the races for the RSFSR congress and local soviets. The bloc came to be known as "Democratic Russia." As a result of their efforts to construct a nationwide electoral coalition, the 1990 elections in Russia had some of the characteristics of a partisan contest.

Generally the election process—nominations, campaign, voting, and counting—was freer and fairer than in 1989. There was more competition for seats (on average, 6.3 candidates competed for each seat as compared with 5 per seat in the USSR races a year before);[8] as a result, given the rule that a candidate had to have an outright majority on the first round to win the seat, very few seats were filled on the first round on March 4. The runoffs held two weeks later filled most of the rest.

The Democratic Russia bloc performed well in the elections: between 30 and 40 percent of the newly elected deputies in the Russian congress were affiliated with it, and the bloc won outright majorities in Moscow and Leningrad. Following the elections, it then sought to consolidate its position. One hundred and ninety deputies met and declared their willingness to form a parliamentary caucus in the impending congress. Several working groups met to prepare draft proposals for the congress and to agree to nominate Boris Yeltsin as their candidate for chairman. As in the case of the 1989 USSR elections, Russia's 1990 elections produced a sharp division between democratic insurgents and the conservative forces. The forces were more evenly balanced, however, in the Russian congress than in its USSR predecessor, and on issues concerning Russia's rights within the union, the camps could sometimes find common cause. Support for the democratic cause, however, was wider than it was deep.

EARLY TACTICAL VICTORIES
FOR THE DEMOCRATS

When the First Russian Congress of People's Deputies convened, on May 16, 1990, neither the democrats nor the conservatives possessed a clear majority. Boris Yeltsin was elected chairman of the Supreme Soviet at the First Congress by a narrow margin on the third round of voting. The voting confirmed the division between pro- and anti-Yeltsin forces, which largely coincided with the conflict between reformers and conservatives. According to the pioneering analyses conducted by the late Alexander Sobyanin and his associates based on early roll-call voting in the First Congress, about 40 percent of the deputies voted rather cohesively in support of the democratic reform positions, and about 40 percent of the deputies opposed them; the remainder formed a wavering center.[9]

Yeltsin's victory drew on his strong support among the democratic reform bloc, therefore, but not on it alone. This is suggested by the sequence of votes for chairman. Yeltsin faced two principal opponents. One was a conservative communist official who was the darling of the newly formed, highly conservative Russian-nationalist Russian Communist Party, Ivan Polozkov. The other was the Russian Republic's chairman of the Council of Ministers, Alexander Vlasov, for whom Gorbachev was lobbying hard behind the scenes. In the first rounds of voting, however, Vlasov withdrew his candidacy. Against Polozkov, Yeltsin received 497 votes to Polozkov's 473. But Yeltsin needed an absolute majority of the 1,060 deputies who had been elected, or 531. Another vote held the next day gave Yeltsin 503 votes to Polozkov's 458. Now Polozkov dropped out and Yeltsin was paired against Vlasov. Yeltsin then won the chairmanship with 535 votes against Vlasov's 467.[10]

How did Yeltsin attract the necessary additional support when the choice came down to Yeltsin versus Vlasov? In the light of a number of later votes at subsequent congresses (such as the Third, when Yeltsin turned the tables on his opposition and won the congress's approval for his plan to institute a presidency; and the Fifth, when Yeltsin persuaded a majority to give him extraordinary decree powers to enact radical market reform), the best explanation is that he won support from some of the deputies who, although not at all enthusiastic about Yeltsin's economic program, saw Yeltsin as their vehicle to appropriate control for the Russian Republic government over economic assets located on the republic's territory. Yeltsin's strong stand in favor of Russian sovereignty and his long battle against Gorbachev made him the logical choice of officials who anticipated increasing their share of power and their economic opportunities by weakening the central government's power over Russia. Yeltsin's ability to win majorities for his power and policies in the first five congresses should be seen in the light of this interpretation. His election as chairman may have been palatable to conservative bureaucratic Russian nationalists who did not want a candidate whom they regarded as a stalking horse for Gorbachev to run the Russian parliament. Certainly Polozkov, who represented the political amalgamation of communist-conservative nationalism, would have been their preferred choice over Yeltsin. But political moderates disliked Polozkov, who was leading the reactionary wing of the communist party into direct opposition to Gorbachev. Once Polozkov dropped out, both the moderates and a certain number of the Russian bureaucratic nationalists must have supported Yeltsin over Vlasov.

Yeltsin's support from a coalition of democrats and moderate Russian nationalists helps explain his successes as chairman of the Russian Supreme Soviet in 1990–91. To be sure, he lost some battles; the balance of forces was very close. On those issues, however, where Yeltsin was a necessary ally both for radical democrats and for republic-level bureaucratic nationalists, Yeltsin could often construct a voting majority at the congresses. And those were above all issues where radical democrats and conservative bureaucratic nationalists both found it expedient to weaken the power of the central union government. After December 1991, with the union dissolved, however, this coalition foundered as the conflict between Russia and the union could no longer structure voting alignments. Moreover, Yeltsin by then had left the parliament and could not wield the powers of patronage. These had been taken over by Ruslan Khasbulatov, his former first deputy chairman. Khasbulatov used them to build his own voting majority in the congress, although ultimately he was unable to sustain enough control to prevent the catastrophic demise of the entire legislative system.

The other crucial vote taken at the First Congress sheds additional light on the two major ideological axes among deputies. On June 12, the deputies voted by an overwhelming margin (907 votes in favor, 12 against, and 9 abstaining) to adopt a "Declaration on Sovereignty." The statement asserted that the laws and constitution of the RSFSR were "supreme" on the territory of the RSFSR and that union-level legal acts that contradicted RSFSR legislation were invalid on Russian territory. The declaration drew near-unanimous support from among the democrats but divided conservatives evenly.[11] The declaration highlighted the fundamental political fact at the heart of the Soviet regime: there could be no USSR without sovereignty over Russia.

Yeltsin was therefore in a stronger strategic position than Gorbachev. Gorbachev found it increasingly hard to unite those who wanted to preserve the union with those who wanted to reform it and ultimately found himself forced to choose between these camps. Yeltsin, in contrast, found it possible to join democratic reformers with moderately conservative bureaucratic nationalists in battles against Gorbachev and the union center. Yeltsin has often been accused of cynical opportunism in exploiting this strategic situation, which ended in the collapse of the union and full power for himself as president.[12] Against this it must be borne in mind that Gorbachev failed to take advantage of opportunities to ally with Yeltsin against his own conservative flank (as in late summer and fall 1990), and that Gorbachev's willingness or ability to make a decisive breakthrough for liberal reform in the face of the powerful opposition of the bureaucracy was very doubtful. Playing the Russian national card may therefore have been the only way of destroying the communist party's hold on power, which seems to have been Yeltsin's principal policy goal. If Gorbachev's aim was to introduce democratic and market-oriented institutions by gradual steps while still preserving the federal union, Yeltsin's seems to have been the more radical one of replacing the communist system with a fully market-governed economy. It is certainly the case, of course, that Yeltsin never neglected his own interest in power aggrandizement over this period. But neither did Gorbachev. For that reason, it is probably more accurate to see the union's breakup—which neither Gorbachev nor Yeltsin wanted to bring about—as a "lose, lose" outcome in a game such as chicken or prisoner's dilemma.

YELTSIN AND THE RUSSIAN PRESIDENCY

Through the fall of 1990 Yeltsin demanded wider powers for himself as chairman of the Supreme Soviet on the grounds that he needed to oppose Gorbachev and the central union government more effectively. Gorbachev at this point had retreated to the embrace of reactionary elements in the union bu-reaucracy, renouncing, among other things, his summer agreement with Yeltsin to carry out the radical 500 Days program. Instead, Gorbachev turned to hard-line conservatives as his allies and returned to traditional Soviet approaches to economic reorganization and won the support of the USSR Supreme Soviet for extraordinary decree powers to fight the crisis in the country (see chapter 2).

Yeltsin capitalized on the democratic and nationalist opposition to Gor-bachev by demanding the creation of a Russian presidency, knowing perfectly well that he was by far the likeliest person to occupy it. He had, after all, won a landslide victory in his race for USSR deputy in March 1989, winning 89 per-cent of the vote in the city of Moscow for Moscow's at-large seat. Then he had taken 84 percent of the vote in Sverdlovsk in his race for RSFSR people's deputy. He had succeeded in winning election as chairman of the RSFSR Supreme Soviet. There was little doubt about the fact that Yeltsin would hand-ily win any direct popular election for the Russian presidency. This contrasted glaringly with Gorbachev's situation. Gorbachev, whose popularity was slip-ping sharply in late 1990 and early 1991, had not subjected himself to popular election for USSR president or, indeed, for any political office. Thus the presi-dential post Yeltsin proposed to create would not only compete directly with Gorbachev's new presidency at the union level, but because it would be filled by direct popular election, its incumbent would have a huge political advantage over Gorbachev.

But the Second Congress, which convened in November 1990, defeated a proposal by Yeltsin to create a directly elected Russian presidency. The commu-nist wing at the congress was slightly stronger than it had been at the First Con-gress, reflecting the backlash against the democratic wave in public opinion and a more aggressive opposition stance on the part of the Communists of Russia. These pressures brought some of the wavering forces of the center over to con-servative camp. Yeltsin's proposal that he be given a free hand to name his own deputy chairmen was defeated as well. Moreover, the communists succeeded in winning passage of a motion for a declaration in support of Iraq in the Persian Gulf crisis and another that weakened the impact of a package of land reform laws.[13]

YELTSIN'S COUNTERATTACK

The resurgence of the conservative forces at the union and RSFSR levels made it all the more urgent for Yeltsin to create a presidency. He justified the constitutional step of creating a presidency by the need for the power to challenge Gorbachev and the union center more effectively, but undoubtedly he sought to free himself of the constraints on his power from the collective decision-making procedures of the Presidium. There, although he enjoyed the support of a majority of the committee chairmen, the deputy chairs of the Supreme Soviet mainly opposed him. Six of the seven deputy chairs of the Supreme Soviet signed a statement in February protesting Yeltsin's unwillingness to consult them in decision making.[14] Undoubtedly he reasoned that as president he would not need to compromise with his opponents in the Supreme Soviet and its leadership in order to set policy.

Meantime, building on their successes at the Second Congress, the communist opposition began gathering signatures to demand that an extraordinary session of the Russian congress aimed at curtailing Yeltsin's power or even removing him. Yeltsin's opponents included communist conservatives at both the union and RSFSR levels. Yeltsin's supporters discerned the hand of Gorbachev and Gorbachev's erstwhile hard-line allies in the union government behind the campaign against Yeltsin. They saw the violent episode in Vilnius, when special Soviet paratroop forces attempted to seize the television tower in the city, along with other events, as evidence that hard-liners were conspiring to mount a coup.

In this tense atmosphere, Yeltsin turned directly to the populace for support. His plan was to piggyback a question on a Russian presidency onto the referendum that Gorbachev had called for March 17, 1991, for the purpose of winning a popular mandate for his efforts to preserve the union. Yeltsin persuaded the Russian Supreme Soviet Presidium in late January 1991 to put an item on creating a presidency by referendum onto the agenda of the next session of the Supreme Soviet. The Supreme Soviet then approved the idea in February, agreeing that on the territory of the Russian Republic, the referendum ballot would include an additional question on whether to institute a presidency in Russia. When the referendum was held in March, around 75 percent of the eligible voters in the Russian Republic took part. Of them, 71.3 percent voted in the affirmative for Gorbachev's ambiguously worded question,[15] and 69.9 percent voted in favor of the question on establishing an elected Russian presidency.[16]

The communists succeeded in forcing the convening of an extraordinary congress, but Yeltsin was able to ensure that it met only after the referendum had been held and had delivered him a significant political victory. Moreover, on the eve of the congress, Gorbachev made the mistake of overplaying his hand. He attempted to intimidate the deputies at the congress by surrounding the Kremlin with armored vehicles on the first day of the congress and banning all public demonstrations. This heavy-handed show of force tended to deepen the split between Russian bureaucratic nationalists and defenders of the union—both groups including liberals, moderates, and conservatives. Once again, Yeltsin successfully rallied both democrats and Russian nationalists against the central government. The congress passed a resolution, by a one-vote margin, denouncing the union government's actions, then suspended its proceedings in protest against Gorbachev's show of force.[17] Gorbachev backed down and withdrew the troops. Yeltsin's victory in the showdown gave him a temporary advantage at the congress, which he skillfully converted into significant institutional victories. Yeltsin's victory at the Third Congress owed a great deal to a split among the communist deputies led by Alexander Rutskoi, who formed a breakaway faction called "Communists for Democracy." Rutskoi's group sided with Yeltsin in his drive for the presidency and his struggle against Gorbachev over economic reform and Russian sovereignty. Yeltsin rewarded him by making Rutskoi his running mate in the presidential election.[18] Thanks to the support for Yeltsin from Rutskoi's faction, the congress voted on April 5 to schedule a presidential election for June 12 (one year to the day after the First Congress passed the Declaration on Sovereignty) and to convene another session of the congress on May 21 to consider the necessary constitutional amendments.[19]

Moreover, the congress voted to give Yeltsin as chairman additional powers to set policy by executive order (*rasporiazheniia*); these powers were to expire once the elected president took office. Yeltsin's rationale was that the country required an effective executive that could take emergency action without waiting for parliamentary approval. But he also made it clear that the special executive powers he sought for himself as chairman were intended to allow him finally to carry out a rapid, far-reaching program of liberalization and stabilization along the lines of the 500 Days program. If Gorbachev were not going to implement such a program at the union level, Yeltsin repeatedly declared, he would do so in Russia.[20]

In the months after the congress, Yeltsin made use of these powers to sign a series of orders granting regions the right to the status of "free economic zones." These orders granted tax exemptions, special customs privileges, simplified import and export procedures, and they allowed wider autonomy to set up enterprises. In effect, they allowed Yeltsin to distribute patronage benefits on his own authority, using the office of chairman of the Supreme Soviet as a source of allocative power for political purposes. Where formerly the Presidium collectively exercised this right of patronage, the new rights granted Yeltsin by the Third Congress were granted to him as chairman of the Supreme Soviet. He then carried these rights over into the presidency after June 12.

PRESIDENTIAL POWERS, TAKE 1

The Fourth Congress convened on May 21 and duly enacted the constitutional amendments creating the presidency. It based the amendments on the Law on the RSFSR President, which the Supreme Soviet passed on April 24 and which formulated the office's powers.[21] Compared with the presidency later established under Yeltsin's 1993 constitution, the 1991 presidency was significantly weaker in relation to the legislative branch; the weakness reflects the tenuous nature of Yeltsin's majority within parliament. The powers delegated to the president were all carefully balanced by countervailing powers for parliament. The president was to be both "supreme official of the RSFSR" and chief executive. He could not occupy any other posts, including that of people's deputy, and he could not be member of a political party. He had the power to reject laws passed by the Supreme Soviet (though he was required to do so within the fourteen-day period specified), but his rejection could be overturned by a simple majority of each chamber of the Supreme Soviet. He had to present an annual report on the situation in the country to the congress, and the congress could demand an early report by majority vote. He named the chairman of the Council of Ministers, but the Supreme Soviet had to vote to confirm the appointment. He did not have the power to dissolve either the congress or the Supreme Soviet. He did have the power to issue decrees (which had formerly been the exclusive prerogative of the Presidium of the Supreme Soviet), but these could not contradict the law or the constitution, and they could be repealed by the congress or Supreme Soviet if the Constitutional Court held that they violated existing constitutional or statutory law. By a two-thirds vote of the congress, the president could be removed from office.

The weakness of the office suggests that Yeltsin made some necessary concessions to win approval for the law and the amendments establishing the presidency by the necessary two-thirds majority.[22] Democrats, bureaucratic nationalists, and moderate prounionists could all agree to a presidency that was aimed at cooperation with rather than disintegration of the union and which was subject to the legislature's control. Yeltsin also benefited from the fact that the campaign for the Russian presidency had already effectively begun; several people had declared their candidacies even though the office itself had not yet been formally established. Clearly, in April and May the political establishment generally supported the plan to create a presidency and assumed that the election would be held on June 12 as scheduled. After a short and vigorous campaign, Yeltsin won a convincing election victory, taking 59.7 percent of the valid votes cast, with turnout at 74.7 percent.[23] It was his third impressive victory in a popular election in as many years—a remarkable achievement for any politician.

The hard-line interests entrenched in the central union government and its bureaucracies could not accept the new treaty between Gorbachev and Yeltsin and eight other republic leaders under which republics would acquire substantially greater economic power at the expense of the union center. As we know, they organized an unsuccessful attempt to seize power. The coup's failure strengthened Yeltsin's political position since he had rallied opposition to the coup. Gorbachev's position was fatally weakened; he could neither command the union-level government bureaucracies nor any substantial popular following. Through fall 1991, all the elements of the central union government reorganized themselves under Russian Republic control—including, crucially, the KGB and army. In September Yeltsin decreed that all fuel and energy resources on Russian territory were the property of Russia. In November, he outlawed the Communist Party of the Soviet Union and the Russian Communist Party and took over the economic ministries, including the Finance Ministry, that had served the union government. By the end of 1991, the USSR state had ceased to exist in reality; Gorbachev's resignation as its president formally recognized this political fact.[24]

PRESIDENT, PARLIAMENT, AND THE STRUGGLE FOR SUPREMACY

Triumph in the battle between Russia and the union center, however, removed the very issue on which Yeltsin had been able to rally majorities—ever thinner, to be sure—for his proposals to the congresses for more power as president. With the disappearance of Gorbachev and the last vestiges of a union, the communist opposition confronted Yeltsin over radical reform. Polarization between parliament and president deepened throughout 1992 and the first half of 1993 as Yeltsin demanded constitutional reforms recognizing his supremacy as president, and parliament adamantly refused to accept any such changes but tried instead to roll back the powers that it had delegated to him. Yeltsin demanded to put the issue before the people in a referendum, but parliament refused to do that as well. Ultimately, the confrontation was resolved by force in September-October 1993.

Deepening disagreements over policy, unresolved constitutional ambiguity, and the temperaments of the principals all contributed to this confrontation. Yeltsin used the expanded presidential powers that the congress delegated him to enact radical market-oriented reform and to protect the Gaidar government from parliamentary opposition. As the economy plunged into depression, Yeltsin's parliamentary opposition gained strength and grew in intensity in its antagonism toward Yeltsin's policies. The parliamentary opposition, in turn, claimed that it was fighting to restore the traditional prerogatives of the Supreme Soviet and its Presidium as the supreme authority in the state. Certainly the constitution was inconsistent on this point. When the constitution was amended so as to establish a state presidency in the Russian Republic, it introduced the principle of separation of powers between legislative and executive branches but left intact the traditional soviet doctrine that the Supreme Soviet was the highest level of state power and had sovereign jurisdiction over any policy issue. Thus the powers traditionally enjoyed by the Presidium of the Supreme Soviet, as a collective head of state, were in dispute, among them the power to award symbolic honors and enact legislation in the name of the legislature.

Moreover, Yeltsin's departure from the parliament and his use of presidential decree power to enact radical policy reform weakened his already diminishing support base in the legislature, allowing his communist opposition to form a majority against him. Before the establishment of the presidency, Yeltsin could use his position as chairman to influence agenda setting, the distribution of committee chairmanships, and the makeup of the membership of the Supreme Soviet. The rather even balance of democratic and conservative elements in the early congresses meant that he lost on some issues, won on others. But once he left the chairmanship, he gave up these institutional prerogatives. This affected both the balance of political forces in the congress and Supreme Soviet and the way the parliament organized itself for decision making.[25] It therefore strongly influenced the development of relations between president and parliament. The result was a deadlock. Yeltsin controlled the executive (as heads of government, Gaidar and then Chernomyrdin remained loyal to Yeltsin, and the army accepted Yeltsin's authority), but Ruslan Khasbulatov expanded parliament's control over the Central Bank and regional soviets and cultivated an alliance with conservative and even extremist groups in society. Both claimed supremacy under the constitution, but neither had the means to resolve the,impasse constitutionally.

EMERGENCY POWERS

After August 1991, the struggle between Yeltsin and the parliament was played out against the background of the disintegration of the union. Economic and political breakdown was a real threat. As shortages of goods spread, some regions went so far as to erect roadblocks to prevent people from other regions from purchasing food on their territories. Yeltsin justified his demands for wider presidential powers by arguing that he needed the authority to fight the deepening crisis. Like Gorbachev one year previously, Yeltsin attempted to win support for emergency decree powers simultaneously from among conservatives who wanted him to exercise police powers to restore order, and from among democratic radicals who wanted him to enact deep economic reform. Yeltsin's plan for emergency powers therefore split the democratic and communist camps. Some democrats were reluctant to delegate dictatorial powers to Yeltsin, while some communist opponents accepted the argument that Yeltsin needed the additional powers in order to fight the mounting disorder in the country and to defend Russia's interests against the union. In place of the former bipolarity between left and right that had marked the First through the Fourth Congresses, the Fifth revealed serious divisions within each camp. These cross-cutting divisions shaped the politics of the Fifth Congress, which was held in two parts.

Initially the congress convened in July 1991, a month after the presidential election, and considered a motion to elect Ruslan Khasbulatov to the post of chairman of the Supreme Soviet. Although Yeltsin had endorsed Khasbulatov, as many as half of the democratic deputies refused to support him.[26] Deadlocked on this issue, the congress recessed after a week and only reconvened two months later, well after the August coup attempt. By this time the political forces were substantially realigned.[27] Now Khasbulatov succeeded in winning election as chairman. Even more significant, Yeltsin won the congress's agreement to sweeping demands for additional powers as president. At his behest, the congress agreed that there were to be no new elections of soviet or executive branch officials at lower levels of government until December 1, 1992, and that until then, President Yeltsin would name new "chiefs of administration" to head the executive branch in regions, cities, and districts.[28] The president also gained special powers to enact emergency economic measures by decree. Yeltsin made it patently clear that he would use this decree power to enact a program of deep liberalizing economic reform—not for Stalinist measures to freeze wages and prices. Nonetheless, on November 1, the congress granted him the powers he sought for the program he outlined. He would have the power to issue decrees (*ukazy*) that carried the force of law even if they contradicted existing legislation, and the power to name a government without seeking parliamentary confirmation for it. His decrees could set policy in a wide range of enumerated policy areas: banking, stock and commodities exchanges, financial and currency regulation, foreign trade, investment, employment, customs, price regulation, taxation, property rights, land reform, and the powers of the executive branch. The act granting Yeltsin these extraordinary powers was not altogether a blank check. The president was required to submit the text of such decrees to the Supreme Soviet (or its Presidium). If the Supreme Soviet failed to reject a decree within seven days, it would go into effect automatically. If parliament did reject it, it automatically became the text of a draft law submitted by the president.[29] Meantime, one supposes, the bureaucracy and society would already have begun to respond to it, creating a fait accompli that would be costly for parliament to reverse.

The congress's actions are hard to explain. There can have been no uncertainty about how Yeltsin would employ his powers or the policy content of his economic program. Already in July and August he had exercised the more limited decree authority granted to him under the Law on the President that the Supreme Soviet and congress had approved. In July he had decreed that political parties could not maintain primary organizations (cells) within state enterprises or organizations, such as factories, institutes, schools, and military units. This was of course a direct blow to the primary level organizations of the Communist Party of the Soviet Union and was intended to free the state and society from the control of the party. It was a profoundly important decree, as communists immediately recognized in denouncing it as illegal. Then, almost immediately after the failure of the August coup attempt, Yeltsin issued further decrees suspending the activity of the Russian Communist Party and confiscating its property and that of the CPSU and demanding a judicial investigation of their role in the coup.[30] Communists at the Fifth Congress could have had little doubt that Yeltsin would use his extraordinary powers to enact a program that would dismantle state ownership, planning, and administration of the Russian economy; introduce private property and market relations; and fundamentally restructure society.

Yet half the communists supported Yeltsin.[31] Undoubtedly one reason was the demoralization and weakness of the communists following the failed August coup; many probably reasoned that it was imprudent to oppose Yeltsin when the tide of events was so strongly favorable to him and they were on the defensive for their role in the coup. Another reason, suggested by Scott Parrish, was that the delegation of policy-making power to the president allowed them to overcome the institutional barriers that they faced as a result of the weak organization of the congress to devise their own majority-supported package of policy measures.[32] Perhaps they reasoned as well that they were retaining the ability to check Yeltsin through their right to reject any of his decrees.

Deliberate delegation of policy power by a legislature as a response to collective action problems is surely part of the story, as it has been in other cases of executive-legislative relations.[33] The communists' unwillingness to oppose Yeltsin too forcefully at a moment when the country faced a grave threat of breakdown must also play a part in any explanation of the congress's generosity.

There is another observation as well that sheds light on these votes. The vote to elect Khasbulatov as chairman coincided with the vote to delegate power to Yeltsin. Moreover, two other developments occurred at the same time: a change in the Standing Rules to expand the rights of political factions, and the election of a slate of deputy chairmen of the Supreme Soviet who were carefully balanced by political faction. The coincidence of all these decisions in time strongly suggests the work of a strategically minded institutional engineer who arranged to solve several contentious problems at once in a grand package. I will develop this supposition in detail in chapter 5. Here let me simply note that the difficulty that Ruslan Khasbulatov experienced in winning election as Yeltsin's replacement (compared, say, with the smooth succession of Luk'ianov to the chairmanship of the union parliament the previous year) prompted Khasbulatov to build a support base different from Yeltsin's. Because many of Yeltsin's radical democratic supporters despised Khasbulatov, he looked for a different way to win election. It is likely that he offered a deal to the faction leaders: in return for their support, he would grant them additional rights within the parliament. At the same time, Khasbulatov evidently believed that he needed to maintain a cooperative relationship with Yeltsin. Whether Khasbulatov himself constructed the deal granting Yeltsin the decree power he wanted in return for elevated rights for factions, or mediated between faction leaders and President Yeltsin, is not clear. But the fact that all of these changes occurred almost simultaneously—the Supreme Soviet adopted the new rules on factions on October 25, Khasbulatov was elected chairman on October 29, the deputy chairmen were elected on November 1, and Yeltsin got his extraor-

dinary powers on November 1—suggests strongly that Khasbulatov and the
faction leaders found their way to a package deal. In return for giving Yeltsin
the powers he wanted to enact radical reform and supporting Khasbulatov and
a carefully balanced slate of deputy chairmen,[34] faction leaders gained new
leverage over their members through the rule that members could belong to
only one faction, and collectively, the faction leaders would be given the opportunity to exercise their influence through a new structure, the Council of
Factions.

GROWING CONFRONTATION

Yeltsin moved quickly after the Fifth Congress to make vigorous use of his new
decree powers. Within days of the congress's end, he formed a new government
of young liberal reformers. He named himself prime minister, Gennadii Burbulis first deputy prime minister, and Egor Gaidar deputy prime minister responsible for formulating and carrying out the economic reform program. On
January 2, 1992, the new team took the first steps of what became known as
"shock therapy" when by decree they abolished fixed prices on all goods and
services except for two categories: fuel and energy, and food and basic commodities. Thereafter, nearly all the major reform measures associated with the
macro-economic stabilization and privatization programs were embodied in
presidential decrees. Only some years later did supporters of the radical reforms
express second thoughts as to whether the heavy reliance on presidential decree
power had weakened democratic institutions.

Soon after the stabilization program had been launched, Yeltsin's opponents
in parliament, including his former ally Ruslan Khasbulatov, began seeking
ways to retract the blanket grant of power they had given him. Yeltsin's vice-
president, Alexander Rutskoi, joined with Khasbulatov in opposition to the
president and government. For his part, Yeltsin renewed his drive to put into
place a new constitution that would institute a "presidential republic" and
floated proposals aimed at dissolving the congress. Khasbulatov responded
with what became a series of counteroffers designed to give Yeltsin a new constitution in return for preserving Khasbulatov's own power as head of parliament. For example, in April 1992, Yeltsin called for a nationwide referendum
on a new constitution in which there would be no congress. Khasbulatov responded shortly afterward with a proposal that the congress adopt a constitution that would replace the existing parliamentary structure with a smaller, full-
time parliament that had a strong Presidium. Clearly he envisioned that he

would control the new parliament through its Presidium. Yeltsin now actively looked for ways to adopt a constitution that would not require the congress's approval and would not be based on the draft developed by the congress's constitutional commission. Yeltsin did not have the right under the current constitution to conduct a referendum on his own authority. The law did permit a referendum, however, if its initiators gathered a million signatures on petitions calling for one. Many democratic supporters of Yeltsin called for a signature drive for a referendum on the principles of a new constitution. Yeltsin also considered joining a question on legalizing private property in land to a question on the new constitution.

The Sixth Congress, meeting in April, reflected the severe disagreements between Yeltsin and his parliamentary opponents and revealed that the latter had a clear majority at the congress. Early on they succeeded in winning several important agenda votes aimed at placing onto the congress's agenda several items aimed at weakening Gaidar's government. One was a motion to debate a constitutional amendment giving parliament greater power to oversee the government. They agreed to debate a proposal to retract some of the powers they had granted Yeltsin the previous November, and another one to require parliamentary approval of major government appointments. They rejected a resolution supporting the government's economic program in favor of a resolution calling for lower taxes and substantial increases in spending. Gaidar and the government submitted their resignations. The confrontation was eventually averted when Yeltsin and the congress agreed to a compromise (worked out by First Deputy Supreme Soviet Chairman Sergei Filatov and the heads of the factions) under which the congress would adopt a new resolution endorsing continued reforms but calling for their "correction" in return for a number of concessions: Yeltsin would appoint new members of the government representing the state industrial lobby; relinquish the post of prime minister and offer a law on the government in which he would be obliged to seek parliament's approval for a prime ministerial candidate; fire the most objectionable members of the government, including Burbulis and Shakhrai; give the government greater authority to set policy and reduce the power of his "state councillors." He also assured the deputies that he had no intention of dissolving the congress. Twice Yeltsin met with the heads of the political factions to work out compromises on the major issues. In the end, although Yeltsin had to make some concessions, he was able to head off the opposition's attempt to curtail his powers or to increase the parliament's influence over the government. But the pattern of votes at the congress demonstrated that Yeltsin could win majority support only at the cost of significant concessions; certainly he could not hope to win the congress's agreement to dissolving itself and adopting a new constitution. Notwithstanding his conciliatory remarks at the congress, shortly after it adjourned, he again commented that it would be a good idea to dissolve the congress and hold elections for a new parliament.[35]

As Yeltsin fought off parliamentary incursions on his power that would interfere with the autonomy of the Gaidar government, Khasbulatov worked within parliament to consolidate and expand his own political support. In August 1992 Khasbulatov upset the interfactional agreement under which the democratic forces gained the post of first deputy chairman of the Supreme Soviet. As first deputy chairman, Sergei Filatov had overseen the parliament's administrative affairs; its organizational and housekeeping responsibilities, including the flow of legislative business; allocation of internal resources; and record keeping. Now Khasbulatov moved to increase his personal control of parliament by stripping Filatov, the first deputy chairman, of all of his responsibilities except for oversight of agricultural policy. This meant that Khasbulatov took personal charge of managing the parliament's budget and the resources it distributed to deputies, such as staff, rights to cars and drivers, apartments, full-time jobs, and other important perquisites. Now Khasbulatov could use his control over staffing, inclusion in delegations traveling overseas, candidacies for committee chairmanships, and the like to punish enemies and reward allies.

When the dwindling forces of the democratic camp attempted to remove Khasbulatov as chairman, the communist and nationalist groups successfully defended him. Nonetheless, Khasbulatov seems to have been uncomfortable in the opposition camp's embrace and attempted to form his own autonomous base of support. This led him to expand the rights of political factions and to rely on the support of the new Council of Factions chaired by Vladimir Novikov. Khasbulatov, relying on the support of faction leaders by giving them new rights and privileges, attempted to make himself the pivotal figure in the struggle between the opposition camp and Yeltsin. Khasbulatov's strategy evidently was to make himself indispensable to President Yeltsin as the leader who could deliver parliament's support for a constitution satisfactory to Yeltsin and obtain, in return, Yeltsin's acceptance of Khasbulatov's control over a future parliament. At the same time, Khasbulatov would be the indispensable bridge between parliament and president, ensuring that the opposition majority in parliament would need him to defend parliament against the president.

For their part, neither the communists nor the Yeltsin forces took much stock in Khasbulatov's overtures. Yeltsin ignored Khasbulatov's repeated proposals to hold early elections for *both* parliament and president, and the opposition tried to remove him as chairman at the Eighth Congress in March 1993. His "pivotal player" strategy led only to disaster when Yeltsin ultimately dissolved parliament, and he found himself hostage to extremist paramilitary forces during the October 1993 uprising.

Khasbulatov also formed his own private army and intelligence service. The commander of the parliamentary security force of five thousand men declared that he was loyal exclusively to Khasbulatov. Khasbulatov sent this force to take over the premises of the newspaper *Izvestiia* to make good his claim that the newspaper belonged to the Supreme Soviet. The security forces refused to surrender when ordered to by the security troops of the Ministry of the Interior. Only the appearance of the special commando forces ("the Alpha Unit") of the KGB resolved the standoff in favor of the Interior Ministry. Within parliament, Khasbulatov appointed General Vladislav Achalov, a former paratroop commander and USSR deputy defense minister who had been an active participant in the 1991 coup attempt, to serve as "head of the analytic center for ties with the regions." Among other duties, Achalov managed a communications network that the chairman used for conference calls with the heads of soviets in the regions. Khasbulatov and Rutskoi named Achalov "minister of defense" in the days following Yeltsin's suspension of parliament the following year when a rump congress declared Rutskoi president of Russia.

IMPASSE

Relations between president and parliament were extremely tense in the months leading up to the Seventh Congress, which convened on December 1. In fall 1992, the Supreme Soviet attempted to increase its leverage over the government by passing a law that would require nominees to other top ministries to be confirmed by parliament as well. Yeltsin had attempted to forestall holding the congress then, preferring to wait until spring, but parliament refused to oblige. Yeltsin would need to name his candidate for prime minister for congressional approval. Yeltsin therefore looked for a way to win support for Gaidar. Khasbulatov, playing the role of pivotal ally, signaled Yeltsin on the eve of the congress that he could deliver the congress's support for Yeltsin's program if Yeltsin agreed to give him more power. Yeltsin, however, refused to go along. Yeltsin's address to the deputies assembled on the first day of the congress was not conciliatory. Yeltsin called for wider powers for himself as president and reduced powers for the congress until a new constitution was adopted. Gaidar's address was also unrepentant and largely defended the stabilization policies his government had pursued throughout the preceding year.

The congress responded in kind and debated an amendment to the constitution that would have required Yeltsin to submit not only the name of his candidate for head of government to the parliament for approval, but also his choices for ministers of defense, security, foreign affairs, and interior (the so-called power ministries). A constitutional amendment was required because the law had been vetoed by Yeltsin. On the first and second votes, the proposed amendment failed. Yeltsin then proposed a deal. In return for the congress's support for Gaidar, Yeltsin would support the proposed amendment giving the Supreme Soviet the right to confirm the power ministers. The deputies, however, accepted Yeltsin's concession but then did not give Gaidar the necessary majority. Gaidar received 467 favorable votes and 486 against, whereas the constitutional amendment passed. So did an even more unpalatable constitutional amendment, which would automatically strip the president of his powers in the event he dissolved the congress. Yeltsin then angrily demanded a popular referendum on the fundamental issue of who should rule—parliament or president? Congress, however, refused to support the referendum proposal. Khasbulatov proposed simultaneous parliamentary and presidential elections, but Yeltsin was unwilling to step down himself.

The difference in the outcomes between the Sixth and Seventh Congresses shows how great the distance between parliamentary majority and president had become. At the Sixth Congress, despite fiery denunciations by president and deputies against one another, meetings between Yeltsin and the faction leaders eventually produced a compromise that averted a direct confrontation. The congress agreed to a qualified endorsement of the government's program, and Yeltsin made some changes in the composition of the government. At the Seventh Congress, in contrast, no one could deliver the necessary majority for a compromise agreement. Yeltsin made several overtures that could have been used, and Khasbulatov seems to have tried to broker a deal. But all attempts failed. Conflict was now too intense to permit concessions aimed at the moderates in the center to work. The radical opposition had the initiative. Compromise was achieved only through the mediation of an outside party, Valerii Zor'kin, chairman of the Constitutional Court. Zor'kin offered to negotiate a compromise agreement between president and parliament. Through his efforts, the congress agreed to call a referendum in April on basic constitutional principles, and Yeltsin agreed to propose another candidate for prime minister.

After testing the deputies' support for several candidates and finding that Viktor Chernomyrdin had the widest support, Yeltsin then named Chernomyrdin as his choice for prime minister. Chernomyrdin was promptly confirmed and went on to serve until March 1998.

THE APRIL REFERENDUM

Soon after the end of the congress, Khasbulatov backed away from the agreement on the referendum. Presumably he and the parliamentary majority recognized that Yeltsin was more popular than the parliament and would win in any direct popularity contest among the electorate. Among the deputies, only Yeltsin's diminishing following of democratic allies supported the referendum, while the communist, nationalist, and centrist factions all opposed it. Yeltsin then proposed another deal. He would drop the referendum plan if the congress would approve a new procedure for drawing up and adopting a new constitution. Under it, the congress would turn over responsibility for writing the new constitution to a constitutional assembly. In addition, Yeltsin demanded that the congress cede full control over economic policy to the government.

Khasbulatov rejected the proposal. The opposition forces pressed forward with their plan to convene another congress, with the goal of impeaching the president. Yeltsin in turn threatened to impose emergency rule. Yeltsin could not hold the referendum until the congress had approved the wording of the questions, and although the date of the referendum had been set for April 11, the law on the referendum required that the wording of the questions be approved and published at least thirty days before the referendum was held. Without congress's consent, therefore, the president could not legally conduct the referendum despite the December bargain. Fear that the president would dissolve parliament and introduce direct rule again intensified as Yeltsin's associates hinted that the president's patience was limited. Foreign newspapers published reports that Yeltsin was sounding out prominent Western leaders about their reaction to such a plan.

The deputies convened the Eighth Congress on March 10 and voted to include on its agenda a motion to consider whether Yeltsin's recent actions were constitutional or not, which participants considered a maneuver that would lead to impeachment proceedings. They also voted to consider restructuring the responsibility of particular government agencies in order to increase parliamentary influence over them. On the latter issue, Khasbulatov and Yeltsin met and negotiated an agreement acceptable to both congress and the president, which made certain functions of government, as well as the Central Bank and the State Property Fund, jointly accountable to both president and parliament. However, the congress also passed decrees stripping Yeltsin of some of his powers—including the power to issue economic and political decrees—and formally canceling the referendum.

One week after the congress ended, Yeltsin appeared on national television to declare that he had signed a decree declaring special presidential rule and suspending the work of parliament. His announcement may have been a kind of trial balloon, intended to test the strength of his support among the public and the key government actors. In any case, when the actual decree was published, it no longer contained the point on special rule. Nonetheless, Yeltsin may well have ascertained that opposition to such a move was relatively limited and that he could probably get away with it as a last resort at some future time. The parliamentary opposition, however, convened yet another congress, the Ninth, to consider impeachment. Khasbulatov again sought to avert a direct collision, meeting with Yeltsin on the second day of the congress and proposing that instead of the referendum demanded by Yeltsin on a new constitution, that early elections be held in November 1993 for both president and parliament. But when he proposed this plan to the congress, the deputies voted on a motion to remove him as well.

Both the impeachment vote and the vote on removing Khasbulatov failed. Each, however, had substantial support. The vote to remove Yeltsin gained 617 votes, 72 votes short of the required two-thirds majority. The vote against Khasbulatov won 339 votes, 178 votes short of the required simple majority. But the outcomes of the two votes had different effects: Yeltsin's position grew stronger, Khasbulatov's weaker. As a result, Yeltsin was able to win the congress's approval of four questions for a referendum to be held on April 25. These included two questions worded favorably for Yeltsin's interests and two favorable to the opposition. The questions were: (1) Do you have confidence in the president of the Russian Federation? (2) Do you approve of the social-economic policy carried out by the president and government of the Russian Federation since 1992? (3) Do you consider it necessary to hold early presidential elections? (4) Do you consider it necessary to hold early elections for people's deputies?

The first reflected the president's desire to win a vote of confidence from the voters, the second was intended by the deputies to tap the voters' dissatisfaction with the government, the "shock therapy" economic program, and the economic hardship the country was undergoing. The third and fourth questions (which the congress voted to consider "constitutional" issues so that they would have legal force only if a majority of all registered voters approved them) balanced the president's interests against the deputies.

The results of the referendum were strongly favorable to the president. 69.2 million (64 percent of all eligible voters) participated. Of those who voted, 58.7 percent expressed confidence in President Yeltsin; 53 percent approved of his economic reforms; 49.5 percent supported early presidential elections, and 67.2 percent supported early parliamentary elections.[36] Support for the latter two items failed to clear the threshold of a majority of all registered voters (approval constituted 31.7 percent and 43.1 percent, respectively, of registered voters). Politically, however, the results represented a significant victory for the president and a defeat for Khasbulatov's strategy of pairing Yeltsin's fate with that of the parliament. Politically, if not constitutionally, Yeltsin now considered himself free to press forward with plans to draft and adopt his preferred constitutional system. Sergei Filatov, whom Yeltsin had recruited from parliament at the beginning of January to serve as his chief of administration, declared that adoption of the new constitution was now Yeltsin's first priority after his victory in the referendum. Yeltsin's strategy shifted to winning over the support of the leaders of the regional governments and building agreement for the principles of the new constitution among a wide cross section of the public. Yeltsin convened a large constitutional assembly, which met in May and June, and, ignoring the parliament, worked out most of the details of a new constitution (see chapter 6).

The parliamentary opposition now found itself with fewer options than ever. It had lost the political initiative, lost the battle for public support, and lost any real ability to use the one constitutional power that Yeltsin had appeared to fear—the congress's exclusive prerogative to amend or adopt the constitution. The last legal lever left to it, albeit a weak one, was its right to adopt the state budget. This it now proceeded to do in such a way as to wreck Yeltsin's economic program and the support of Western public and private financial institutions. Through the summer, the Supreme Soviet sought to use what legal authority it had to undermine Yeltsin. It passed a law giving it the right to overturn any international treaty retroactively. It lowered the quorum requirement so that pro-Yeltsin deputies could not paralyze its work by boycotting Supreme Soviet sessions. It approved a request by the procurator general to investigate the first deputy prime minister. It approved the text of a constitutional amendment, to be taken up by the next session of the congress, which would strip the president of his powers as chief executive and make him into a ceremonial head of state. When the president vetoed the budget that parliament had passed, with projected expenditures twice the volume of projected revenues, the

Supreme Soviet overrode the veto. The parliament's actions seemed to reflect a desire to provoke Yeltsin into suspending parliament and perhaps instigating an armed uprising.

That this is not a fanciful explanation for the tragic events which followed is suggested by the actions of the extremist anti-Yeltsin forces outside parliament. Although Yeltsin had outlawed the National Salvation Front, the Constitutional Court had reversed his decision. The National Salvation Front, spearheaded by a fiery young deputy named Ilya Konstantinov, was a loose alliance of opposition groups formed in October 1992. Konstantinov sought to unite a diverse array of communist and ultranationalist elements, ranging from paramilitary formations to factions of parliament, in the anti-Yeltsin cause. Some of the constituent elements of the alliance were very extreme in that they called for an armed revolution to overthrow state power.[37] Besides extremist rhetoric, some elements of the front were willing, even eager, to use violent tactics in order to provoke police suppression, as they had done in their May Day demonstration in Moscow in 1993. The front had strong support within the congress through a close link with the bloc "Russian Unity." In July, however, the front intensified its confrontational tactics. It adopted a decision requiring disciplined adherence to its leaders' decisions on the part of members, while at the same time consolidating its alliance with Khasbulatov and Rutskoi. One of the leaders of the front, for instance, was Khasbulatov's chief of security, General Achalov. The front's turn to greater militance in summer 1993 seems to have spurred the actions by the Supreme Soviet that were aimed at provoking a coercive response by the government.

Whether Khasbulatov had become dependent upon the extremists or thought he was using them in a last-ditch desperate effort to force Yeltsin to accept his terms for a constitutional agreement, or both, Khasbulatov grossly miscalculated the actual balance of forces. Yeltsin's decree of September 21 "terminating the activity of the congress and Supreme Soviet" (as the decree put it) did result in an armed uprising by forces claiming to support the parliament. Certainly once Yeltsin had issued his decree, and the parliamentary opposition holed up in the White House, many of the extremist groups were in a triumphant spirit, gratified, apparently, that they had succeeded in instigating the long-anticipated crackdown they hoped would widen into a revolution or civil war.[38] For ten days a diminishing body of deputies refused to submit to Yeltsin. Two of the groups within the building affiliated with the National Salvation Front proclaimed the siege to be the beginning of the "proletarian revolution." Moderate deputies were marginalized as the extremists gained the initiative;

some left the White House voluntarily, others were expelled by the militants within. Yeltsin ordered water and electricity to be cut off. Mediation by the Church failed. On the afternoon of October 3, a group of a few thousand demonstrators, some armed with hand grenades, broke through the ring of federal troops stationed around the White House and went on to attack the building next door, which housed the offices of the mayor of Moscow. Vice-President Rutskoi addressed the crowd from the balcony of the White House and called on them to seize the Ostankino TV station, and Chairman Khasbulatov appealed to them to attack the Kremlin. Khasbulatov and Rutskoi issued a joint appeal to the Russian people, calling on them to "defend the motherland." Federal troops suppressed the uprising and arrested the leaders, Khasbulatov disclaiming any responsibility for the violent actions of the protesters and Rutskoi protesting that he had never used his weapon. Federal units lobbed artillery shells into the White House building, killing many who remained inside. Yeltsin subsequently issued decrees mandating elections for a new parliament and a nationwide vote to approve the text of the new constitutional draft based on the product of the summer's constitutional assembly.

SUMMING UP

As had happened at the union level in the 1989–91 period, the competition of the major political actors for constitutional supremacy resulted in strategic deadlock and, ultimately, violent breakdown of the regime. In the RSFSR, the transitional parliament was modeled on that of the interim Gorbachev period, but the electoral mobilization of 1990 had produced a very different balance of forces among the newly elected corps of deputies. The Russian congress initially was composed of a roughly even balance of democrats and conservatives, whereas the union predecessor was dominated by its conservative majority. After his narrow margin of victory in his election as chairman, then, Boris Yeltsin was able to use the chairman's prerogatives to forge some crucial majorities for his preferred policies and institutional reforms. In particular, he was able to mobilize enough support from among conservative bureaucratic nationalists in RSFSR state structures, along with his support from democrats, to win approval for his plans to establish a presidency in the RSFSR. The basis for this alliance was the desire to expand Russia's prerogatives at the expense of the union center. Yeltsin took advantage of this support base to increase his own powers as president and to prepare a program of radical economic liberalization for Russia.

After the failure of the August 1991 coup and the final collapse of the union state, however, Yeltsin's strategic situation changed. Now he could not rally support against the central union government. His departure from the chairmanship of parliament deprived him of many of the levers that he had used to win majorities in the congress. His successor as chairman, Ruslan Khasbulatov, forged a highly conservative support base comprised of communists and nationalists who strongly opposed Yeltsin's economic reforms. As Yeltsin used his presidential powers, however, to enact radical reforms in 1992, the distance between his position and that of the majority in parliament widened, and the majority grew more cohesive in opposition to both his powers and his policies.

Policy conflict between parliament and president deepened into a contest for constitutional supremacy. Khasbulatov and Yeltsin pushed the powers of their respective offices beyond constitutional limits, Khasbulatov creating his own private army and intelligence service; Yeltsin ignoring parliament's acts. The strategic deadlock could not be resolved peacefully because there was no way Yeltsin could compel parliament to relinquish its exclusive control over constitutional reform. Before the violent denouement of this impasse, however, the use that Yeltsin, and later Khasbulatov, made of the powers of the chairman to reorganize parliamentary procedures led to some significant and lasting institutional innovations.

Chapter 5 Deputies and Lawmaking in the RSFSR Supreme Soviet

As Yeltsin and Gorbachev, and then Yeltsin and Khasbulatov, battled over the distribution of constitutional powers, their choices affected parliamentary operations; in particular, the deputies elected to the new Russian parliament devised rules and procedures for their legislative activity reflecting the changing constitutional landscape. In this chapter I will focus on four features of parliamentary organization—deputies' mandates and their parliamentary rights and obligations; committees and the legislative process; the Presidium's powers of governance; and the emergence of deputy groups and factions—and how deputies used these institutions to achieve their political and legislative ends.

ELECTORAL MANDATES AND PARLIAMENTARY REPRESENTATION

Mandates and Membership

The new Russian parliament closely resembled its counterpart body at the union level in organizational structure and constitutional powers. As at the union level, the RSFSR Congress of People's Deputies

Table 5.1. Apportionment of National-Territorial Districts in the Russian Congress

Type of Unit	Number of Units	NTIOs per Unit	Total
Autonomous republic	16	4	64
Autonomous oblast	5	2	10
Autonomous okrug	10	1	10
Total			84

(CPD) was formally defined by the newly amended RSFSR constitution as the "highest organ of state power of the RSFSR."[1] It was given the right to "take under consideration and decide any question pertaining to the jurisdiction of the RSFSR." It had the power to adopt constitutional amendments or a new constitution, to elect the Supreme Soviet from among its members, to pass laws or to nullify laws passed by the Supreme Soviet. The Supreme Soviet, in turn, was a "permanently operating legislative, dispositive [*rasporiaditel'nyi*], and supervisory [*kontrol'nyi*] organ of state power of the RSFSR." But the Russian congress did differ from the union congress in size and composition. The Russian CPD was composed of 1,068 deputies, 900 of whom were elected in single-member territorial districts, and another 168 elected in national-territorial districts (NTIOs, or *natsional'no-territorial'nye izbiratel'nye okruga*).[2] Of the latter, half were assigned to the ethnic-national territorial units of the Russian Republic (see table 5.1).[3] Note that the RSFSR was the only Soviet republic to be formally designated as federal.

The distinction between regular territorial districts and the national-territorial districts affected the formation of the Supreme Soviet. The congress was to elect members to two chambers of the full-time, quasi-professional Supreme Soviet. The two chambers, the Council of the Republic and the Council of Nationalities, each had 126 deputies and were formally equal in powers although they were intended to specialize in somewhat different areas of legislation. They differed in the mandates possessed by their members. The deputies serving in the Council of Nationalities would be drawn entirely from among the deputies elected in national-territorial electoral districts, while those in the Council of the Republic would be elected from among deputies elected in regular territorial districts.[4]

The bicameral principle was an innovation for the RSFSR, taken over from the USSR model. The old RSFSR Supreme Soviet had gotten by with a single chamber consisting of 975 deputies, all elected in single-member districts. The new Russian congress and Supreme Soviet system also differed in some respects from the structure used at the union level. Apart from the different numbers of mandates in the congress and two chambers of the Supreme Soviet, Russia's parliament lacked seats directly filled by public organizations, such as the communist party, the trade unions, the Academy of Sciences, and the like. But, as we have seen, it carried over the centralized leadership and staff structures of the old Supreme Soviet.

Full-Time and Part-Time Service

The original distinction between deputies who were members of the Supreme Soviet and those who were not presumed that members of the Supreme Soviet would work on a full-time basis. As had been the case in the union parliament, however, this expectation raised a number of serious difficulties. Were Supreme Soviet members *required* to give up outside employment in order to work full time in the parliament? Such a rule was actively opposed by many deputies, who argued, reasonably enough, that they were not willing to give up their regular employment for service as a full-time parliamentarian for a year or two. The other side argued that unless Supreme Soviet members were required to relinquish outside employment as a condition of assuming their seats, the parliament would be dominated by state officials.

In 1989, in the amendments originally creating the new parliament, the RSFSR constitution had simply provided that deputies who were elected from the congress to the Supreme Soviet "*could* be released" from their outside jobs and did not specifically *oblige* them to give up their jobs;[5] the provision was presumably meant to require their employers to grant them unpaid leave if they sought it. A year later, the constitution was amended again to provide that deputies who were elected to the Supreme Soviet "were released" from their regular employment in order to participate in the parliament's work.[6] Similarly, the Standing Rules of the Russian Supreme Soviet adopted in October 1990 stated that members of the Supreme Soviet were obligated to attend sessions of the individual chambers and joint sessions.[7] The constitutional ambiguity reflected the deputies' unwillingness to require themselves to choose between taking a seat in the Supreme Soviet and keeping their jobs, just as was the case with the union parliament.

Yet, as was also the case at the union level, Russian deputies who were not members of the Supreme Soviet *could* work full time in the Supreme Soviet. That is, if the Supreme Soviet Presidium and a committee chair agreed, they had the right to come to work full time as a member of a committee or com-mission and be paid a full-time salary. Such deputies had full legal rights to work on legislation and vote in committee, served in factions, and attended Supreme Soviet and chamber sessions. They lacked only a vote on the floor, al-though of course they had full voting rights at the congress. The ability to offer full-time employment as committee member to a deputy seeking a job in the Supreme Soviet, and still more a leadership position such as a committee chair-manship, became a significant source of patronage power for the Supreme So-viet chairman. Undoubtedly it was one of the considerations leading Khasbu-latov to take these powers from his first deputy chairman, Sergei Filatov, in August 1992.

By late 1991, most deputies in the Russian parliament had come to agree that Supreme Soviet membership should carry with it the obligation to serve full time. According to Sergei Filatov, who was then in charge of day-to-day opera-tions of the parliament and its staff, all deputies were polled by telegram over the summer recess of 1991 and asked whether they thought that all deputies who were members of the Supreme Soviet should have to work on a permanent basis. Just over half the deputies replied, and of these 92 percent answered affir-matively.[8] Filatov himself interpreted the new constitutional wording to mean that deputies had a "constitutional obligation to attend sessions."[9] In Novem-ber, the Fifth Congress rotated out a number of deputies who were flagrant nonparticipants and named new ones from among those who had already been working actively in committees.[10] The net total of Supreme Soviet members who were not full time dropped from about 80 to about 70 as a result.

But just as deputies were forever exhorting each other to work conscien-tiously in the Supreme Soviet if they were members of it and to serve full time, and passing rules and constitutional amendments to bind themselves, they just as regularly inserted loopholes through which to escape the obligation. The amendment adopted by the Fifth Congress of People's Deputies requiring members of the Supreme Soviet to participate on a full-time basis was offset by a provision in the implementing resolution that gave deputies a grace period until April 1, 1992, before the rule took effect. Even then the parliament chose not to enforce the rule. As of May 1992 only 72 percent of the deputies who were Supreme Soviet members had given up outside employment. On the other hand, a nearly equal number of deputies who were not Supreme Soviet members were working full time in it. Therefore the pool of full-time deputies was larger than the pool of Supreme Soviet members (see table 5.2).

The decision whether to work in the Supreme Soviet on a full-time basis had

Table 5.2. Russian Deputies by Type of Participation,
Estimates as of Spring 1992

	Supreme Soviet Member	Nonmember
Full-time deputy	180	160
Non full-time deputy	70	640

several significant implications. One had to do with the deputies' material circumstances, another with the parliament's ability to attain a quorum and pass legislation. In one sense, of course, the attendance problem reflected the awkwardness of the parliament's disjoint structure, which prevented the Supreme Soviet from working without continually looking over its collective shoulder at the congress. Because the congress could always overturn or amend the Supreme Soviet's decisions, debates in the Supreme Soviet were sometimes inconclusive, as deputies urged that a particular decision be referred to the congress. Moreover, the constitution gave the congress the right to shape the political arena in which the Supreme Soviet worked by defining its powers through constitutional amendment. Likewise, the congress acted as if it were reluctant to relinquish full lawmaking power to the Supreme Soviet even though it lacked the organizational capacity to serve as a working legislature. Neither, then, could function autonomously, but they were harnessed together in an inefficient arrangement. Yet, even though nearly all deputies and officials agreed, almost from the beginning, that the two-tiered legislative structure had outlived its usefulness, the deputies at the congress could never agree to relinquish their powers.

Incentives for Service

For many deputies, parliament was an inviting source of employment and career opportunity, one reason that even deputies who were not members of the Supreme Soviet looked for paying jobs in its committees. Full-time deputies were compensated at a level moderately higher than the average wage in industry; committee chairs received a salary twice that of rank-and-file deputies.[11] Fully two-thirds of all full-time deputies held some leadership position, as committee chair or deputy committee chair, and so were being compensated at higher than the base rate.

Russian deputies were drawn to full-time parliamentary work for the same kinds of reasons as parliamentarians elsewhere: the opportunity to shape public policy; hopes for further career advancement; the perquisites that came with holding public office, such as the opportunity to reside in Moscow. Many of those who worked in the Supreme Soviet—a higher proportion than their counterparts in the USSR Supreme Soviet—anticipated making political careers. According to Timothy Colton's survey data, 21 percent of the members of the Supreme Soviet whom he interviewed and 29 percent of those who were not members but were working full time in its committees planned to run again for election (as compared with only 3.8 percent of the USSR Supreme Soviet deputies in his survey). Moreover, the RSFSR Supreme Soviet deputies were far more likely to feel that they were able to influence legislation: almost three quarters of the Russian Supreme Soviet members responded that they were able to affect legislation most or all of the time, as compared with only one-third of their counterparts in the USSR Supreme Soviet.[12]

But compared with their counterparts in Western democracies, the Russian deputies had few independent political resources. Inflation eroded the value of their salaries and the prospects for other employment if they lost their mandates were poor. There were not enough apartments in Moscow to go around: as of September 1991, more than half the Supreme Soviet's members were living in hotels.[13] Insecurity made deputies that much more dependent on the chairman, who rewarded friendly deputies with higher-paying leadership posts and apartments. Other deputies became beholden to outside sponsors or left to take jobs in the executive branch. Corruption was widely believed to flourish in this environment; deputies often assumed that their colleagues were on the payroll of one or another organization.

Deputies were insecure not only because their pay and benefits did not keep up with inflation, but also because the surrounding political environment was insecure. They feared losing everything—their mandates and privileges as deputies, their Moscow residency permits and apartments, their career prospects. For many, therefore, a position in the executive branch offered significant attractions, both for material and security reasons. Working and living conditions were better, and there was less chance of suddenly losing their mandate. Between 1990 and 1993, a large number of deputies took jobs in the government or with the president. By summer 1993, more than 200 deputies worked in the executive branch. More than half were presidential appointees— 55 as chiefs of administration in regions and cities, 25 as presidential representatives in regions, 25 in staff and ambassadorial posts.[14]

As this practice grew widespread, the Supreme Soviet passed a law in November 1991 prohibiting deputies from holding paid positions both in the

Supreme Soviet and in government. Deputies also legislated benefits for themselves. In July 1993, evidently foreseeing that Yeltsin would soon dissolve parliament as he had been threatening to do, deputies passed (in first reading) a law amending the Law on the Status of the Deputy so as to provide some postdissolution insurance. It provided that they could keep and even privatize the apartments they had received as deputies if they had worked in the Supreme Soviet on a full-time basis for at least three years. It also stipulated that they received separation benefits equivalent to half a year's pay, a full year if their place of employment was reorganized or liquidated. Moreover, deputies would be entitled to receive their medical and vacation benefits for three years after their service ended, and if the term of their mandate expired within five years of retirement age, they were eligible to receive a pension equal to 70 percent of their salary.[15] When Yeltsin, just two months later, did dissolve parliament, he carefully ensured that the deputies' material interests were secure, decreeing that they would be entitled to keep their Moscow apartments and would be paid to the end of their elected terms. Undoubtedly this softened the blow substantially.

Attendance Problems

Another consequence of the freedom deputies had to decide how conscientiously they wished to take part in parliament was the difficulty in reaching a quorum. Absenteeism made it more difficult to satisfy the requirement that a majority of the deputies who were members of each chamber had to vote in favor of a bill in order to pass it into law, a requirement written into the constitution as well as the rules.[16] Since (as of May 1992) 126 deputies were members of the Council of the Republic, and 122 of the Council of Nationalities, passage of a bill or amendment required 64 affirmative votes in the first chamber and 62 in the second. The majority requirement was slightly easier to meet to the extent that not all seats of each chamber were occupied but was nonetheless a high hurdle because of the problem of nonattendance. When a vote was held, nonattendance, attendance but nonregistration at the day's session, nonvoting, and abstention were all equivalent to voting "no." Members were strongly frustrated, therefore, by the fact that absenteeism made it difficult to pass even routine legislation. As a result of these problems, deputies found themselves pressed by multiple competing responsibilities, then frustrated by the low efficiency of Supreme Soviet sessions. An exchange in the Council of Nationalities in December 1991 captured the dilemma well. The chamber was debating the rule that required attendance except when an absence had been excused. A deputy named Yakovlev challenged the chairman to clarify the reasons that would excuse nonattendance:

YAKOVLEV: Today I spent the day, after coming here and registering at the Supreme Soviet, at the Ministry of Foreign Trade, interceding on a question of Italian credits to my city. No one else could handle this issue and the chairman of the executive committee of the city asked me to intercede. I want to know if this would be considered an extenuating circumstance.

CHAIRMAN: No.

YAKOVLEV: Here at the session I sit and listen. We fail to meet most of our goals. Compared to working on constituency problems, which does more good for the voters? It is the voters that elected me, and I am accountable to them. So I want to know what you consider extenuating circumstances. The voters in my city are who elected me, not you. All the more since we decide almost nothing here.

(Shouts arise from the floor. Deputy Murav'ev then supports Yakovlev.)

MURAV'EV: Often I sit here and don't understand a thing because the bill is not in my specialty. It wouldn't help that problem if attendance were required. It would be better if the quorum were one-half rather than two-thirds and if voting went by a majority of those present. Then it would really matter if my vote were cast or not. I'd have an incentive to come and vote. Also, we could provide other incentives, like paying deputies for their attendance on floor, and planning the agenda better, and setting aside particular time periods for voting.[17]

This exchange accurately indicates that it was not officially acceptable for deputies to miss sessions. But it also sheds light on the problem of weak institutional mechanisms for accomplishing legislative business. Frustration at spending, as a rule, three days a week sitting in session (in the Fourth Session, from September 1991 through July 1992, the chambers normally met one day a week and the Supreme Soviet in joint session two days)[18] but accomplishing so little left many deputies demanding more central control over the proceedings so that they could plan their time better. Deputies depended on the Presidium to plan the agenda of each session and of each day's proceedings. As was the case at the union level, the Presidium developed the session agenda on the basis of proposals from committees, from particular deputies, and from the government, as well as the leadership's own reading of the urgency of various problems confronting the country. Although they constantly complained that the Presidium was too powerful, the deputies leaned heavily on it to enable them to accomplish their collective ends.

STANDING COMMITTEES
AND THE LEGISLATIVE PROCESS

The constitution granted the right to propose matters for consideration to a very wide range of individuals and organizations,[19] but it was easier to put an item into the legislative hopper than to ensure that it would receive priority consideration. Deputies constantly found legislative business piling up faster than they could dispose of it. The Supreme Soviet could vote at any time to add an item to its agenda. Indeed, debate over the day's business often occupied the first hour, and sometimes the first hour and a half, of every day's session. Interviews indicated that some deputies were frustrated with the efforts of certain of their colleagues to politicize the proceedings; one deputy in an interview said that these deputies were trying to turn the Supreme Soviet into a "circus." It was relatively difficult, however, for one or a few deputies to persuade a majority to expand the already overstretched agenda, so most motions to amend the agenda failed.

The rules and established practice built in a number of filters to keep the agenda manageable and to achieve wide agreement about what matters should be taken up and in what order, but the rules also protected the rights of individuals to take up scarce time with agenda proposals and motions to amend pending legislation. The most important screening points were the weekly Presidium meetings. Here each committee chair proposed and defended a set of items to be included into the calendar for the coming days and weeks. Over and over, interviewed deputies agreed that the main operational criterion for approving an item to be reported out to the floor was its state of "readiness," a criterion reflecting whether the draft was in a sufficiently polished state to be given its first or second reading by the floor. Readiness was more than a matter of technical preparation, of course; it also represented an assessment of the level of support for the bill. Among other criteria were a matter's urgency in the eyes of deputies and of the president and government.

In most cases, committees were the sponsors of legislation. Deputies who introduced bills tended to avoid seeking personal credit for a particular version. Although self-sponsored bills were entirely in order (and were called "author's drafts" and "initiative drafts") they were rare in comparison with the collective and officially authorized versions sponsored under committee auspices. It was also uncommon for factions to propose bills in their own name. Almost always, alternative conceptions of a piece of legislation were either rejected or integrated into a working document that gained the status of official draft. Although political factions were the main channel through which deputies took positions on the great political conflicts of the day, deputies used committees to conduct their legislative business.[20]

Deputies were generally free to join committees according to their own preference, but the committee chairs and parliamentary chairman tried to ensure that no committee had too few or too many members. Members also may have consulted with their factions in deciding which committees to enter. It was considered bad form for a committee chairman to exercise arbitrary authority in selecting members, but many deputies referred approvingly to the principle that members should sit on committees where their educational and occupational backgrounds gave them particular expertise. Almost universally, interviewed members cited the principle of professionalism in discussing committees and their legislative work: it was considered proper for members to treat committee work as the domain of serious, professional, nonpolitical legislative business and to leave their political and factional passions for other venues. The regularity with which this axiom has been emphasized by parliamentarians in the union, RSFSR, and post-1993 parliaments suggests that members do indeed operate with it as a working norm. Moreover, a few committees were heavily tilted toward a particular partisan or sectoral interest. The most conspicuous example was that of the Committee on Agricultural Policy, which was largely a legislative extension service of the agrarian deputy group.

Once introduced, draft laws were referred by the Presidium to committees according to jurisdiction. Committees were influential sources of initiative. They could hold hearings, launch investigations and studies, form working groups to draft legislation and recruit outside experts to participate in such groups, actively push legislation that they wanted to adopt, or bottle up legislation that their members opposed. There were no provisions in the rules to force an unwilling committee to report out a piece of legislation. Because the Presidium worked as a committee of committee chairs, the Presidium was normally reluctant to upset the working relations among its members by violating the gatekeeping powers of a committee. Because there were always more legislative items ready to be scheduled than there was time to consider them, a committee chairman's stated judgment about a a bill's readiness to be considered on the floor was generally the operating criterion members used in deciding whether and when to schedule a bill for floor debate. Committee chairs and members considered themselves rushed and overworked, in view of their heavy workload and the critical conditions in the country, but the deputies' reluctance to streamline their operating procedures meant that work continued to accumulate faster than it could be completed.

Committees worked to build consensus for the legislative measures they sponsored. Within committees, chairs tended to seek consensus among their members rather than making decisions by majority vote. They also worked to ensure that the opinion of other committees and of the factions was brought to bear on each piece of legislation that they considered. Highly divisive measures tended to remain in the committee until and unless substantial agreement could be found. A bill was only brought to a vote in the first reading once the committee believed that it had sufficient support to warrant further work. The vote in first reading was a vote to accept the bill *za osnovu,* meaning to take the bill "as the basis" for further work. Once passed in first reading, the item returned to the sponsoring committee and deputies submitted proposals to the committee for revision. Once the committee had sifted through the proposed changes, agreeing to accept some and reject others, the committee reported it out again and the Presidium scheduled it for a vote on the floor in the second reading. It was the second reading that passed the bill into law. The 1990–93 Russian parliament, unlike the union parliament and unlike the State Duma, dispensed with a third reading although sometimes the deputies discussed whether to add this stage as well. The steps of the basic legislative process are outlined in table 5.3.

Before both the first and second readings, a complex process of consultation took place. Even to submit a bill, the rules specified that certain criteria be met: the bill's authors had to possess the "right of legislative initiative" and the authors were required to submit an accompanying statement justifying the bill, laying out its purposes, giving a detailed description of the tasks it sets, outlining the legislative principles it includes and their relation to current legislation, forecasting anticipated social and economic consequences, listing the persons who took part in drafting it, and explaining what costs it would entail.[21] The Presidium had the right to turn back any bill lacking such attachments (although in practice many bills were submitted that lacked them).[22] Around 40 percent of bills introduced were submitted by the executive branch, while nearly all the rest came from within committees.[23]

Bills judged unlikely to win a wide consensus tended to be screened out quickly, usually well before they reached the floor for a first reading. It made sense, therefore, for a deputy interested in pursuing a particular cause to work through his committee because no other parliamentary forum carried as much weight as the committee in dealings with other committees and on the floor. This point is especially important in understanding why factions played a relatively minor role in the legislative process. Factions did take stands on particu-

Table 5.3. The Legislative Process in the Russian Supreme Soviet

1. Introduction of a bill. Bill registered. Presidium approves it for further consideration or not. If not, it goes back to authors. If approved, Presidium examines it, may seek informal opinion from committees.
2. Assignment: Presidium assigns it to a lead (*golovnoi*) committee and legislation committee.
3. Lead committee report: recommends/not for first reading.
4. Legislation committee report: recommends/not for first reading.
5. Presidium discussion. Approval/not. If approval, Presidium schedules first reading; if not, sends it back to committee, forms special working group, or suspends action.
6. First reading. Approval/not. If not approved, bill returns to lead committee, which may decide to revise it and submit it again for first reading.
7. If approved, returns to lead committee for preparation for second reading. Lead committee receives proposals for revisions from committee members, other deputies, other committees, factions.
8. Lead committee decides which proposed amendments to recommend for approval and which to recommend for rejection; legislation committee may also review the proposed amendments.
9. Other committees review the lead committee's report and sign off on it to signify approval.
10. If other committees have serious disagreements, Presidium may form agreement commission to iron out intercommittee differences.
11. Presidium schedules bill for second reading.
12. Second reading: floor vote on amendments.
13. If in second reading, the two chambers vote differently (e.g., one fails to approve the bill), Presidium forms an agreement committee to reconcile differences.
14. If part or all of bill fails to pass on second reading, Presidium forms an agreement commission or working group to find compromise language.
15. Once passed, bill is "polished" by Editorial-Publishing Department and Juridical Department of Supreme Soviet apparatus to eliminate technical errors and smooth out style and approved by lead committee.
16. Bill goes to president for signature. (Note: This provision only applied once the presidency was created).
17. President signs bill, making it law, or returns it to parliament with his objections.

lar pieces of legislation, but only if they could command a majority of support in a committee or could they hope to undertake the process of building support on the part of other committees.

A consistent theme in deputies' accounts of the legislative process was the constant involvement of multiple committees in working up bills, a process that required very heavy reliance on staff experts and outside consultants, since each committee referred each bill that came before it to one of its members, who in turn referred it to specialists. The Presidium always designated a principal committee but its jurisdiction was never exclusive, and often the working group that the principal committee formed to work on the bill included deputies of other committees as well as hired experts. And the Legislation Committee screened all bills for technical quality.

Of course some bills generated serious policy disagreements, no matter how much effort was made to incorporate the views of opponents. In a committee, when all else failed, a vote was taken, and the majority viewpoint prevailed. But a committee that backed a particular bill did not simply wait to see how it would fare on the floor. One reason committees expended so much effort consulting with other committees was to determine how serious the opposition to a bill was so that they could revise the bill to meet the opposition's objections and prevent its defeat on the floor. A committee unhappy about the shape of a piece of legislation (or unhappy at having been left out of the deliberation process) was usually mollified when the Presidium or lead committee recruited its representatives to the working group that was marking up the bill.[24] Likewise, it could happen that a difference developed between the two chambers on a legislative matter, although this too was surprisingly infrequent. When it occurred, the Supreme Soviet chairman formed an agreement commission composed of an equal number of representatives of the two chambers to reach a compromise and report back to the Supreme Soviet. The same procedure was adopted when serious differences developed between two or more committees charged with managing the same bill.

It appears that to a great degree, in fact as well as in the deputies' ideal, partisan conflict was muted in handling legislation. Deputies widened support for legislation by depoliticizing issues. When serious conflicts arose, numerous mechanisms were used to ensure that conflict did not defeat a bill that had been taken as the basis for legislation. Conflict resolution procedures included extensive cross-committee consultation, reliance on the advice of policy experts, formation of new or expanded legislative working groups, and, to some degree, consultation within and among factions.

At the same time, the Russian parliament also followed its union predecessor by delegating responsibility for the most contentious issues to the president; but then like the union parliament it complained that the president was overstepping the bounds of his authority. In the process of considering legislation, far more support was built for most bills than was strictly necessary for their passage. Usually both the vote in first reading and the vote on final passage, which was taken section by section and sometimes on the whole bill after each amendment has been dealt with, were passed by such wide margins that they were equivalent to passage by acclamation. This was because committees took care to ensure that most contentious issues had been removed. As a result, many bills either turned into declarations of good intentions ("slogans," the representative of a major business association called them) or were internally self-contradictory.

The consequence of vague legislative language was to perpetuate the the profusion of regulations promulgated by administrative agencies specifying how a law was to be applied. The consultative, consensual style of lawmaking helps explain the toothlessness of so much of the legislation that passed: many laws were depoliticized during the consensus-building process as divisive provisions were replaced with anodyne language and specific, binding statements of right and obligation replaced with statements of desired outcomes and legislative intent. Although the insufficiency of resources, including information, through which the legislature could enforce bureaucratic compliance with its will was certainly a problem, the character of the laws themselves also contributed to the inability of the legislature to cope with the deepening crisis in Russia. This character reflected the rules and practices that governed the legislative process.

These consensus-building procedures also made lawmaking extremely time-intensive. Deputies found it easier to pass declarations and resolutions, where the stakes were lower and the thresholds for passage more relaxed. From May to November 1992, for instance, the Supreme Soviet passed only 53 laws but 268 decrees (*postanovleniia*), and its chambers passed another 71. In its final scssion—January to July 1993—the Supreme Soviet passed 98 laws and 104 decrees.[25]

Although I have emphasized the many obstacles to effective legislative work in the Russian Supreme Soviet, including the tendency to water down bills in the course of building broad support for them, the delegation of power to the Presidium and the president, and the preoccupation of parliament with constitutional crisis, we should not leave this phase of parliamentary evolution without taking note of the serious legislative accomplishments of the Supreme Soviet in 1990–93. It passed laws regulating a number of entirely new spheres of economic and political activity as a result of the transition from the Soviet state planning system. Among these were laws on taxation and budget formation, privatization and property relations, banking, bankruptcy, and land relations. Other legislation reformed regional government and the state's territorial-administrative structure. Perhaps of still greater importance were the laws reforming the justice system, including the law creating the Constitutional Court and the legislation transforming the old system of state arbitration (*gosarbitrazh*) into a new system of courts for commercial disputes (*arbitrazhnye sudy*). The Supreme Soviet also passed legislation on social welfare, creating a mandatory medical insurance system, as well as on civil liberties, including a law guaranteeing freedom of religious practice. Experts found fault with much of this legislation. The scope of the legislative record of the Supreme Soviet suggests, nonetheless, that the deputies took their lawmaking responsibilities seriously and used the institutional resources at hand to fulfill them.

THE PRESIDIUM

Under the Russian parliament's Standing Rules, the Presidium consisted of the chairman of the Supreme Soviet, the first deputy chairman, three deputy chairmen, the chairmen of the two chambers, and the chairmen of the joint standing committees of the Supreme Soviet and the standing commissions of each chamber—some thirty-five members altogether (see table 3.6). Part of the Presidium's great power stemmed from the fact that it managed both chambers of the Supreme Soviet as well as the joint sessions of the Supreme Soviet and the congresses. It was the central coordinating body for the entire legislative system. It assigned legislation to committees; planned the agenda for the Supreme Soviet, its two chambers, and the parent congress; oversaw the sizable staff machinery of the Supreme Soviet; managed the extensive physical resources of the Supreme Soviet (which included, besides the White House itself, apartment buildings and dachas, a large car park, and such administrative support services as the parliamentary library and the computer center); and issued orders and policy decisions in its own name. The Presidium was headed by the chairman of the Supreme Soviet. This position was filled by Boris Yeltsin until he became president, then, after the Fifth Congress in October-November 1991, by Ruslan Khasbulatov. Khasbulatov had in effect been acting chairman for most of the time since Yeltsin had held the post of chairman.[26]

Developing the legislative agenda was one of the principal tasks of the Presidium. The floor had the power to reject, accept, or alter the proposed agenda by a majority vote of the members of each chamber. The Presidium was both a forum where differences about legislative priorities were thrashed out and a governing authority over the Supreme Soviet. As in the new union parliament, the Presidium dominated agenda setting by virtue of the fact that it served as a committee of committees. The chairmen of the four commissions of each chamber and the twenty committees of the Supreme Soviet as a whole were members. The chairs thus were the main channel of communication between the body of deputies and the leadership. Therefore when the committee chairs could reach agreement on the calendar and agenda, the Presidium had considerable power to steer the chamber. It worked rather like a parliamentary government where cabinet ministers voice the particular interests of their respective organizations before their peers and in turn relay the collective authority of the cabinet to their departments. And as in cabinet government, the chairman had a great deal of opportunity to steer the discussion and influence its outcome. In the Russian parliament, as in the union-level system, when the first chairman of the Supreme Soviet chose to become the country's president and chief executive, his first deputy chairman moved out from under his former boss's shadow to become a strong and independent figure in his own right, building his personal power base on the power of the parliament as an institution.

In response to objections from deputies about the excessive power of the Presidium, the leaders argued that a strong Presidium was required in view of the huge workload it faced. The volume of legislative business sent up by committees required a great deal of coordination and organization so that the parliament could act, and to prepare for each day's session. As Sergei Filatov explained during floor debate: "The Presidium strongly filters [*fil'truet*] all the documentation required for a session of the Supreme Soviet."[27]

Across a wide spectrum of political opinion, deputies resented the power of the Presidium and disliked Khasbulatov in particular. But the deputies had no other means for coordinating their work than the Presidium and chairman, and the powers of the Presidium and the chairman were never curtailed throughout the 1990–93 period. Interviewed deputies both of the left and right were equally vehement in their view that the Presidium had usurped the rightful powers of parliament, and each group thought that the Presidium served the interests of the other. Over and over, deputies called for strengthening the role of the individual chambers at the expense of the power of the Presidium, as did the deputies in the Supreme Soviet of the USSR. Indeed, Khasbulatov and Filatov themselves repeatedly urged the deputies to do the main work of deliberation on laws in the separate chambers, and then to convene for joint sessions simply to ratify the chambers' efforts. In fact, at one point, Khasbulatov went so far as to comment that ideally, the first reading of all bills should be done in the separate chambers and the second reading at joint sessions. But move the second reading along more quickly, he urged the deputies, and skip unnecessary discussions. Why repeat debate held in the chambers? Let the chambers examine bills thoroughly, so that the second reading takes only half an hour.[28]

Well into the Yeltsin period, the Presidium acted as the equivalent of a collective chief executive. It issued decrees (*postanovleniia*) with policy consequences, as when it granted tax exemptions to regions or firms. In some cases it issued decisions jointly with the Council of Ministers, such as a decision in March 1991 providing for the acquisition of farmland by private citizens and one in May 1991 introducing inflation-based price indexes and subsidies on products of the agro-industrial complex. In February 1992, the Presidium expanded the assets under its direct control when it passed a confidential decree simply appropriating for its own use all the property formerly belonging to the Central Committee of the Communist Party of the Soviet Union, the Supreme Soviet of the USSR, and the Council of Ministers of the USSR.[29]

Both under Yeltsin and Khasbulatov, the Presidium routinely approved requests to create free economic zones in particular territories, a decision effectively freeing the government of that jurisdiction from paying taxes to the central government. Yeltsin opposed efforts to enact a law regulating how such zones were to be formed, perhaps because a law would have tied his hands by requiring Supreme Soviet approval. Thus major policy decisions sometimes bypassed the Supreme Soviet and were enacted by the Presidium alone or the Presidium in conjunction with the government. The Presidium continued to serve as a site for decisions allocating special distributive benefits to favored bureaucratic interests. This patronage power was a resource that successive chairs of the parliament were loath to relinquish. The chairman could also reward friendly committee chairs this way, allocating parliamentary funds for their constituency interests.[30]

Some idea of the volume of decisions that the Presidum and its chairman made on their own authority is suggested by the fact that over the period from May to November 1992, a period during which the Supreme Soviet produced more than one thousand official acts, only 53 were laws. Fully two-thirds (671 of 1,073) were orders and decrees of the Presidium and its chairman, including 390 decrees of the Presidium (both *postanovleniia* and *ukazy*) and 281 orders (*rasporizheniia*) of the chairman and his deputies.[31]

Over 1992 and 1993, as drafts of a new constitution were circulated and discussed, parliamentarians debated how a future parliament could be governed. Many sought a way to avoid creating a Presidium again, and it was generally taken for granted that the bifurcation of a large, part-time congress and smaller Supreme Soviet would not be repeated. But members had a hard time imagining how to steer parliament without some presidiumlike body because they had no other way of formulating agenda items for legislative business. The challenge was to make the Presidium accountable to the deputies and prevent it from becoming, once again, all powerful. Most deputies accepted that one solution to the problem was to ensure that the future parliament would be bicameral in fact, and that each chamber would govern itself. In interviews, some deputies went further and predicted that some body like the Council of Faction, composed of the leaders of the political factions, would replace the Presidium as the governing body in the future parliament.

GROUPS, FACTIONS, AND BLOCS

In contrast to their union-level predecessors, the RSFSR deputies entered the new parliament with much more sharply articulated proto-partisan affiliations rooted in the 1990 elections. One reason was that the spring 1990 races in the Russian Republic had been organized by partylike movements and more deputies entered the RSFSR parliament with factional affiliations. A coalition of radical democrats had formed to compete in both republic level elections as well as races for lower soviets. Another was that the experience of group activity in the union parliament enabled political activists to transfer the knowledge about parliamentary organization and strategy to their ideological counterparts in the Russian parliament. Perhaps most important was the fact that once the democrats succeeded in gaining Boris Yeltsin's election as chairman of the Supreme Soviet, parliamentary governance was taken over by a team of outsiders with a political agenda rather than remaining in the hands of the former staff, whom the democrats regarded as agents of the party-state bureaucracy. Yeltsin and his associates attempted to seize control of the levers of power within the parliament, granting greater rights for organized deputies' groups as part of their strategy for asserting political control over decision making. As radical democrats organized to challenge the apparat's control over parliamentary organization, the communists countered by forming their own factions. A system of groups and factions thus formed much earlier in the Russian parliament than it had in the union parliament, held together by the mutual rivalry of faction leaders and their common interest in expanding the rights of parliamentary factions.

Initial Rules Changes

Even before the congress convened, the parliamentary staff drafted a provisional set of Standing Orders intended to accommodate a wider definition of deputy group activity; this was undoubtedly prompted by the changes that the union parliament had made in its rules so as to provide for political and other nonterritorial deputy groups. Article 6 of the provisional Standing Orders of the RSFSR Congress of People's Deputies, like the union congress rules, provided that *both* territorial *and* nonterritorial groups were permitted and set a threshold of fifty for the minimum number of deputies required to register as an officially recognized group. (An exemption for groups representing non-populous ethnic minorities was added; such groups did not need to meet a minimum size threshold.) Registered groups were entitled to have the Presidium distribute their materials among the deputies and could publish their programs in the mass media. Moreover, the Russian congress's rules significantly expanded the rights of groups by granting them the same rights as those enjoyed by individual deputies in addressing inquiries (*zaprosy*) to government officials and other organizations. Groups also were to enjoy certain floor privileges: a registered group could demand to speak on an issue even after debate ended so long as this demand was supported by 20 percent of all deputies. Finally, the revised rules of the Russian parliament in 1990–91 eliminated the institution of the Council of Elders.

Ideological Polarization
in the Russian Congresses

From the start, decisions over the new Russian parliament's leadership, committee staffing, and agenda were the object of contention between organized political forces. The opposing sides had formed during the spring 1990 electoral campaign, as democratic reformers mobilized to fight the communist party-state bureaucracy. Therefore, when the new congress and Supreme Soviet convened, deputies' positions on questions of organization and agenda were polarized between radical democrats and conservatives identified with nationalist, statist, and communist values. Reformers wanted to place onto the Russian parliament's agenda such fundamental issues as property rights, privatization, political reform, and radical macroeconomic stabilization, which sharply divided democrats from communists. Votes on these issues revealed a clear axis of conflict. On other issues, to be sure, secondary alignments formed. Factor analysis of voting on some issues reveals a "centrist" position interested in preserving traditional universal entitlements but supporting some economic reform; another division appeared over the issue of creating a powerful executive presidency for the Russian Republic; another cleavage was apparent between those preferring greater uniformity and centralization within the Russian Republic and those advocating more rights for regions and republics within Russia; and finally, later in this period, a foreign policy division developed between those who supported restoration of the union, although not necessarily under communist party rule, and those preferring a "little Russia."[32] But the left-right cleavage was strongly felt throughout the 1990–93 period because it was so closely linked to the issue of presidential power.

One reason for this was that in the Russian parliament, the communist faction was more conservative from the start than its counterpart at the union level had been. This was because in the Russian congress, the communists were the parliamentary branch of the breakaway, ultraconservative Communist Party of the Russian Federation, whereas in the union congress the communists were divided between reformers and conservatives. The more disciplined communist faction in the republican parliament asserted its positions aggressively and effectively and stimulated the radical democrats to develop an effective organization to oppose them.

The voting blocs defined by the left-right axis were rather evenly matched for the first year or so of the parliament's existence. The Democratic Russia coalition could count on no more than around 40 percent of the votes, and a roughly similar number of deputies opposed them.[33] Neither side possessed a secure majority. At the beginning, democrats held a slight advantage because they were able to appeal to many conservative officials who favored greater autonomy for the republic in controlling the resources on RSFSR territory. I have argued that "bureaucratic nationalist" support for Yeltsin against Gorbachev and the union bureaucracy was an important factor in producing the narrow majority for him in the election to the chairmanship of the parliament (see chapter 4). The democrats possessed several resources that proved important: a radical ideological program that captured the support of the wave of popular discontent and resentment that had built up in society; a popular antiunion, anticenter program that identified greater autonomy for Russia within the union with the attractive prospects of material and political prosperity; a vigorous, popular leader in the person of Boris Yeltsin; and dedicated, energetic activists working behind the scenes.

The communist camp had a number of advantages as well, however, so long as it was united in opposition to radical economic and political reform. To the extent that they could control it, the centralized, staff-dominated organizational structure of the Supreme Soviet was a significant asset that could be used to block the initiatives of the antiestablishment democrats through its access to the process of preparation of options on such matters as chamber leaders, committee chairs and members, Supreme Soviet members, drafting the rules, and drafting legislation. Long-established links between the communist deputies and members of the parliament staff were also useful, and the communists filled parliamentary staff positions with individuals who had formerly worked in the CPSU Central Committee staff structures. Finally, the communists drew upon ties with deputies and officials who worked in soviets in the regions, sharing with them a growing antipathy to Boris Yeltsin's power and policies.

In this polarized environment, each side made use of its resources to seek organizational advantages but neither could count on a stable majority among the deputies at the First Congress. The democrats won a very important victory when Yeltsin was elected chairman, but the conservatives came out ahead in the election of members of the Supreme Soviet.[34] On several occasions early in the parliament's history, therefore, the two camps proposed power-sharing arrangements as a way of resolving paralyzing deadlocks, rather than adopting a winner-take-all, majoritarian principle. The rough equality in their relative strength made it reasonable for their leaders to agree on a parity rule rather than proportionality in distributing key positions between them.

From the start, then, bipolarity and factionalism characterized the Russian congresses. The ideological division took a partisan cast as coalitions of deputies, formed in the heat of the election campaign, fought for organizational advantages in the new parliament. Occasionally the leaders of opposing factions agreed to put aside their competition and to share power as a way of resolving or preventing procedural battles. Early on, organized factions fought over the basic organizational questions of selecting a chair and deputy chairs of the Supreme Soviet, electing deputies to serve in the two chambers of the Supreme Soviet, and selecting committee chairs and members.[35] On all of these matters, the democrats were unwilling to relinquish decision-making power to the bureaucratic apparatus inherited from the old regime, as had happened a year previously at the union parliament. It required some effort for the outsiders to wrest control of the parliament from the apparat, however.

Nonetheless, initial preparations for the First Congress were firmly controlled by the inherited staff of the Supreme Soviet.[36] Following traditional procedures, the parliamentary bureaucracy processed the documents that were to be taken up by the "preparatory commission," which was composed of deputies who had also been selected for this work by the apparat. Unwilling to ease the newly elected deputies' task of forming independent organizational structures, the apparat even refused to distribute a list of newly elected deputies with their telephone numbers. However, the blocs that had formed to contest the elections, Democratic Russia and the Communists of Russia, held their own organizational meetings before the congress convened. On March 31 and April 1, around 200 newly elected RSFSR deputies who were affiliated with Democratic Russia met to form a parliamentary bloc; about 190 deputies agreed to join. They formed into several working groups that drafted organizational and legislative proposals to submit to the congress for its first meeting, scheduled for May 16; their most important proposal was the nomination of Yeltsin for the chairmanship. The Communists of Russia also met, supported by elements of the Central Committee of the CPSU.

In contrast to the proceedings of the union congress the previous year, at the Russian congress the democratic reformers succeeded in winning several early procedural and substantive victories, notably Yeltsin's election to the chairmanship. After winning, Yeltsin formed a conciliation commission, inviting each group to delegate two representatives to meet with him and discuss candidacies for deputy chairs of the Supreme Soviet: some 200 people gathered.[37] The commission produced a package slate of candidates that included both communists and democrats and reflected an evident balancing strategy.[38] The careful ticket-balancing proposals of the commission, however, were not supported on the floor. The candidates it proposed often failed to receive the necessary minimum number of votes, even those who ran as the only candidate nominated for a post.

Factional conflict also surrounded the election of members to the Supreme Soviet. The analogous issue at the union level the previous year had been handled by allowing territorial delegations to determine their own slates of candidates for the two chambers. Although territorial delegations were still given the right to propose slates of candidates for each chamber, now intense political competition surrounded the nomination of candidates and the voting on the floor. Each camp attempted to agree on its positions about whom to nominate and whom to support. The communists were generally more effective at reaching and adhering to a group position. They drew up lists of deputies whom they would support for election to the Supreme Soviet and deputies they opposed. The research done by the opposing political teams enabled deputies to coordinate their voting. But the leaders of the opposing camps could not always deliver the votes of their followers on the floor; some communist deputies refused to vote for some of the radical democrats from Moscow and Leningrad. Many seats therefore remained vacant even after several rounds of voting. Even when the leaders agreed to present slates with no more candidates than there were seats in the Supreme Soviet, some candidates failed to win election for want of a sufficient number of votes. Factional conflict was able to produce mutual vetoes more effectively than successful package deals.

As a result of the protracted impasse, the leaders of the communist and democratic factions met and agreed to present a unified, uncontested slate of candidates for election to the Supreme Soviet. Yet even then, the deputies often did not go along with their leaders and refused to support some nominations. Democratic Russia, unable to win sufficient numbers of votes for some of their candidates, had to find candidates more acceptable to the communists.[39] The distance between reformers and communists was too great, and voting discipline too slight, for leadership pacts to work well. Yet it is of considerable significance that from the beginning of the Russian transitional parliament, faction leaders agreed on an informal rule of power sharing through parity representation of different political forces in internal bodies as a way of generating stable agreements.

At the same time, Yeltsin and his supporters used the powers of the chairmanship to the advantage of the democratic camp as much as possible. In particular, Yeltsin's team proposed a set of committee chairs who were proreform. They evaluated the voting records of deputies to figure out who their friends and foes were by using methods of vote analysis worked out by a research team of democratic activists associated with Academician Sakharov in the union congress. A group of analysts headed by the late Alexander Sobyanin, working under the direction of Gennadii Burbulis, who headed Yeltsin's advisory council, devised a scoring system to assess support for and opposition to Yeltsin and reform based on the analysis of roll-call voting in the congress. This group enabled Yeltsin to nominate moderate democrats for committee chairs who could be confirmed in floor voting, and to give the committees a slightly proreform majority. According to the Sobyanin group's rating system, where a score of +100 indicated a voting record that took the proreform, pro-Yeltsin side 100 percent of the time in a selected set of bellwether votes, and a score of −100 denoted a voting record that took the diametrically opposed positions, the average score of Supreme Soviet committee chairs was +30 (data from March 1991), and the average committee member's score was +23. Meanwhile the average Sobyanin score for all deputies was +7 at the First Congress, and +3.5 and +4.0 at the Second and Third Congresses.[40] Yeltsin therefore used the advantages of chairmanship to gain some political leverage in running the parliament, but his control was tenuous, in part because his supporters did not have a stable majority and he had to cede some organizational power to his opponents.

We should not overemphasize the cohesion of the political groups in the new parliament. Neither democrats nor communists possessed strong levers to enforce voting discipline. But neither camp had a majority. For both reasons, therefore, group leaders stood to benefit from negotiated power-sharing arrangements among organized groups when they lacked the means to swing clear majorities. Apart from the benefit such arrangements conferred by ensuring political representation for minority interests, they also had the advantage of giving group leaders leverage to strengthen group discipline.

Interest Groups

Explaining how new institutional arrangements come into being requires an account both of the demand side and the supply side. In this case the establishment of recognized, organized groups, and later factions, was a significant innovation in the way Russia's parliament operated. It is not enough to say simply that the demand—the ideological polarization of the deputies produced by the 1990 elections and the struggles over reform—produced corresponding organizational forms. For one thing, such an explanation would fail to explain the immediate fragmentation of groups once the congress convened. Likewise political leaders' interest in possessing instruments to attract and hold together fellow partisans would not suffice to explain the growing factionalism in the Russian parliament because by themselves, the political leaders lacked the means to change the rules to their benefit. Thus we need to consider the way the new arrangements were supplied as well. Earlier I suggested that the early factional forms in the union parliament represented modifications of the old "territorial delegation" and "CPSU group" features of the pre-Gorbachev Supreme Soviet that were adapted to serve the goals of the newly elected democratic radicals, the Baltic nationalists, the agrarian lobby, and other organized interests. I observed as well that Anatolii Luk'ianov had skillfully proposed rules changes to accommodate these and other groups in such a way as to strengthen his own hand in the parliament.

In a similar way, the supply problem in the Russian setting was partly solved by Boris Yeltsin's strategy of encouraging groups to form and represent coherent interests. Again, the supply of institutions to meet a demand took the form of a clear exchange of rights: Yeltsin traded an agreement to grant representative rights to groups in return for their political support and the information that groups could provide him about the political temper of the deputies.

The point also illustrates another aspect of the process by which new institutions are adopted. The development of groups and factions was strongly affected by the rules of the game, both constitutional and parliamentary. The first set a ceiling on the growth of partisanship, the other put a floor under it. The constitution limited parliament's influence over government, while parliament's Standing Orders set the minimum threshold number of deputies that had to be registered as members before a group could gain recognition at fifty. If there were no direct link between a government's mandate and its support in parliament, then there was little point for deputies in forming into party teams and trying to form a majority coalition. In contrast, if deputies found it more advantageous to be a member of a registered group than not to be a member, groups were likely to be able to recruit at least the minimum number of deputies required for registration.

These considerations help to explain the sequence of rules changes concerning group rights in the Russian parliament. Although ideological polarization characterized the early battles over the chairmanship, agenda, and election of the members of the Supreme Soviet, with the opposing camps organizing behind the Democratic Russia and Communists of Russia factions, the new Russian deputies quickly formed a variety of other organized groups that reflected more particular interests. At the same time, the big polarized blocs, the communists and democrats, split up into multiple small political groups. Although the incentives to remain allied, such as might have existed if a majority coalition could form the government, were weak or nonexistent, the inducement of possessing just enough members to enjoy procedural rights sufficed to motivate smaller groups to coalesce.

The greater rights for groups and factions in the Russian parliament by comparison with the union parliament gave deputies in the Russian parliament stronger incentives to affiliate. By the end of April 1992, 850 of 1,045 elected Russian deputies (81 percent) were registered in deputy groups of a political type, that is, factions. Of 348 full-time deputies in the Supreme Soviet (including those who were formally members of the Supreme Soviet as well as those working in it full time), 298 were members of factions (86 percent).[41] In comparison, in the union parliament, as of the end of 1990, only two-thirds of all deputies were members of any group, and just half belonged to political groups.[42]

As chairman, Boris Yeltsin encouraged the formation of regional caucuses and occupational and professional groups. As noted above, after he was elected chairman, he created an ad hoc commission formed of representatives of groups to nominate candidates for deputy chair of the Supreme Soviet. Similarly, on the eve of the Second Congress (November–December 1990), Yeltsin convened group representatives to discuss the congress's agenda. At this meeting some deputies urged Yeltsin to put the organization of the agenda onto a more strictly political footing and to give greater weight to political groups or factions in reaching agreements about the agenda. This proposal was supported by several politically oriented groups, including the communists and the Radical Democrats. A centrist deputy, Vladimir Novikov, took it upon himself to call the joint meetings of the political groups.[43] Eventually he created an organized form to coordinate the work of the factions, called the Council of Factions.

At the opening of the First Congress in May 1990, twenty-four groups registered. They included seven regional groups, eight occupational or sectoral groups, four cause-oriented groups, a generational group, and three political groups (see table 5.4).[44] Soon, however, the large political groups splintered. Although Democratic Russia and the Communists of Russia remained the two largest factions at the First Congress, by early June some thirty-two deputies' groups in all had registered. These included interest-based caucuses and territorial groups, as well as more explicitly ideological groups. Ideological differences within the major camps pushed members to differentiate themselves organizationally. But the rules also influenced the way groups formed, making it desirable for smaller groups to recruit members until they could reach the threshold of fifty, while tempting ambitious leaders of wings of oversize groups to break off and form their own groups. Much as was the case at the union level, the fact that weak benefits accrued to groups that could hold fifty members together, but that there were no additional marginal benefits from having more members, produced an incentive for organizational entrepreneurs to form groups with the bare number of members. It would certainly have been in the interest of the leaders of such groups to change the rules further to give political factions more rights within the parliament (for instance, by introducing a rule of exclusive membership, such that a deputy could only be a member of one group) as a way to increase their own leverage over their members, but a rules change required both agreement among the group leaders and the cooperation of the presidium leadership. Therefore at the Third Congress, along with a few oversize politically oriented groups, there were some whose membership hovered tellingly close to the threshold of fifty (see table 5.5). Multiple membership was permitted until the rules change of October 1991.

Context, Rules, and the Formation of Factions

Two events in 1991 ended the trend toward fragmentation of deputies' groups in the Russian parliament and encouraged political forces to coalesce. One was

Table 5.4. Registered Deputies' Groups at First RSFSR Congress of People's Deputies, as of May 25, 1990

Group	Number of Members
Generational	
Smena	51
Sectoral and Occupational	
Food and Health (later Agrarian)	183
Questions of Upbringing, Education, Science, and Culture	71
Medical Employees	97
Federation of Independent Trade Unions	89
Armed Forces, KGB, and Reserve Officers	55
Chernobyl'	69
Workers-Peasants Union	72
Judicial Employees	65
Employees of Transport, Communications, and Information Services	51
Specialists on the Economy and Management	61
Political	
Communists of Russia	355
Nonparty Deputies [i.e., non-CPSU]	61
Democratic Russia	66
Cause	
Glasnost'	51
For Returning Citizenship to Solzhenisyn	53
Ecology	83
For the Problems of Refugees and Defense of the Rights of Russian Countrymen	51
Regional	
Deputies from Autonomous Republics	83
North	83
Urals deputy group	65
Moscow deputy group	64
Far East and Trans-Baikal	62
Central Russia	126

the breakup of the Soviet Union with its far-reaching ramifications. The other was the change in the congress's rules in October 1991, which encouraged deputies to affiliate with political groups, or factions, and factions to join together in blocs.[45] As noted in chapter 4, Khasbulatov's election to the chairmanship coincided, intriguingly, with the congress's approval of emergency

Table 5.5. Political Groups at the Third RSFSR Congress of People's Deputies, April 1, 1991

Group	Number of Members
Agrarian Union	215
Nonparty Deputies	61
Democratic Russia	205
Communists for Democracy	103
Communists of Russia	216
Left Center	80
United Faction of Social-Democrats and Republicans	52
Fatherland	145
Industrial Union	158
Radical Democrats	54
Russian Union	51
Russia	102
Smena	51
From the Republic and National-Territorial Units of the RFSFR	83

decree powers for President Yeltsin and a rules change in the congress that elevated the status of political factions.

In chapter 4, I suggested that Khasbulatov succeeded in winning election to the post of chairman by offering a bargain, tacit or explicit, to the faction leaders: in return for their support, he would grant them additional rights within the parliament. To what degree Khasbulatov himself constructed this deal is not known. But as a result of the rules change, faction leaders gained new leverage over their members through the rule that members could only belong to one faction, and collectively, the faction leaders would be given the opportunity to exercise their influence through a new structure, the Council of Factions.

The new rules that went into effect at the end of October 1991 led to changes in the relations between deputies and their groups and factions. The rules now distinguished among three categories of deputies' associations: ordinary deputy groups, factions, and blocs. Groups were organized along territorial, occupational, or other nonpolitical principles, whereas factions were created on a political basis. Factions were further allowed to coalesce into blocs. Groups were still required to have fifty members unless they were organized on behalf of a nonpopulous ethnic group. Factions also had to have fifty members, but, most significant, a deputy could be a member of only one faction. This change gave leaders additional leverage over their members because it raised slightly the costs and benefits of membership. Factions gained the right to delegate a representative to any body of the congress, and the rule further allowed the congress to determine whether an organ of the congress was to be formed on a parity basis or a proportional basis.[46] Already faction leaders were looking for ways to erase differences in relative influence arising from small differences in size, suggesting an agreement among faction leaders that they preferred to seek influence for themselves collectively rather than to organize for majority control.[47]

In turn, blocs were also recognized and given precedence in floor procedures over factions, much as factions took precedence over ordinary groups.[48] Representatives of blocs, fractions, and groups had priority right to recognition on floor for debate, but representatives of blocs were to have first priority, then representatives of fractions outside blocs, then representatives of groups and individual deputies.

The rules change had a substantial effect on group membership. Deputies left some groups in order to affiliate with a single faction. In turn, factions sought to increase their influence in decision making by forming blocs. In spring 1992, as Yeltsin's government of young reformers pursued the shock therapy program, two of the radical democratic factions, Democratic Russia and Radical Democrats, which supported the government, joined with four other groups in an alliance called "Coalition for Reforms" aimed at giving economic reform a base of political support in the parliament. The new coalition could not gain registration as a deputy bloc, because only two of the members of the coalition were recognized as factions. The coalition disintegrated over the course of the year.

Meantime, some new moderately proreform factions—the Nonparty Deputies, Left Center, and Free Russia—formed a bloc called "Democratic Center." The Democratic Russia and Radical Democrats factions did not join it. Probably Ruslan Khasbulatov took a hand in forming this Democratic Center bloc because it served two purposes for him: it isolated the radical democrats by positioning the bloc toward the center of spectrum, and it provided him with a bloc of support that he could use to play off against the more conservative forces in the congress. His partner in engineering this new alignment of blocs was Vladimir Novikov, leader of the Council of Factions. Novikov was a leader of the Nonparty Deputies (referring to the fact that they had not been CPSU members) and had helped create the bloc Democratic Center, which he also chaired.

Chairman Khasbulatov found it useful to turn to the Council of Factions when he needed help putting together politically difficult packages. An example was an episode in spring 1992. Hard-liners in the Supreme Soviet were threatening to vote no confidence in the Gaidar government;[49] democrats were threatening to retaliate by walking out and denying the Supreme Soviet a quorum. Khasbulatov's leadership was in jeopardy. Novikov then forged a cross-factional agreement among conservative, moderates, and democrats that resolved the deadlock, exacting promises from both sides that they would defer any no-confidence motion or walkout at least until the upcoming Seventh Congress in December 1992.[50] Both Khasbulatov's and Gaidar's positions remained secure for the time being. The agreement had the effect, presumably not unforeseen, of making both Khasbulatov and Gaidar dependent on Novikov's pivotal position as the chairman of the Council of Factions.

The Council of Factions never gained official recognition in the rules as an arm of parliament; it was a competitor with the committee chairmen for political influence. Generally it was active only at moments when Khasbulatov turned to it as a counterweight to opposition among the committee chairs. It arose because it served complementary interests: the leadership's desire for information and for a capacity to forge political agreements over contentious issues, and the interest on the part of faction leaders in gaining recognition for their status and the material rights and benefits that followed from recognition. A similar confluence of interests led to the gradual expansion of rights of organized political groups in the union-level congresses and Supreme Soviet. And much the same intersection of interests underlay the arrangement reached in 1993–94 through which the political factions won the right collectively to govern the Duma in return for their acceptance of a constitutional formula heavily tilted in favor of the president. At each point we can observe a reciprocity of interests at work between forces that were deeply divided over policy: the executive won support for autonomous power in exchange for granting institutional rights to political factions. At each point, the executive strengthened its own freedom of action by expanding the formal rights for factions and their leaders.

Factions and Blocs in the Parliament's Final Year

The rough balance between left and right that characterized the parliament's first year of existence shifted after Yeltsin left parliament. The effects of the radical economic reform program and the dissolution of the union drove many waverers into the arms of the communist-nationalist alliance. Khasbulatov sought to build up his own support base and replaced most of the liberal committee chairs with conservatives. Therefore, in the course of 1992, the bipolarity in parliamentary alignments remained sharp, and it continued to be defined by the opposing stances of the democratic and communist political factions. But the median position shifted substantially toward the communist-nationalist end of the spectrum as the number of deputies opposing Yeltsin and his policies burgeoned.

By fall 1992, factions were aligned symmetrically in three blocs, three factions to a bloc. The Bloc of Constructive Forces, with a moderate statist but not communist orientation, was composed of Industrial Union, Workers' Union, and Smena-New Policy.[51] The conservative alliance of communist and nationalist forces united in the Russian Unity Bloc, made up of Agrarian Union, Communists of Russia, and Russia. In early 1993 a further shift in alignments occurred. The Nonparty Deputies recruited some new members and formed the faction Rodina. A new faction was registered, called "Accord for the Sake of Progress," aimed, according to its leaders, at occupying the political space between the centrist blocs and the radical democratic forces. The Workers' Union faction united with the Reforms without Shock group. The Left Center faction allied with the group Cooperation. By March 1993, the factions and their bloc affiliations were as indicated by table 5.6. An ideological position score based on a dimensional analysis of electronically recorded votes at the Seventh, Eighth, and Ninth Congresses is also listed in the table.[52]

Note that the groups vary considerably in the degree to which members adhered to the faction position on this dimension. The communists' score is at the anti-Yeltsin extreme, with a standard deviation of only .3. The Radical Democrats faction, at the other end of the spectrum, has almost as low a standard deviation. Deputies who are not members of any faction have a mean factor score of .059 and a standard deviation of .8, higher than nearly any faction. Thus factions whose political positions are farthest from the mean tended to be more cohesive, a finding we observed among the union deputies as well.

Intrafactional and Interfactional Agreement

Factions articulated the opposing political positions of deputies and, given the high polarization of positions on the major issues before the parliament, factions were reasonably cohesive with respect to the members' ideological preferences in the left-right axis. From time to time, the faction system was also able to produce compromises or logrolls that enabled parliament to overcome a collective choice problem. For both leaders and rank-and-file deputies, political

Table 5.6. Factions and Blocs in the RSFSR Congress, as of March 1, 1993

Bloc or Faction	Number of Members	Mean Ideology Score (standard deviation)
Bloc Russian Unity	303	
Agrarian Union	130	−.80 (.53)
Communists of Russia	67	−1.05 (.30)
Fatherland	51	−.81 (.55)
Russia	55	−.86 (.38)
Bloc of Constructive Forces	157	
Smena–New Policy	53	−.16 (.61)
Industrial Union	51	−.40 (.66)
Workers' Union–Reforms without Shock	53	−.02 (.62)
Democratic Center	165	
Left Center–Cooperation	61	.72 (.70)
Free Russia	54	.33 (.81)
Sovereignty and Equality	50	−.26 (.63)
Outside the blocs		
Democratic Russia	48	1.60 (.42)
Radical Democrats	50	1.49 (.32)
Accord for the Sake of Progress	54	1.47 (.44)
Motherland	57	.17 (.72)

factions supplied valuable information as well as a capacity to broker agreements that could win majority support on the floor. In fact, these properties of factions have repeatedly been cited in interviews with deputies in all three parliaments during this decade. Committee chairs and others interested in building support for a measure sounded out faction leaders to determine its chances of passage and turned to them as well to help locate compromises that would enable it to win a majority.

The formalization of faction rights in the interim Russian parliament seems to have had some effect in increasing the legislature's ability to aggregate preferences in a highly polarized environment. Deputies themselves entered the Russian parliament with a more widely held and sharply articulated factional orientation than their union parliament counterparts had done one year before, and they sought recognition for factional groups in the Standing Orders. As was the case in the union-level parliament, however, those deputies who were members of political factions had a stronger interest in using the parliament to serve their political interests, including lawmaking and reelection. This tendency was distinctly more pronounced among members of radical democratic factions, members of which were far more likely to want to seek reelection.[53] As at the union level, it was the democrats who saw parliament as an instrument of political change, and who therefore pressed for structural changes that would allow deputies to be active and effective as legislators. Their greater strength as parliament convened and Yeltsin's support for factionalism produced a series of rules changes that encouraged factional membership and the differentiation of political factions from ordinary interest groups. As Colton observed of this process, "to the extent that the liberal groups have been the embryos of modern parties in the post-USSR, the implication is that one key to professionalization of *legislative* careers will be professionalization of *political* careers."[54]

In turn, the existence of a system of factions, and of the Council on Factions, sometimes allowed deputies to reach negotiated agreements on political issues, preventing the paralysis of parliamentary decision making through the mutual vetoes of the democrats and communists. But we should not overestimate the importance of organized factionalism at this point. The stakes in the power struggle were too high for the opposing camps to confine their power struggle to parliamentary politics. On both sides, many deputies were perfectly willing to use extraconstitutional means to settle their scores. By early 1993, democratic factions were boycotting the Council of Factions in protest against its manipulation by the opposition. When Yeltsin met with the democratic factions at the time of the Eighth Congress (March 1993), deputies urged him to dissolve soviets throughout the country and establish direct presidential rule.[55] At the same time, the opposition had formed an alliance with the extraparliamentary, antidemocratic National Salvation Front. The Council of Factions system could succeed only as long as the camps were still committed to playing by the constitutional rules.

SUMMING UP

Parliamentary structure and process in the Russian congress and Supreme Soviet combined inherited features of the old, pre-Gorbachev system with the new constitutional elements introduced under Gorbachev. The political battles between Russia and the union, and later between parliament and president, also strongly influenced parliamentary processes. The first enabled Yeltsin to win some important early victories over staffing and organization and to establish a strong presidency, and the latter prompted Khasbulatov to create his own, opposition-oriented political base in the parliament with which to contest Yeltsin's presidential prerogatives. Constitutional deadlock followed.

Still, despite the constitutional crisis, the deputies in the Russian parliament got a great deal done. They retained the highly consultative, collegial style of lawmaking that the old Supreme Soviet had used but adjusted it by including a wider range of interests, including, informally, political factions. As was the case at the union level, the Presidium became both more powerful and more representative than it had been in the old days. Operating as a committee on committees, it dominated the agenda-setting process. Through the Presidium's agenda-setting power, committee chairmen could sometimes achieve their legislative purposes, and through them, so could rank-and-file deputies. In order to build consensus and retain their support, the Supreme Soviet chairman had to know when to accommodate committee chairs' demands. But the chairman's powers of patronage and his ability to manipulate floor proceedings allowed him, as time passed, to stack the committees with chairs who supported him.

Consequently, despite these innovations in parliamentary institutions, there were severe limits on deputies' ability to use parliament to serve their collective interests, and deputies were too deeply divided to be able to enact any major organizational changes. Parliament could not solve the problem of controlling a runaway chairman. Having surrendered sweeping legislative powers to the president, their ability to set policy on major issues was limited. Pro-Yeltsin deputies defected from parliament or fought from within to weaken it, while anti-Yeltsin deputies opposed all constitutional reforms acceptable to Yeltsin. Likewise the ad hoc consensus-building processes managed by committees were relatively inefficient mechanisms for aggregating the preferences of deputies over legislation; a standing partisan majority would have been able to construct majorities over a much broader range of issues and thus accomplish much more legislative business. These and other organizational features of both the union and Russian Supreme Soviets reflected the premise that policy making could be separated from legislative decision making as it had been in the Soviet era.

But such an institutional framework worked reasonably well only when members were willing to check their politics at the door when they went to work in committees and other lawmaking arenas of the parliament. In a world in which legislation mattered for policy, political differences could not be separated from legislative procedures so neatly. Every choice the deputies made implied the choice of a policy preference, including the selection of a chairman; agreement over the priority of one set of laws over another; the selection of members for the chambers and committees; the rules regarding property rights, privatization, land, banking, collective bargaining, taxation, and spending; and the balance of power between president and parliament. Both the inherited norms of lawmaking and the inherited institutional arrangements acted to eliminate the element of political choice from lawmaking.

The centralized, Presidium- and staff-dominated organizational structure that Russian deputies had at their disposal was poorly suited to identifying plausible policy alternatives. The parliamentary staff was uncertain in its loyalty and inconstant as an agent of the committees and deputies who were nominally its principals. (The parliament's chairman seems to have been the actual principal for the staff.) The committees and committee chairs worked well to aggregate preferences in their policy domains, but they were dependent on information provided by other committee chairs and by faction leaders about political and policy considerations outside their jurisdictions. Factions were another instrument through which agreements could be constructed on legislative business and played a key part at several junctures, but factions had too few resources for maintaining discipline among their members for their leaders' backroom deals and prevote nose counts to be entirely authoritative.

Still, there is evidence that factions came to play a larger role in parliamentary decision making with time as a consequence of a series of explicit and implicit bargains struck between executive leaders and heads of organized deputy groups. As factions acquired more standing, faction leaders collectively gained greater influence in building political support for package agreements over both institutional and policy issue problems. Their ability collectively to deliver political support to leaders in time of need made it more advantageous for the leadership to expand their institutional rights further. Several times, in fact, a chairman in search of a political base or a compromise agreement that would resolve an impasse turned to the faction leaders to hammer out a deal. The most significant example of this kind was the agreement among faction leaders in October 1991 that gained them greater rights and privileges while enabling parliament to break a logjam and elect Khasbulatov chairman. In turn Khasbulatov granted the Council of Factions various kinds of recognition, using it as a counterweight to the collective power of the committee chairs and to the hardline communist-nationalist opposition that was increasingly defining the parliament's position. Once the political center of gravity had shifted sufficiently far from the center point between Yeltsin and the opposition to render the Council of Factions useless, neither it nor any other structure could prevent the extremists from provoking Yeltsin to shut parliament down. The institutional innovations of the union and Russian interim parliaments did not dissolve with it, however. Rather, the precedent of a council of faction leaders was directly incorporated into the Standing Rules of the new parliament that formed in January 1994 and, under the name "Council of the Duma," became its central governing body.

Chapter 6 Framing
a New Constitution

The innovations to the USSR constitution during 1989–91 and to that of the RSFSR during 1990–93 took the form of amendments and accompanying legislation, but they did not involve the adoption of a new, fully consistent constitution. Within both the USSR and RSFSR parliaments, rules changes that recognized procedural rights for political factions represented a relaxation of the CPSU's former monopoly on power, but there were no corresponding innovations in the relations or powers of the two chambers of the Supreme Soviet: bicameralism remained entirely formal.

The confrontation between Yeltsin and his parliamentary opposition over the proper balance of legislative and executive power prevented an agreement on the text of a new constitution. The quieter but no less serious contest between the central government and Russia's regions was another obstacle. Just as a new constitution required resolution of the problem of executive-legislative power, so also did it require a decision on how to give federalism real institutional form. Examining the issues at stake in the effort to frame a new constitution requires us to link the struggle over economic reform and legislative-executive relations to the federalism issue of center-regional power.

THE CONSTITUTIONAL DEBATE, 1990–1993

Two Dimensions of Conflict

The design of the Federal Assembly did not spring fully formed from Yeltsin's pen like Athena from Zeus's brow. Most of its major features had been worked out in the course of three years of constitutional debate and deliberation within the political elite. Yeltsin had the final word on most of these issues, but not the only word. On the matters that were most contentious, he had his way. These were not necessarily the most important issues, however, in structuring the new parliament or shaping its relations with external actors. Several crucial principles, such as bicameralism and a mixed electoral system for the lower chamber, were widely accepted. Even the replacement of the Presidium as the instrument for governing the new lower chamber with a council of political factions was acceptable to a wide range of political leaders.

On other key issues there was deep disagreement. The most contentious points in the constitutional debate were the balance of power between president and parliament and the relation between the central government, ethnic republics, and regular territorial divisions of the state. Generally Yeltsin had his way on those points, adopting arrangements that he considered favorable to his political interests. Some matters, however, were not resolved by the new constitution but were left to future federal and constitutional legislation. There is no question about the fact that Yeltsin devised a constitution that would serve his institutional purposes and that he took action outside the old constitution to put the new one into effect. But he did so in a way that gave his opponents a reason to go along with the new arrangements and that made it unlikely that they would unite to overturn them.

Most discussions of the new constitutional structure have focused either on the contest between Yeltsin and the communist-nationalist opposition, based in the parliament, for control over the executive or on the problem of reconciling the competing interests of republics, ordinary regions, and the central government.[1] But the crucial point is that these struggles went on simultaneously, forming two cross-cutting dimensions of conflict with different stakes. One complex of issues revolved around the struggle for control over Russia's productive assets between the federal government and the regional and republic governments; the other concerned the degree to which private property and market relations should govern the economy. Left and right could agree on the desirability of a uniform federal legal order but fought over whether that order should be socialist or capitalist. Regional leaders took different sides on the left-right issue but united in demanding greater control over the assets on their territories at the expense of the central government. Both conflicts had immediate implications for the relative balance of power between president and parliament. The left opposition to Yeltsin defended parliamentary prerogatives against a president who demanded greater power to force through market-oriented reform. The regional leaders took advantage of the paralyzing impasse between the Supreme Soviet and president in 1992 and 1993 as Yeltsin and Khasbulatov bid for their support by offering concessions to them that strengthened regional autonomy. Therefore Yeltsin's violent suppression of the parliamentary rebels in October 1993 fortified his position in dealing with the regions and republics, both because it demonstrated his willingness to use force to preserve order and because regional leaders no longer had the opportunity to win leverage over the center by playing parliament off against president.[2]

These cleavages have been an enduring feature of Russia's political development in the transition era. They could be seen in the Gorbachev period when Gorbachev was unable to formulate a market-oriented reform program that eliminated central controls over production and exchange without conceding administrative autonomy to republics. The conflict over market reform divided democrats from conservatives, but each camp was itself divided by the conflict over the issue of central power vis-à-vis the republics. These dimensions were not aligned; indeed they cut across each other cleanly. In spatial terms, their alignment was orthogonal.

After the union's breakup, these axes of conflict reproduced themselves in the Russian Republic, as the center faced the problem of reconciling state integrity with the claims to autonomy and even independence on the part of many of its constituent republics and regions. These strains had been intensified by the Gorbachev-era struggles to preserve the union while reforming it. Recall, for example, that Gorbachev had attempted to undermine Yeltsin's power by appealing to the heads of Russia's internal republics to sign the union treaty as equals with the constituent republics of the union. Yeltsin had countered with his famous appeal to the republics that they should "take as much autonomy as they could swallow." The relation between center and regions had become the object of a power struggle between the union and the Russian Republic, and specifically between Gorbachev and Yeltsin. Thus the newly independent Russia confronted the challenge of rebuilding a political order that reconciled the competing demands of central and regional leaders.

The institutional setting in which these conflicts were played out made a great deal of difference to the country's ability to make policy decisions. Any major policy issue arising from economic reform affected interests in both domains. Property rights, privatization, the elimination of price controls, the reduction of state subsidies, and other fundamental policy issues, for instance, all raised the question of the degree of control regional governments would have over economic policy in their regions. As was the case at the union level in 1989–91 with the problem of economic reform and central relations with the republics, so too in Russia, many regional leaders welcomed the relaxation of the center's economic levers because they sought greater regional control, not because they hoped to benefit from countrywide market reform. Indeed, the political benefits of bureaucratic control over the economy made many regional leaders into conservatives on the left-right axis and at the same time opponents of central power. We can therefore characterize the political arena in 1992–93 as consisting of three political camps: the Yeltsin forces, which sought to push Russia in the direction of a market-governed economy; the communists, who wanted to strengthen centralism and block radical market reform; and regional leaders, who sought greater autonomy vis-à-vis the central government and took a pragmatic, instrumental view of the economic reform issue. Some favored market-oriented institutions, while others, doubtless a larger share of them, simply wanted to replace the center's administrative control with their own. But all agreed on the priority of conceding more control over economic decision making to regional governments so that they could decide how much foreign investment and market competition to allow.

It is helpful to employ a spatial model of these conflicts. Let us imagine that these three camps were roughly equal in strength in the Russian congresses and that any alliance of two of the camps could command a simple majority of deputies. In figure 6.1 the location of these camps are depicted in a two-dimensional space. Yeltsin and the Democratic Russia forces (and like groups) are positioned in the upper left quadrant, much as were the academic liberal economists in the Gorbachev period. But then, the radical democrats tended to favor autonomy for the republics because this, they reasoned, was the only way to break the stranglehold that the union bureaucracy had upon economic institutions. Now that Russia was independent, the radical democrats favored

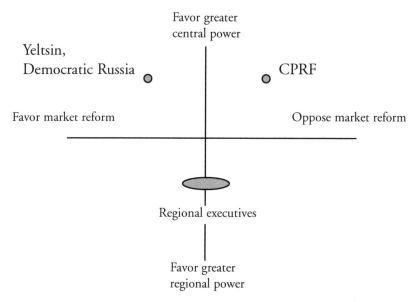

6.1. Dimensions of RSFSR Political Conflict, 1992–1993

central control precisely for the sake of enacting radical economic reform. In the upper right-hand quadrant are the Communist Party of the Russian Federation (CPRF) and other centralizing conservatives who oppose both Russia's disintegration and far-reaching capitalist transformation. Spanning the lower quadrants are regional leaders, with the median actor at the mid-point on the axis.

For each major policy issue that arises, each camp has a preference defined by its underlying views on the left-right and center-region dimensions of conflict according to whether the proposed change from the status quo would alter policy in the direction of the camp's preferred outcomes. The status quo, too, can be located in the same two-dimensional space, so that any shift away from the status quo will move policy in some direction along those two dimensions. Let us characterize the status quo with respect to the issue of property rights in 1992–93, more specifically the right to private ownership of business and industry. Property rights were gaining legal and political recognition, but only partially; for the most part, there was still no private ownership of land. Still, owing to the legalization of small-scale enterprise, and the rapid sell-off of state-owned firms, we can set the status quo point to the west of the communists' preferences, although still well to the east of the reformers' ideal point; regional authorities had also acquired rights over privatization and the regulation

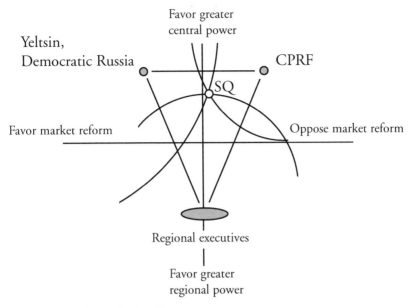

6.2. Political Conflict and Policy Choice, 1992–1993

of private business, so that the new status quo also lay somewhat to the south of the old. Accordingly we can suppose that the status quo in property rights lies west and south of the CPRF's ideal position, east and south of Yeltsin's, and north of the regional elite's preferences.[3]

For any particular proposal to change policy from the status quo, the preferences of our three major players can be mapped according to an indifference curve where their ideal point in two dimensions defines the center of a circle (or arc), with the curve running through the status quo.[4] An actor is indifferent as between any two policy changes lying along the curve since none is better nor worse than any other point along it: a gain in one dimension is offset by a loss in another. The player prefers any policy change located within the arc and opposes any change that would push policy to a point outside the curve. Let us imagine the positions, then, of the three camps in relation to a policy issue where the status quo is located in the upper right-hand quadrant—close to the communists' position but already somewhat shifted south and west of their ideal point. For each camp, the indifference curve is represented by an arc running through the status quo. Such a situation is depicted in figure 6.2. The three players' indifference curves all intersect at the status quo (SQ). There are petal-shaped zones demarcating proposals that would be acceptable to any two of the three camps because they would be improvements over the status quo for both. But note that there is no point common to all three sides' indifference curves other than the status quo: any proposal requiring the consent of all three would therefore be blocked. The communists are willing to concede slightly on the market reform axis if they could increase the centralization of state power; Yeltsin would concede slightly to the communists on market reform if he could increase central power; the governors would accept considerable changes in the area of market reform if they could win greater autonomy for the regions.

Any two of the three camps can theoretically agree on a new policy located somewhere along the straight line connecting them as long as it is in the petal-shaped zone common to their indifference curves. But there is no point that all three prefer to the status quo. Any policy change that suits both the communists and Yeltsin (and note that this model suggests that there are some points of this kind that are slightly more market oriented than the status quo and would move control further toward the central government) is more centralist than the regional executives can accept. They therefore oppose any such proposals. Any proposal that Yeltsin and the regions prefer to the status quo is more market oriented and decentralizing than the communists can accept. And whereas the regional leaders and the communists may be able to agree on a policy change that is slightly decentralizing and definitely market restricting, Yeltsin will oppose it. Although any two of the camps can find a zone of agreement lying between them in which they can agree on a policy and win a majority, social choice theory demonstrates that there is another alternative which could defeat it. Indeed, Josephine Andrews has demonstrated that cycling indeed occurred in the Russian congresses at points when the issue agenda was clearly multidimensional and there were no institutional barriers to prevent it.[5] Moreover any decision that any one side was in a position to veto would also be blocked. Such might be the case with a constitutional decision allowing one-third of the deputies plus one to defeat a proposed alternative to the status quo.

It is reasonable to explain the constitutional deadlock as an extension of the fights over economic policy: giving Yeltsin as president more power under a new constitution meant giving him more power to enact radical reform. The dilemma of constitutional choice thus "inherited" the distributional conflict over policies.[6] Therefore, in the above two-dimensional scheme, any proposals to alter the constitution in a way that gives the president, parliament, or regions significantly more power over policy making will also fail because each side will oppose constitutional amendments that weaken its power to block unwanted policy changes and any side can prevent such an amendment from passing.

When we examined the effect of the combined problem of two-dimensional issue conflict with institutional structure in the transitional Gorbachev and RSFSR parliaments, we pointed out that both parliaments simply punted: they chose to delegate emergency powers to the president rather than to take responsibility themselves for making major policy decisions that affected both the economic reform and center-region problems. Neither could find solutions to the grave constitutional and economic issues on their agenda. Even the immense agenda power that the parliaments' leaders held could not overcome the ability of any of these camps to frustrate action by the parliament. Recall what happened when Gorbachev plus the regional leaders worked *outside parliament* to negotiate a new union treaty—the communists and Luk'ianov then also went *outside the constitution* to block it. In this transition period, veto players did not feel obliged to confine their political action to constitutional means.

In their recent study of bicameralism, George Tsebelis and Jeannette Money address exactly this type of dilemma and relate it to the characteristics of bicameral parliaments. Their analysis of bicameralism as a solution to decision making in multidimensional space may be compared to related models of institutional solutions to collective choice dilemmas. Committee systems in parliaments, the allocation of portfolios to coalition partners in parliamentary governments, and majority party control of agenda setting have all been modeled as solutions to the dilemma of unstable decision making in settings where multiple dimensions of conflict structure the alignments of actors.[7]

Bicameralism, Tsebelis and Money have shown, can work similarly to reduce the complexity of decision making in such a way that only one dimension of conflict is dealt with at a time. The conditions under which this can occur require that the alignments of preferences in the two chambers differ (which can readily arise if the electoral rules governing the formation of the two bodies of members differ) and that both chambers must jointly agree to any decision for it to be adopted. Like other institutional mechanisms, such an arrangement is a way of reducing the complexity of issue space to a single dimension. This then permits majority voting to produce coherent and stable decisions, consistent with the median voter theorem.[8] Outcomes lie along the dimension defined by the different medians of the two chambers in relation to each other. The dilemma of aggregating preferences in multidimensional issue space remains for each chamber. But to the extent that each chamber is able to formulate its preferred position in relation to the other's preference, the chambers can prevent alternatives lying off the single axis separating them from undermining the chamber's agreement on its desired outcome.

Bicameralism had an effect in Russia consistent with the Tsebelis-Money

model in that it aided in reducing the propensity for policy decisions to deadlock or cycle. As we have seen, before the 1993 constitution, Russia's (and the
USSR's) legislature was not in fact bicameral. Differences in the behavior between the nominal chambers of the Supreme Soviet in the USSR and RSFSR
parliaments were trivial and were almost always overcome by the tight central
control over them exercised by the chairman of the Supreme Soviet, the joint
nature of most standing committees, and the Presidium (which was composed
of the chairman of parliament and the chairs of the joint committees). So
nearly merged were the two chambers in the general hierarchy of parliamentary
institutions that the alignments of preferences in each were very similar, and
the Presidium could generally control decision making in both.

In effect, bicameralism in the 1993 constitution compartmentalized the left-
right and center-region dimensions of conflict, making each chamber an institutional arena dominated by one major axis of policy disputes. The bicameral
structure of the Federal Assembly provided direct representation for the constituent territories of the federation in one chamber of parliament, while the
other, popular chamber, gave representation to organized political and party
forces that competed with the president for control over the executive. This
made it probable that members in the lower chamber would be aligned along
the dominant left-right cleavage dividing supporters and opponents of a market economy, and that the members of the upper chamber would have similar
regionalist perspectives.

Yeltsin's design overcame the constitutional deadlock, where a majority of
organized political forces were dissatisfied with the existing arrangement of
congress and Supreme Soviet and president but had no way to reach agreement
on an alternative framework that could command a stable majority. The essential elements of a constitutional reform that most groups could accept were well
known: a mixed presidential-prime ministerial executive, a mixed electoral law,
and a two-chamber parliament giving privileged representation to regions in
one house and direct popular election in the other. Many of the crucial features
of such a model were hotly disputed, including the relative balance of presidential and parliamentary power and the degree to which regional leaders
would be able to set or veto federal policy. But so long as the old institutional
formula remained, in which *only* the Congress of People's Deputies could
adopt a new constitution and then *only* by a two-thirds majority of all deputies,
it proved to be easy for some coalition of opponents to find at least one-third
plus one votes to defeat any alternative scheme.

Thus Yeltsin needed to find a constitutional model that no majority coalition of opponents could defeat, and, even more important, to find a mechanism for putting such a new scheme into place that did not depend on Khasbulatov and the congress. A constitutional arrangement that favored presidential power over parliamentary power too much would alienate regional and republican interests and fuel the separatist pressures that were strongly felt in 1990–92. But an arrangement favoring parliamentary power over presidential power would give Yeltsin's political opponents the means to reverse reform. Yeltsin had to find enough common ground with his left opposition on the preservation of Russia's integrity in the face of territorial separatism, and with the leaders of republics and regions on issues of executive power, to prevent the different flanks of opposition from allying to overturn the new constitutional order.

In spatial terms, this was equivalent to placing the new constitution's bundle of institutional features at a location near the notional midpoint in the spectrum of elite preferences along each of the two dimensions of policy conflict. Of course Yeltsin had to reckon with substantial uncertainty both about where that hypothetical two-dimensional median point lay, a problem in view of the absence of clear indications of the relative strength of the major camps; but he also had to fear that if he located his constitutional scheme too far toward one side or the other, the disadvantaged side would take to the streets. He would have assumed that somewhere between his preferred outcome (say, a tsar-like presidency and a rubber-stamp parliament) and the imaginary midpoint of all the organized political forces, there was probably a breakpoint where his opponents would refuse to go along: political order would break down and a revolution or civil war would follow. Structurally partitioning the two dimensions and imposing a new way of adopting the constitution were essential, however; so long as the congress had the power to reject any new constitutional draft, there would always be at least one-third plus one of the deputies opposed to a new constitution. Some set of deputies would always want to amend the draft along one dimension or the other. By bundling his solutions on both issues into a single unamendable package and putting it to a straight up-or-down national vote in December 1993, Yeltsin made it unlikely that any group of opponents could build a coalition strong enough to overturn it.[9]

The Parliamentary Constitutional Commission

Some issues concerning the structure of the new parliament were uncontroversial. One, the elimination of a two-tiered parliament, was generally supported

by political leaders.[10] From the point that the Russian congress met and established a commission to draft a new constitution, deputies, party leaders, and
experts generally agreed that the current two-tiered form represented a temporary feature of the transition period and would not be employed in a future
constitution. No serious constitutional scheme proposed a two-tiered parliament and nearly everyone anticipated that the new parliament, at least its lower
house, would be made up of full-time professional parliamentarians. The real
problem was how the existing congress would dissolve itself into the new,
smaller professional parliament of the future, since the deputies were reluctant
to relinquish their powers and privileges as deputies. But the Gorbachev-
Luk'ianov parliamentary model featuring a grand assembly that would serve
as an outer parliament that in turn elected a full-time inner parliament almost
immediately dropped from further discussion.

Yeltsin created a constitutional commission under the auspices of the Congress of People's Deputies shortly after he was elected chairman.[11] He named
himself chairman of the commission, but for the most part he did not take part
actively in the commission's work. Actual management of the commission was
vested with a young deputy, Oleg Rumiantsev, who headed a smaller working
group of deputies and legal experts.[12] Initially Rumiantsev and the commission were sympathetic to the president's outlook, with the result that their first
draft, published in November 1990, was unacceptable to the communist wing
of the congress and was not debated at the December congress.[13] A year later
the commission produced a second draft, but the Fifth Congress refused to
consider it and demanded that the commission prepare another version. The
commission duly returned to the drafting board and drafted a third version,
which it published in March 1992, on the eve of the Sixth Congress in April
1992.

By the time the commission's third draft was published, momentous constitutional and policy change had occurred. The union had fallen apart and Russia was independent; Yeltsin had been elected to a new presidency; the congress
had granted Yeltsin emergency decree powers, which Yeltsin was using to enact
shock therapy and privatization. The old constitution had been amended and
revised to the point of incoherence in order to accommodate these changes.
The widening chasm between Yeltsin and the parliamentary opposition prevented a wholesale revision of the old constitution, still less the adoption of a
new one. Yeltsin's departure from parliament reduced his influence over the
constitutional commission, much as it limited his ability to build support
among deputies for his policy program. The commission grew increasingly

hostile to Yeltsin's demands for a constitution that enshrined his conception of a "presidential republic." Rumiantsev himself drew closer to the nationalist-communist opposition.

The constitutional conflict over the balance of power between president and legislature directly reflected the confrontation between radical reformers and communist opponents of Yeltsin's policies. Ardent Yeltsin supporters in parliament wanted to maximize presidential power and minimize parliament's ability to block Yeltsin. Their thinking about constitutional architecture was focused almost exclusively on the immediate political struggle between communists and reformers over radical political and economic change.[14] But the issue of presidential-parliamentary power was also affected by another set of closely linked problems concerning the constitutional status of regular territorial administrative units of the republic (oblasts, krais, and the two cities that were considered to have equivalent status, Moscow and St. Petersburg) and the ethnic republics. These issues were extremely delicate in 1990–92 because the contest between Yeltsin and Gorbachev had led each to encourage the republics' aspirations for sovereignty. Several republic leaders were demanding outright independence or at least full control over all economic resources on their territories. Leaders of regular territorial units, in contrast, strongly opposed the special privileges and rights of republics. On issues such as the rights of ethnic republics, the equality of all subjects of the federation vis-à-vis the central government, and preventing the breakup of the Russian state, Yeltsin and his parliamentary opposition stood much closer together.

Recognizing that it was impractical to abolish the special legal privileges that the Soviet constitution had granted to ethnic-national territories, a parliamentary majority agreed to preserve the inherited hierarchy of territorial units and to recognize the upgrades in status that many of the units' governments had unilaterally declared. Autonomous republics all became "republics," and four autonomous oblasts were promoted to republic. On March 31, 1992, President Yeltsin signed a Federal Treaty with all but two of the constituent territories of the Russian Federation, Tatarstan and the Chechen Republic. The Federal Treaty was a set of three somewhat different agreements—one with republics, one with ordinary oblasts and krais, and one with autonomous oblasts and okrugs—demarcating spheres of jurisdiction between the central government and the regions.[15] Republics were given broader rights than other territorial units, although still not enough to satisfy the leaders of several republics.[16] The treaty enumerated responsibilities exclusively assigned to the federal government, those that were exercised jointly by the federal and regional governments, and those that fell exclusively to regional jurisdiction. The treaty left so many major policy issues in the ambiguous zone of "shared jurisdiction" that its significance was more honorific than effective. It did, however, resolve a few basic issues. It left intact the existing structure of territorial units, it confirmed that the old Soviet-era inequality in constitutional status between ethnic republics and ordinary territorial units would be reproduced in the future, and it created the concept of a "subject"—"constituent member"—of the federation under which each territory, ethnic or ordinary, would have equal representation at the center. This principle soon became the basis for many proposals for constitutional representation in the upper house of a future parliament, most of which provided that two members would be elected to the upper house from each territorial subject. By equalizing the constitutional status of the different kinds of territorial units, this model departed significantly from the old hierarchical system of territorial administration.

The president and the parliament's constitutional commission alike accepted the Federal Treaty as a significant political agreement, on a par with the constitution. Perhaps surprisingly, in view of the intensity of the confrontation between Yeltsin and the parliament over economic policy, the Sixth Congress approved the treaty by an overwhelming margin. Although the Federal Treaty left a great many important issues unresolved, it defined certain agreed principles for future constitution making and was widely considered, even by Yeltsin's enemies, to be the best outcome that the central government could get in its relations with the constituent territories under the circumstances. The same could not be said for the issue of presidential-parliamentary power, where the distance between Yeltsin and the parliamentary opposition widened over 1992 and 1993. The draft constitution published in March 1992 by the parliament's constitutional commission went some way to satisfying Yeltsin's demands but still left the president weaker than Yeltsin wanted.[17] It provided for a popularly elected president who appointed a prime minister, and it preserved the president's power to issue decrees (and was silent on what if any power parliament had to rescind or confirm them). However, it gave parliament the ability to override a presidential veto of legislation with a simple majority of each chamber; gave parliament but not the president the right to call a referendum; and gave the president no means to dissolve parliament, although parliament could remove the president.

If it is reasonable to suppose that Rumiantsev and his colleagues on the commission sought to frame a constitution that could win the support of at least two-thirds of the deputies and that their draft accordingly was placed at least somewhere close to that point, then their proposal shows most deputies had moved well away from the old communist-era constitutional model. The draft eliminated the Presidium or any form of joint governance of the two chambers (although it did preserve the existing Presidium until the next elections). It envisioned that the current congress would dissolve itself into a new bicameral Supreme Soviet, with different modes of election for the two chambers, and a sequential process for legislation: first a bill would be approved by the lower house, the State Duma, and then it would move to the upper house, the Federal Assembly, before being sent to the president for his signature. The Duma would have 450 members, all elected for four-year terms in single-member constituencies, while the upper house would be composed of 2 elected deputies, with six-year terms, from each of the constituent territories of the federation (except that only one deputy each would be elected from the autonomous districts [*okruga*]). The chambers would not be governed by a presidium and would have separate rules of procedure and leadership.

The Sixth Congress debated the draft and decided finally to approve its "general principles" and "concept" but to defer the issue of adopting it to a later date. Although it was not rejected, a constitutional majority of two-thirds could not be found to pass it in toto. Yeltsin was dissatisfied with it as well because it did not give him as much power as he sought. Even before the Sixth Congress convened, he began to seek a different way to enact a new constitution. He charged Sergei Shakhrai (who had recently left the parliament to become head of the new chief legal administration of the presidential administration) to draft a constitution more consonant with Yeltsin's preferences. Shakhrai's draft occasioned protests at the Sixth Congress since it bypassed the president's own constitutional commission (of which, anomalously, Yeltsin continued to be chairman). Through the spring and summer Yeltsin attempted to press the parliamentary commission to rewrite its version more to his liking, but it failed to go as far in the direction of a presidential republic as he demanded. Therefore, he shifted strategy again, demanding at the Seventh Congress in December 1992 that his conception of constitutional reform be put to the voters in a referendum.[18] Initially the congress refused to go along, then agreed to a allow a referendum on the principles to govern a new constitution, then reneged again. Following the failure of the congress's effort to remove Yeltsin, however, the deputies agreed to a general referendum on support for Yeltsin. Yeltsin, however, declared that he would interpret popular endorsement of his leadership as support for his plan for constitutional reform.

On April 24, the day before the referendum was held, *Izvestiia* published the elements of Yeltsin's own desired constitutional model. The accompanying note explained that Yeltsin intended to put this constitution into effect if he won the referendum. The draft created a bicameral Federal Assembly and gave Yeltsin the powers he had been demanding to name the government and the members of the highest courts, both subject to parliamentary confirmation, and to dissolve parliament in the event of a political crisis. Yeltsin won a re-sounding vote of confidence in the referendum and proceeded to build politi-cal support for his constitutional scheme.

The full draft of his model constitution—drafted by a committee chaired by Sergei Alekseev, a legal scholar sympathetic to the democratic camp—was pub-lished shortly after the referendum.[19] In many respects it incorporated points that the parliament's constitutional commission had elaborated, such as the long section outlining the rights of citizens. But it differed from the commis-sion's product in the powers that it granted the president. It provided for a lower chamber, the State Duma, with 300 deputies elected in single-member districts, and an upper chamber, the Council of the Federation. Although the State Duma would consider laws first before sending them on to the Federation Council and could override the Federation Council in case of disagreement, it was the latter chamber that had the power to confirm the president's choice of prime minister and to bring down the government through a vote of no confi-dence. The president could dissolve parliament not only if it failed to confirm his choice of prime minister, but also "in other cases as well, when a crisis of state power cannot be resolved on the basis of procedures established by the current constitution."[20] The president could call a referendum, a right that the parliamentary commission reserved for parliament, and the presidential draft eliminated the post of vice-president. Whereas the parliament's commission would have given parliament the power to confirm the deputy prime ministers and most other ministers, the president's draft gave parliament the right to con-firm only the prime minister. The presidential draft enumerated many more re-sponsibilities for the president than did parliament's draft constitution.[21]

The president's concern with satisfying the demands of the ethnic republics is manifest in the draft.[22] The voters of each subject of the federation would elect two members to the Federation Council. But each ethnic republic and au-tonomous oblast or okrug would also elect additional members—in accor-dance with a law yet to be drafted—such that "in the Council of the Federation deputies from these subjects of the federation would make up no less than 50 percent."

The presidential draft was attacked from two sides. Many criticized it for granting the president open-ended power and reducing parliament to a decorative appendage, while others, particularly republic and region leaders, accused it of granting too much power to the republics or of failing to equalize the powers of republics and regions.

The Constitutional Assembly

On May 12 Yeltsin decreed that a constitutional convention was to convene to refine the draft and adopt a new constitution in final form. On May 21 he issued a second decree to the effect that the constitutional assembly would debate and revise the draft, but he dropped the provision that the assembly would formally adopt it.[23]

Yeltsin's use of a large national constitutional assembly as a forum for drafting a new constitution posed a dilemma for the parliament's leadership. The assembly had no legal standing, but Yeltsin's political position had been strengthened, and that of the parliamentary opposition weakened, by the results of the April referendum. Several anti-Yeltsin parliamentary leaders concluded that it was better to take part in the proposed constitutional assembly than to be left without influence over the subsequent course of events. Yeltsin refused to commit himself to the idea that the congress would be the vehicle by which the new constitution would be adopted, but in fact, by the time the assembly convened, the issue of center-regional relations had become even more problematic for a new constitution than the fight between Yeltsin and the left opposition. At the same time, the competition between the presidential draft constitution and the parliament's version prompted a number of other groups to circulate their draft constitutions, among them several political parties and movements. A draft published by a group of communist deputies, for example, would have returned to the soviet model of the pre-Gorbachev era.

Notwithstanding its doubtful constitutional status, Yeltsin succeeded in persuading virtually all sections of the political leadership of the country to send delegates to his constitutional assembly. Its 750 members met in five parallel working groups, each assigned responsibility for drafting a particular section of a new text. Yeltsin initially took a conciliatory line in his opening speech to the assembly, urging it to consider the good points of both the presidential and the parliamentary drafts and referring to the assembly as a consultative body. He then made his own political position very clear, however, by categorically denouncing the very doctrine of soviet rule, declaring flatly that "soviets and democracy are incompatible." Moreover, since the current soviets were the "direct heirs of those soviets that usurped power in 1918," the entire system of soviet power was illegitimate.[24] Yeltsin was referring to the doctrine under which all state power was fused in the soviets, as opposed to a separation of powers system, still less a system with a dominant presidency. The doctrine of soviet power, of course, was the theoretical justification for the resistance to Yeltsin by Khasbulatov and the parliamentary opposition because it made the congress the highest body of state power. As soon as Yeltsin finished, Khasbulatov demanded the floor, was given it, was shouted down by listeners, and stalked out of the hall.

After four weeks of deliberation, the constitutional assembly approved by a large majority a new constitutional draft somewhat different from the president's original draft.[25] Their version envisioned a weaker president: he could issue edicts, but these were not to contradict federal law or constitution; he would not have the broad power to dissolve the parliament if it was unable to overcome a crisis in state power; and he could no longer be the "arbiter" of disputes in relations between the central government and lower governments or among lower governments. Instead, he was now to use "conciliation procedures" to settle such disputes, and if the dispute could not be settled by mediation, he was to refer the issue to the courts. Still other major issues, such as the president's power to call a referendum, were finessed by being referred to future legislation.

The assembly's draft gave the president the right to dissolve the Duma under only two circumstances: its refusal to confirm, on the third attempt, the president's nominee for head of government, and after a second vote of no confidence by the Duma in the government within three months. With slight modifications, these provisions survived into the December draft that was approved in the referendum.

On September 21, 1993, Yeltsin's Ukaz no. 1400 dissolved the congress and Supreme Soviet and established instead a new framework of state power based on the constitutional assembly's July 12 draft.[26] The parliament—called the Federal Assembly—would consist of the State Duma and the Federation Council. Deputies would be elected to the Duma for a term of four years while the Federation Council would be composed on an ex officio basis of the heads of the executive and legislative branches of each subject of the federation. Elections to the Duma were to be held on December 12.

On October 11 Yeltsin changed this plan with a new decree, which provided that the members of the Federation Council were to be elected and that both Federation Council and Duma elections would both be held on December 12. Still later, on October 15, Yeltsin decreed that there would also be a national vote on a new draft constitution, also on December 12. The text of the draft constitution itself, however, was not published until November 10.[27] The confusing and inconsistent series of decrees about the structure of the new parliament, the manner of its establishment, the nature of the new constitution, and the procedure for its ratification shows a high level of improvisation and indecision within the presidential administration. Most of this was caused by the sensitive and unresolved nature of the political contest between Yeltsin and the heads of the republics and regions over their constitutional powers. Yeltsin's team continued to tinker with the draft adopted by the constitutional assembly until the final version was published on November 10 as the text to be voted on in December. These modifications tended to increase the power of the central government vis-à-vis the republics and to strengthen the power of the president's control of government at the expense of parliament's power. The decision to put the final draft to a national referendum rather than to submit it to the Federal Assembly also suggests that Yeltsin was unwilling to give either parliament or the regional leaders any opportunity to debate or alter his decisions in these two crucial respects.[28]

When the final version of the constitution was finally published, it revealed that Yeltsin had again changed his mind about the procedure for forming the upper house. In a series of transitional provisions added to the end of the text, he proposed that the first Federation Council was to be elected for a two-year transition period and that its members would serve on only a part-time basis. Likewise the first Duma would be elected to serve only two years. After that, the Duma would be elected for its full four-year term under a new election law, and the Federation Council would be composed under a law to be enacted for its formation. Yeltsin's revision of October 11 was undoubtedly prompted by the fact that his decrees dissolving local and regional soviets left many regions without any legislative body, and his decree making the heads of the executive branches in the regions and localities appointed officials would have meant that half the members of the Federation Council would have been his appointees.[29]

This left a discrepancy, however, between the provisional structure established by presidential decree and the text of the constitution that Yeltsin was proposing for ratification. Under the latter, the Federation Council was to be "formed" from representatives of the legislative and executive branches of each subject of the federation, although the constitution does not specify how such representatives are to be chosen; the language suggests, however, that the membership of the upper chamber is ex officio rather than elective. The language left open, for instance, the crucial question of whether Federation Council members would work on a full-time basis in parliament or not, and how they were to be chosen as "representatives" of their respective branches. These issues had provoked acute conflict. The central government's influence over the governments of many of the subjects was already tenuous. Automatic representation for their senior leaders, by insulating them from Russia-wide electoral tides, would have weakened the center's hold over the regions and republics still further and given the latter substantial influence over federal policy. The issue had been debated over the summer by the constitutional assembly without being resolved, and it continued to be thrashed out in the following two years as the Duma and Federation Council debated the law on forming the Federation Council.

The "Presidential Republic"

The draft Yeltsin put to the nation for ratification settled a number of issues bearing on the structure and powers of the new parliament. Compared with the assembly's model, Yeltsin's final version veered back toward the president's side in the question over the relative balance of presidential-parliamentary power and closer toward the centralist position on the center-region axis. It thus put more power in the hands of the popular chamber vis-à-vis the upper house. Yeltsin's draft did not make the chambers equal in power, as had been the case in the Soviet era, and they were not to be governed jointly by a superordinate presidium that could serve as the instrument of the executive bureaucracy or of a dominant political faction. Each chamber was given a distinct jurisdiction, and the Federation Council was given unique and crucial powers in regard to confirmation of the president's choices for procurator-general and the judges serving on the three highest courts—the Constitutional Court, the Supreme Arbitration Court, and the Supreme Court—as well as other fundamental issues.[30] The Duma could override the Federation Council, however, on routine legislative issues, and it had the power to refuse to confirm a presidential nominee for prime minister, as well as to vote no confidence in the government. Yeltsin's powers to control the executive were stronger than parliament's and were generally unambiguous.

Yeltsin's vision for the post-Soviet Russian state was a "presidential republic," and his constitution went far to realize that model. Under the constitution, the president was made head of state, the commander in chief of the armed forces, and the chairman of the Security Council. He could declare a state of war or state of emergency on Russian territory subject to the requirement that he immediately notify parliament (he could declare war on another state on his own authority, however). He was given responsibility for directing foreign policy and protecting national security, and overall responsibility for both domestic and foreign policy. He was to appoint the prime minister who then must be confirmed by the State Duma and to appoint the deputy prime ministers and other ministers at the initiative of the prime minister. The Duma could not vote to approve or remove individual ministers; it could only vote on confirmation of the prime minister and on motions of confidence and no confidence in the government. The president also appointed a number of other government officials, among them the chairman of the Central Bank, the procurator-general, and the members of the three highest courts. In each case, his appointments were subject to parliamentary consent (for the justice officials, the Council of the Federation had the right to approve the appointments; the Central Bank chairman appointment was confirmed by the Duma). The president did not need parliamentary consent to appoint the top military commanders, the presidential administration, regional presidential representatives, and the members of the Security Council.

The president enjoyed extensive lawmaking prerogatives. He could introduce legislation or instruct the government to draft and introduce legislation, he could submit amendments to bills under consideration by parliament, and he could withhold his signature from a bill. Parliament, however, had the right to override a presidential veto by a two-thirds vote in each chamber. And parliament was given the right to remove the president through impeachment.[31]

Of course the president would have the power to enact edicts (*ukazy*, or decrees) without parliamentary consent and thus to make law. In his decree power, though, the president again faces important limitations, which have become clearer as precedents and court rulings accumulate. Under the constitution, presidential edicts could not contradict existing law or the constitution. In November 1995 the Constitutional Court ruled that parliament had no authority directly to block a presidential decree, but the court has also ruled that a law passed by parliament may supersede a presidential decree. In April 1996 the court ruled that even in matters where the constitution requires that policy be set by federal legislation, the president may use his decree power to "fill gaps" in the law until such time as parliament has acted.[32] The understanding that presidential decrees fill gaps and are superseded by legislation became widely accepted among both parliamentarians and executive officials. The threat of a presidential decree always hangs over the heads of the parliamentarians, more often as an unspoken but clear reality than as an explicit club, and on some occasions it does spur parliament to act more quickly and to move closer to the president's position.[33] It is widely accepted by officials in both branches that the president's field of discretion is growing narrower with time as parliament passes more fundamental legislation.[34]

The 1993 constitution left a number of significant issues open. In some cases it called for ordinary or constitutional legislation to define necessary procedures; among these were laws on elections of deputies to the Duma and on "forming" the Federation Council, election of the president, conducting a referendum, how to declare a state of emergency and the rules governing civil rights under a state of emergency, the structure of the judicial system, the scope of competence of the government, and how to convene a constitutional assembly. Still other issues were ambiguous as well, although the constitution did not specifically demand new legislation to resolve them. Among these were the limits of the president's decree power and parliament's rights to check it, and the relation between president and government. The open-endedness of the issues pertaining to federalism, above all the lack of closure on how the new upper house was to be established, suggests that these issues were more contentious than those bearing on the relative powers of president and parliament in controlling the executive.

According to the official report of the Central Electoral Commission (CEC), the constitution was approved by popular vote under the rules that Yeltsin had put into effect.[35] The final figures published by the CEC claimed that 54.8 percent of the electorate had participated and that of them 58.4 percent had voted in favor of Yeltsin's constitution. Thus both criteria were met and the constitution was considered to have been ratified. All political forces accepted the result and chose to treat the constitution as ratified. Claims to the contrary by several researchers were denied indignantly by CEC officials and studiously ignored by the communists and other opposition forces.[36] All camps tacitly agreed to accept the new constitution as ratified. Yeltsin's strategy had been to put the constitution to the citizens by plebiscite so that it could not be further modified: although his opponents were able to form a negative majority against any alternative new constitution so long as the arena for choice was the parliament, once Yeltsin had gone over the heads of parliament and put the issue to the populace in an up-or-down vote, his opponents had no chance to pose alternatives or amendments.

THE NEW ELECTORAL SYSTEM

The stream of contradictory decisions that Yeltsin issued over the course of 1993 concerning the constitutional framework also affected the choice of an electoral mechanism for the two new chambers of parliament. Although it was widely agreed across the political elite that the two chambers were to be elected in different ways, with the lower house using some combination of territorial and party-list representation and the upper house providing equal representation to each federal subject, a number of issues continued to be debated. There was a broad agreement that a mixed system that would combine the advantages of single-member-district (SMD) and party-list (PL) representation, but there was disagreement over the appropriate proportions of seats to be filled by each method. Meantime, some politicians still preferred the old all-SMD electoral system for the lower house, while others proposed establishing an all-PL system. Those supporting a mixed system differed, with most preferring a system of two-thirds SMD, one-third PL and others proposing equal proportions. The proper number of seats in the lower house was discussed, as was the problem of apportionment: would the 900 territorial seats created for the 1990 RSFSR election be collapsed into 300 new seats, or 400, or 450? And what would be the relation of these territorial seats to the existing network of administrative-territorial boundaries? In retrospect, it is odd that there was so little debate over the proper electoral threshold to use for the PL share of lower house seats; the 5 percent threshold ultimately chosen was adopted with almost no public discussion or dissent. Much more contentious was a different problem: whether to use an "against all" or "none of the above" option on the ballot and, if so, whether a candidate or party had to receive more than the number of votes cast "against all" to win.

The question of the electoral system for the upper chamber, as noted above, was even more difficult. Yeltsin's decrees contradicted themselves on this point, and the issue continued to be a heated point of dispute into the 1994–95 period as the Duma and Federation Council debated the new law on the "formation" of the Federation Council. Here the issue for Yeltsin was whether he gained more from a chamber that granted automatic representation to the leaders of republics and regions, or one whose composition would be affected by national electoral forces. The concept of a Federation Council made up of the heads of the constituent territories of the federation had been proposed several times under Gorbachev and Yeltsin and had even been brought into being once. Gorbachev in December 1990 created a Federation Council consisting of the heads of the union republics to serve him in his capacity as president as an advisory body. Yeltsin had created a "Council of Heads of Republics" in October 1992 and a "Council of Heads of Administration" in March 1993. In the same month the heads of the soviets and the executive branches in seventy-three of the eighty-nine territories had proposed a new "Federation Council" to be the upper chamber of the future parliament. The proposal was rejected by the Congress of People's Deputies, but the concept continued to be reflected in a number of the constitutional proposals then in circulation.

Moreover, Yeltsin himself created something of the sort when he convened the constitutional assembly in June. Each subject was to send the heads of its legislative and executive bodies, along with two experts, to the assembly.[37] This rule on the automatic delegation of the two leaders of each unit was then incorporated into the constitutional framework that Yeltsin enacted by his September 21 decree. But when it became evident that not all of the regional and republic leaders supported him in the confrontation with the parliamentary opposition October 3–4, he changed his position and decreed, on October 11, that the first Federation Council was to be elected.

Over September and October, Yeltsin also changed his mind about the size and structure of the Duma. His September 21 decree provided for a chamber of 400 deputies, 300 to be elected in single-mandate districts and 100 by proportional representation from party lists. But a number of members of the constitutional assembly working on electoral legislation urged Yeltsin to change this plan so as to increase the number of seats in the new chamber to 450, and to make 225 of them party-list seats. Yeltsin agreed, and in a decree of October 1, he enacted the new model for the Duma. Yeltsin may have hoped that this would give the opposition forces more reason to accept his dissolution of parliament because at the time he changed the formula by increasing the number of list seats, he declared that it would help stabilize the political situation if the communists and "national-patriots" were competing for election to the Duma instead of standing at the barricades.[38] For the most part, Yeltsin was adopting in its entirety the draft law that a group of deputies under the leadership of Viktor Sheinis had proposed at the Constitutional Assembly in June, which had proposed the 225–225 mixed electoral system.[39]

Because the electoral system that Yeltsin decreed for the December 1993 Duma elections was taken with little change from the proposal made by the Sheinis group, we can draw on the memoranda the group circulated and interviews with some of the participants to gain insight into the political objectives that the designers of the law hoped to achieve.[40] The objectives pursued by the Sheinis group combined policy and structural goals. Some members of the group intended for the law to maximize the number of seats that would be won in the next parliamentary elections by adherents of radical reform. Their assumption was that a clear majority of the voters supported radical reform, an assumption based on the results of the April 1993 referendum, the 1991 presidential vote, and the 1990 RSFSR parliamentary election. Local political elites, however, they were convinced, were obstacles to reform and would distort the outcome of the election to the extent they had influence over it. Single-member-district elections would give local power holders the opportunity to manipulate apportionment, candidate selection, the election campaigns, and the processes of voting and tallying the results. National party-list voting would produce less distorted, more representative results than would elections in districts. It was consistent with this premise that the party-list part of the chamber be elected from a single federalwide district, so that all the votes favoring the reform cause could be concentrated and not wasted. Likewise, a political group would have to collect at least 200,000 signatures, of which no more than 15 percent were taken from any one federal subject, to win the right to run candidates. This condition reflected a fear that fissiparous regional parties could get on the ballot, win seats, and push for regional separatism.

Maximizing anticipated seat share for radical reformers was not the only objective of the framers of the new law, and it was certainly not at all the objective of many other groups that favored a mixed system. Like supporters of proportional representation everywhere, the Sheinis group argued that to the extent that the new parliament was based on party lists, it was more likely to represent the diversity of political opinion in the country than was one where winner-take-all races left minority opinion underrepresented.[41] Even more pertinent to the Russian situation was the widely echoed sentiment that a party-based parliament would lend some stability to the extremely and dangerously unstable political environment in Russia. In a crisis, deputies not tied to political forces with some electoral support would run opportunistically for shelter to whatever power centers could protect them, as they had done in the 1990–93 period, with disastrous consequences. Deputies linked to national political forces, in contrast, would give major social strata political voice, encouraging them to seek constitutional solutions to their differences and reducing the polarization in society.

A party-oriented political process, the group argued, would make the political arena more structured, stable, and orderly, qualities sorely absent from the present political system: "As a result of the elections, moreover, a parliament should take form with political factions that will represent not clubs according to interests and tastes, as at present, but organized representation of politically organized social forces, searching for support outside parliament."[42] The law, in turn, would spark the formation of parties, making the new parliament better structured, more accountable, and more orderly.[43]

To these policy-oriented and structural arguments we may add yet other immediate political considerations on the part of other actors. Various political
parties and organizations, such as Zhirinovsky's Liberal-Democratic Party of
Russia, the Congress of Russian Communities, and Civic Union, professed
strong support for a PL system, undoubtedly on the grounds that only in that
way would they have a realistic chance of winning parliamentary representation. President Yeltsin, as we have seen, chose to increase the number of party-
list seats in the proposed new Duma through his October 1 decree, surely cal-
culating that the opportunity to enter into the electoral competition would
weaken the resolve of some of the groups participating in the tense standoff at
the White House, causing them to yield peacefully to Yeltsin's decreed new order. The CPRF's very half-hearted commitment to the rebel cause before and
during the October 3 uprising, and its almost immediate decision to join the
electoral campaign for the December elections, suggests that Yeltsin's calcula-
tion may have been right.

In short, the mixed electoral law for the State Duma won the support of a diverse array of political actors, who differed in their policy, institutional, and
electoral objectives. Much as in the case of the constitution's provisions on the
structure and powers of the new parliament—where there was evidently no
coalition of forces strong enough to adopt it, but also none able to block it because of the separation of the dimensions along which political forces disagreed
about it—so the electoral law was accepted by a broad range of political forces
because it gave each the prospect of attaining something it valued.

SUMMING UP

The 1993 constitution and the electoral law used for the Duma elections were
put into effect through Yeltsin's extraconstitutional decrees; but their staying
power attests to the fact that they provided institutional solutions to severe political conflicts arising from the breakdown of communist rule. It is not too
fanciful to model them as median positions in two dimensions of conflict—
the struggle between democratic reformers and communist conservatives, and
the competition between centralizers and regional leaders. The relative stability
of both the constitution and the mixed electoral system may be explained by
the difficulty for any majority of opponents to agree on an alternative system.

Yeltsin's bicameral model of parliament broke the impasse over a new constitution by separating the struggle over economic reform from the issues of federalism. Compartmentalizing these conflicts into different arenas, a party-gov-

erned lower chamber to fight with the president over control of the executive branch in areas of national economic policy and an upper chamber composed of all the heads of government in the federal subjects, made it unlikely that any coalition of opponents could unite to overturn the new constitution. The solution to the problem of the *supply* of new institutional arrangements thus came about through Yeltsin's efforts to consolidate a new political order that gave him the powers he demanded but also provided a measure of stability by providing other political forces with institutional resources that gave them a reason to stay in the game. Such arrangements as an upper chamber with automatic representation for regional leaders and a closed party-list system for the Duma elections were a form of compensation to Yeltsin's rivals that traded off representative rights and influence for a constitution where he was the pivotal player.[44] But they had enduring consequences for the subsequent actions of all the players in the game, including Yeltsin himself.

Chapter 7 Organizing
the Federal Assembly

THE 1993 ELECTIONS

THE 1993 ELECTIONS

The general outlines of the Federal Assembly's structure were determined by the constitution and the electoral law. It fell to the deputies elected in December 1993 to determine specific rules and procedures to govern each chamber. The two chambers organized themselves very differently, reflecting their different constitutional status and electoral bases. The Duma chose a system of party-based power sharing, while the Federation Council preferred a simplified system of chairman and committee chairs. In devising these arrangements the deputies drew on their experience with similar models developed in the predecessor union and Russian Supreme Soviets. Each chamber's organizational arrangements were preserved with only minor adjustments when new members entered in 1996.

Election Results and Deputy
Factions

The 1993 election gave no single political party or camp an outright majority in the Duma. If the election had turned out differently and one party or coalition had won a clear majority, the initial structure of the Duma might have been constructed very differently, with rules that converted a relative advantage into absolute control. The fact that power was distributed rather evenly across opposition, centrist, and reformist forces, and across eight different organized parties, facilitated the development of a system of power sharing across all the winning parties.[1]

Parties opposing Yeltsin and market-oriented reform policies won about 43 percent of the vote in the party-list ballot. Around half of these votes went to the Liberal-Democratic Party of Russia, led by Vladimir Zhirinovsky. Prore-form parties won about 34 percent of the party-list vote, with about half of that going to Russia's Choice, the party led by former Prime Minister Egor Gaidar. The actual balance of forces in the Duma was affected by the outcomes in the single-member-district races, which partly offset the strong showing of the op-position groups in the party-list voting. All the same, there was great uncer-tainty following the election about how the actual balance of political forces in the Duma would turn out because deputies from single-member districts were free to affiliate themselves with any faction or group, and many changed their political affiliations between the elections and the first days of the parliament's session.[2] Around one-third of the district deputies chose to affiliate with one of the reform-oriented factions and 29 percent affiliated with one of the opposi-tion groups, such as the Communist Party of the Russian Federation (CPRF) or Agrarian Party of Russia (APR) factions.

How the 1993 election results translated into the distribution of deputies by faction is indicated in tables 7.1 and 7.2. None of the five parties that failed to clear the 5-percent threshold was able to form a group of its own on the basis of single-member-district deputies. The eight parties that did receive more than 5 percent all formed factions, and these varied in the proportions of list and SMD deputies making them up. Such factions as Liberal Democratic Party of Russia (LDPR) and Women of Russia relied almost exclusively on the deputies elected from their party lists, whereas Russia's Choice and the communists were much more evenly distributed across district and list members. Deputies could and did run both in single-member-district races and on party lists. Some deputies elected in single-member-district races had been nominated or sup-ported by electoral associations that were also running party lists. For the most part, however, the single-member-district races were contested with little refer-ence to party. Candidates' party affiliations were not listed on the ballot. So, both from the standpoint of interpreting the voters' preferences, and from that of knowing how SMD deputies identified themselves once elected, figures on

Table 7.1. Initial Factional Affiliation of State Duma Deputies by Electoral Category, January 1994

Party	Party-List Vote (%)	List Seats Received	District Deputies Elected
Reform parties			
Russia's choice	15.51	40	24
PRES	6.73	18	4
Yabloko	7.86	20	7
RDDR	4.08	0	5
Centrist parties			
DPR	5.52	14	0
WOR	8.13	21	2
KEDR	0.76	0	1
BRNI	1.25	0	2
Civic Union	1.93	0	10
DiM	0.7	0	3
Opposition parties			
Agrarian	7.99	21	16
CPRF	12.4	32	10
LDPR	22.92	59	5
Against all lists	4.22		
Total		225	89

Abbreviations: PRES: Party of Russian Unity and Accord; Yabloko: the bloc Yavlinsky-Boldyrev-Lukin; RDDR: Russian Movement for Democratic Reforms; DPR: Democratic Party of Russia; WOR: Women of Russia; KEDR: Constructive-Ecological Movement "Cedar"; BRNI: The Future of Russia—New Names; DiM: Dignity and Charity; Agrarian: Agrarian Party of Russia; CPRF: Communist Party of the Russian Federation; LDPR: Liberal Democratic Party of Russia (Zhirinovsky's party).

the "party affiliations" of deputies elected in districts mean little. A much clearer indication of the deputies' own preferences is their decisions on affiliation once in the Duma. On this issue, as indicated in tables 7.1 and 7.2, there was a great deal of movement in the initial months. At the moment that the Duma convened in January, 1994, the initial distribution of mandates by party faction was as indicated in table 7.1.[3] Note that the political parties that failed to meet the 5-percent barrier did have some associated deputies who had been elected in districts. The parties that did well in the party-list races generally were much less successful in winning district races. And the great majority of SMD deputies had no clear affiliation.

Table 7.2. Factional Membership in the State Duma by Electoral Mandate, 1994–1995 (in absolute figures and percentages)

| | April 1994 | | | October 1995 | | |
Faction	Single-Member District	Party List	Total	Single-Member District	Party List	Total
Russia's Choice	33 (45.2)	40 (54.8)	73	22 (46.8)	25 (53.2)	47
PRES	11 (37.9)	18 (62.1)	29	4 (30.8)	9 (69.2)	13
Yabloko	8 (28.6)	20 (71.4)	28	8 (29.6)	19 (70.4)	27
Dec. 12	23 (100)		23			
DPR	1 (6.7)	14 (93.3)	15	1 (9.1)	10 (90.9)	11
WOR	2 (8.7)	21 (91.3)	23	2 (10)	18 (90)	20
NRP	65 (100)		65	36 (100)		36
Agrarian	34 (60.7)	22 (39.3)	56	30 (58.8)	21 (41.2)	51
CPRF	13 (28.3)	33 (71.7)	46	16 (34.0)	31 (66.0)	47
LDPR	5 (7.9)	58 (92.1)	63	5 (9.3)	49 (90.7)	54
Russia's Way	10 (100)		10			
Stability				31 (83.8)	6 (16.2)	37
Rossiia				25 (69.4)	11 (30.6)	36
Total	219	227[a]	446	216	221	437

Abbreviations: PRES: Party of Russian Unity and Accord; Yabloko: the bloc Yavlinsky-Boldyrev-Lukin; Dec. 12: Liberal Democratic Group of December 12; DPR: Democratic Party of Russia; WOR: Women of Russia; NRP: New Regional Policy; Agrarian: Agrarian Party of Russia; CPRF: Communist Party of the Russian Federation; LDPR: Liberal Democratic Party of Russia (Zhirinovsky's party).

[a]This figure exceeds 225 because it includes deputies who entered the Duma after January. As some deputies elected on party lists chose to take a single-member district-mandate instead or decided not to assume their parliamentary mandates, other deputies moved up on the party lists and took their places.

During the first days and weeks of the session, therefore, district deputies chose sides, and a few deputies elected on party lists changed factional affiliation. By April, nearly all deputies had joined one or another faction, most of them joining factions that were represented in the Council of the Duma.

Three deputy groups initially formed on the basis of district deputies: December 12, New Regional Policy, and Russia's Way. Of these the first two were able to register, while the third never recruited the necessary thirty-five members to register as a faction. By the fall session of 1995, substantial change had occurred in factional affiliations, much of it connected with deputies' interests in the impending December 1995 elections. The December 12 and Russia's Way groups faded away. Two new groups formed—called Stability and Rossiia (Russia)—in the spring of 1995. Both were moderately progovernment and proreform, and both were composed almost exclusively of SMD deputies. As indicated in table 7.2, the three groups of "independents"—December 12, Russia's Way, and New Regional Policy—along with Russia's Choice and the Party of Russian Unity and Accord (PRES), saw the most pronounced outflow of members. In all, almost one-quarter of the Duma deputies changed faction affiliations at least once.[4] In table 7.2 figures on faction strength are presented at two points—one after the initial affiliations had stabilized, and one close to the expiration of the Duma's term, as members had decided on the affiliations they wished to have as the election campaign began. For each faction, both absolute figures and the percentage of each faction's membership in the two categories of electoral mandate are given.

New Rules for the State Duma

Soon after dissolving the old parliament, President Yeltsin formed a set of teams to manage the transition to the new parliament. Overseeing several of the groups was a body called the "Commission on Legislative Proposals under the Administration of the President of Russia" (*Komissiia zakonodatel'nykh predpolozhenii pri administratsii prezidenta Rossii*). Yeltsin named Mikhail Mitiukov, a legal specialist and former deputy chairman of the legislation committee, to chair it and recruited several other prominent legal experts of the democratic camp who had been active in the previous parliament (including Viktor Sheinis, Fedor Shelov-Kovediaev, Boris Zolotukhin, and Igor' Bezrukov) to serve as deputy chairs. In all some sixty former deputies received jobs in the commission.[5]

After the December elections, the pace of preparatory work speeded up. The commission divided up into seven subcommissions and recruited representatives of the victorious parties to its work. The adoption of the constitution meant that the drafters of the new Standing Rules of each chamber had to be guided by the constitution, but for many of the most important issues, they were also guided by their own judgment and experience.[6]

The most immediate influence on the drafters of the new rules for the Duma was the sorry precedent of Ruslan Khasbulatov's reign in the Supreme Soviet. Few if any political groups—whether democrats or communists—defended his use of the powers of the office of parliamentary chairman. All agreed that his behavior was sometimes erratic, authoritarian, and self-aggrandizing. It was generally accepted that no future chairman should be given the temptation or opportunity to accumulate so much personal power. Therefore, they felt, a collegial structure should hold governing power so that the chairman could not manipulate the organizational resources of the institution to build a personal power base. The designers of the new parliamentary structure accordingly, explicitly aimed to limit the future chair's power. As participants in the design process put it, power in the new chamber should be organized horizontally across deputy factions rather than vertically from a chairman through a presidium and committee chairs.

But democrats and communists differed in their diagnosis of what had gone wrong in the previous parliament and how the new parliament should be run. Democrats blamed the communist model of soviets itself—the hierarchical arrangement of chairman, Presidium, and apparat—for fostering centralization and depriving deputies of the capacity to control their own proceedings. Communists emphasized the importance of collegial leadership over personal and still preferred some type of presidium model, in which power in the chamber would be centralized in a collective governing body. The Mitiukov commission, composed exclusively of democratically leaning former deputies, rejected the presidium model in favor of a body where opposing organized political forces could check each other. They debated whether the new governing body should be a committee of committee chairs or a council of party leaders, or both. In one of the most significant decisions by Mitiukov's commission, the draft rules it proposed vested governing power over the new Duma in a council of political factions that did not include committee chairs. The commission's members were well familiar with the Council of Factions that had operated in the previous Supreme Soviet and took it as a model. Mitiukov's commission also proposed creating a committee on organization to oversee the staff and material resources of the chamber as another way to reduce the potential power of the new chairman.

As to specialized committees, the commission proposed a system of regular specialized standing committees for each chamber, rather than, as under the Supreme Soviet, ad hoc commissions for the separate chambers, and a system of more powerful joint committees for the Supreme Soviet as a whole. Again, the goal was to avoid recreating the centralized type of parliament of the old Soviet model by separating the two chambers. For the same reason the Mitiukov commission proposed that the Duma and Federation Council should be governed differently, each with its own rules of procedure. The Federation Council would not be party run or party oriented. Instead, it would be overseen by a chairman and deputy chairmen, and its legislative processes would be organized around its standing committees. These early proposals proved to be highly influential. All were embodied into the rules adopted by each chamber. Like the mixed electoral system and the dual executive, these arrangements have stuck: opposing political forces have been willing to work under an arrangement that they could probably not have adopted without Yeltsin's intervention.

The election results gave the organizational process a significant impetus. As soon as the results were in and the victorious parties knew how many seats they would hold in the Duma, the party leaders began horse trading for positions of influence in the new parliament. Factional alliances began to form. Faction leaders took over the process of working out agreements on the structure and agenda of the new chamber, modifying the draft rules proposed by Mitiukov's commission in a series of informal negotiations at the Parliamentary Center building. Mitiukov's proposal had called for a very small number of standing committees, so that the chamber would be less susceptible to ministerial lobbying. But during the month between the election and the day that the Duma convened, as the faction leaders bargained over their demands for committees to control, they gradually increased the number of committees in order to accommodate their different legislative and political interests. By the time the factions had worked out the final distribution of committee chairmanships, the number of committees nearly tripled, from eight, in the original proposal, to twenty-three.[7]

The structure of the new Duma was powerfully influenced by the fact that much of of its leadership had served in the previous Supreme Soviet. Although the great majority of the new deputies elected in December were new to parliamentary politics, a sizable group of experienced deputies returned. Such prominent figures as Viktor Zorkal'tsev, Ivan Rybkin, Vladimir Isakov, Sergei Baburin, Mikhail Lapshin, Alexander Dzasokhov, Boris Zolotukhin, Viktor Sheinis, Bela Denisenko, Vladimir Lysenko, Alexander Pochinok, Nikolai Travkin, Mikhail Mitiukov, Georgii Zadonskii, Gleb Yakunin, Sergei Yushenkov, Sergei Shakhrai, Ekaterina Lakhova, and Nikolai Kharitonov had all served in the 1990–93 Russian transitional parliament. These individuals had worked with one another in interfactional and committee settings, and, despite deep ideological differences, generally agreed on the desirability of making the new parliament an effective instrument for political representation and decision making. In all, sixty-eight members of the new Duma had served in the RSFSR Congress/Supreme Soviet system. Another twenty-five had served in the union congress and Supreme Soviet, among them Anatolii Luk'ianov, who had been the chairman of the union parliament and now was one of the more hard-line members of the communist faction. The only major outsider was Zhirinovsky.

The returning deputies became the leadership core in the new Duma. One-third of those deputies who had previous legislative experience in either the Russian or USSR Supreme Soviet took leadership positions in the Duma as faction heads, committee chairmen and deputy chairmen, and chamber chairman and deputy chairs. One-quarter of the new leaders in these positions had had prior legislative experience. Of the committee chairmen, one-third had parliamentary experience. Given this rather high degree of continuity in leadership between the old and new parliaments, it is not surprising that the returning deputies used their knowledge of parliamentary organization to adapt the new parliament's structure to their interests and desires. They retained those features of the old legislative system they considered viable, such as a system of exclusive political factions, a system of specialized standing committees, a bill procedure employing three readings, working groups and special purpose commissions to draft legislation and settle differences, and a council of factions to work out compromise positions across factions on politically difficult issues. Likewise, they discarded those forms that they considered harmful, especially those associated with the excessive centralization of the chairman-presidium system of governance.

The prior experience of many of the faction leaders who returned to office helped them to settle several organizational questions during the month of bargaining before the new Duma convened on January 11. Although they had been unable to agree on the choice of a chairman, they had agreed on the concept of a package deal for the distribution of other leadership positions for their factions and had discussed whether to choose a chairman, the deputy chairs, and the committee chairs sequentially or as part of a single grand agreement.[8] They had begun to discuss the rules of procedure and the structure of the governing body. They had a considerable advantage, therefore, in determining the structure of power in the new parliament over deputies opposed to giving parties such advantages. As soon as the Duma convened, therefore, unaffiliated deputies responded by attempting to form their own deputy groups or joining party factions.

On the first day of the proceedings, the question immediately arose of how many members a group needed to have in order to enjoy the same privileges as a party faction.[9] The issue was heatedly contested because of the importance the new chamber placed on structuring its proceedings by faction. Through a sequence of votes the Duma settled on a compromise figure of thirty-five, representing a midpoint roughly midway between the preferences of the two dominant wings, reformers and conservatives. Thirty-five was higher than the point of departure of fourteen and lower than the counterproposal of fifty, but it was closer to the preferences of the LDPR-APR-CPRF wing than to the position of the democrats. The sequence of voting revealed that the two wings defined by the left-right axis were approximately equal in size, but that the left was slightly stronger.[10]

The Duma also held a series of "rating" votes to determine which of the six final candidates nominated for chairman could win the largest number. Ivan Rybkin, a member of the communist party who had been elected on the list of the Agrarian Party and an experienced politician regarded as having a moderate and pragmatic temperament, won the most votes. The Duma postponed the final election in order to allow the factions to decide how they would line up on the final vote.

At the same time that they were deliberating over their governing arrangements, deputies were also deciding on their factional affiliations. During breaks in the sessions of the first two days, independent deputies from single-member districts caucused and formed their own "independent" groups. Three nuclei appeared, one with a reform orientation, and another with a conservative and nationalist orientation. A third, avowedly centrist, group formed of deputies close to industrial, and particularly oil and gas industry, interests. Only this third group attracted enough members to register under the thirty-five-member rule. Led by the chairman of the oil workers union, this group, "New Regional Policy" (NRP), also brought in some twenty deputies representing autonomous republics and districts. Eventually they had about sixty-five members. The other two groups, however, Russia's Way (the conservative group) and December 12 (the reform group) failed to recruit enough members to meet the thirty-five-member threshold. Each appealed to friendly party factions to lend it some members so that it could obtain registration, but neither succeeded.[11] However, in April, the December 12 group, now renamed the Liberal Democratic Union of December 12, did attain the required number of members and was registered.[12]

By the end of the second day of proceedings, most decisions about factional affiliation were made. There were eight political factions and one registered group, and two other unregistered groups. The nine factions (we shall henceforth treat the NRP as a faction) divided neatly into three camps, each with three factions: the democrats (Russia's Choice, PRES, and Yabloko), the centrists (Women of Russia, Democratic Party of Russia, and New Regional Policy), and the opposition (the communists, the agrarians, and the LDPR). Now the real test of left-right strength came with the second round of voting on the speakership as the factions formed coalitions backing alternative candidates. The left factions rallied around Ivan Rybkin, and he won by a single vote.[13]

The Interfactional Power-Sharing Agreement

Once Rybkin was elected, the reform forces changed tack.[14] Previously Russia's Choice—the largest faction in the Duma—had been reluctant to take part in the negotiations on distributing leadership positions, evidently believing that it had more to gain by attempting to build its own majority coalition. The election of Rybkin revealed, however, that when it was united, the left opposition was stronger. Now Russia's Choice stood to gain more from participating in proportional arrangements than from losing everything in majoritarian arrangements. For its part, the tenuous left coalition, which had just produced the thinnest of margins for a moderate chairman, evidently lacked the cohesiveness to press its advantage too far and consolidate its control over parliament.

Therefore, as soon as Rybkin was elected chairman, the Duma recessed to allow faction leaders to complete work on a negotiated agreement over the distribution of deputy chairmanships of the Duma, committee chairmanships, and other leadership posts. Rybkin's election occurred on Friday, January 14. Over the weekend the faction leaders met and reached agreement on a package deal to be put to the floor for a straight up-or-down vote. They used an ingenious auction procedure for arriving at the agreement. The elective positions in the chamber were appraised according to their value. The chairmanship, which had already gone to the Agrarian Party, was the most valuable post; deputy Duma chairmanships were worth more than committee chairmanships, and these in turn were worth more than deputy committee chairmanships. The value in points of all the positions at stake was added up and divided by the number of seats in the Duma to yield a point value for each seat. Each faction was allotted bidding rights based on the number of seats it possessed. Factions then bid for the combination of positions they desired according to the number of seats they possessed. Not all demands could be satisfied in this way, however, so adjustments were made. Russia's Choice and the LDPR ended up with the same number of committee chairmanships and deputy chairmanships after the initial distribution, so Russia's Choice was given a specially created post of first deputy chairman of the Duma. The LDPR demanded, but was refused, the chairmanship of the foreign affairs committee, so a new committee on

Table 7.3. Committee Assignments by Party Faction Membership in the State Duma of the Federal Assembly of Russia, as of January 19, 1994

Faction	As % of All Committee members ($N = 425$)	As % of All Deputy Committee Chairs ($N = 70$)	As % of All Committe Chairs ($N = 23$)
Agrarian	10.1	12.9	8.7
CPRF	10.1	10.0	8.7
LDPR	14.6	15.7	21.7
NRP	15.3	20.0	13.0
Russia's Choice	17.4	17.1	17.4
WOR	5.2	1.4	4.3
PRES	6.4	8.6	13.0
Yabloko	6.4	8.6	8.7
DPR	3.5	5.7	4.3
None	11.1	0.0	0.0

Abbreviations: Agrarian : Agrarian Party of Russia; CPRF: Communist Party of the Russian Federation; LDPR: Liberal Democratic Party of Russia (Zhirinovsky's party); NRP: New Regional Policy; WOR: Women of Russia; PRES: Party of Russian Unity and Accord; Yabloko: the bloc Yavlinsky-Boldyrev-Lukin; DPR: Democratic Party of Russia.

"geopolitics" was created that it could control.[15] The deputy chairmanships of the chamber were spread across factions. After Mikhail Mitiukov was given the position of first deputy chairman, the next three deputy chairmanships went to the CPRF, Women of Russia, and LDPR factions. A fourth deputy chairmanship was later given to the New Regional Policy group. The position of human rights commissioner went to the longtime democratic activist, Sergei Kovalev, from Russia's Choice.[16]

When the Duma reconvened on Monday morning, the interfactional power-sharing agreement to allocate deputy chamber chairmanships and committee chairmanships was put to a vote and passed with 290 votes. The resulting distribution of posts is listed in table 7.3. An attempt the next day by a communist deputy to reopen the agreement was overwhelmingly defeated, winning only eighty-eight votes.[17] The success of the package agreement in turn made it easier for the Duma to settle the next open question, the structure of the Council of the Duma. The preference of the communists for proportionalism in distributing leadership positions rather than trying to form a majority coalition with the LDPR and control the chamber as a bloc gave the democratic factions confidence that an all-factions governing arrangement was possible; it showed that other alignments beside simple left-right ones were likely to appear. The communists, in turn, were willing to form the Council of the Duma on a parity basis, that is, one representative from each faction. Small factions would have disproportionate influence, but Russia's Choice and the LDPR, the two largest party-based factions, would have only one vote each. The faction leaders agreed to the parity rule for forming the Council of the Duma; the motion passed on the floor over the objections of representatives of the unaffiliated deputies and unregistered deputy groups, who complained that the decision on the Council of the Duma and the package agreement on distributing committee posts represented an unfair aggrandizement of power by the party factions at the expense of independents.[18] The adoption of a party-dominated power-sharing arrangement for distributing leadership positions came at the expense of deputies with weak partisan affiliations.

Factionalism in the State Duma

Recall that after October 1991, Russian Supreme Soviet deputies could join only one faction but could join as many groups as they wished. Under the rules of the new Duma, the membership restriction was extended to *all* deputy associations, whether faction or group (and whether the group was registered or not): a deputy is not required to join a faction or group but may be a member of only one. Nearly all deputies do in fact join a faction or registered group.[19] They affiliate for both policy-based and office-based reasons; factions, in fact, may be characterized by whether they tend to emphasize one or the other set of interests. More ideologically oriented factions have positions on the left-right policy voting axis that are farther away from the mean, and, more tellingly, the dispersion of their members around that mean position is narrower. Factions more oriented toward office goals alone (that is, the rights to committee chairmanships, staff, office space, and the like) have ideology scores closer to the mean, with wide variations around the mean. These differences are clearly reflected in table 7.4 and (for 1996–97) table 7.8.

In 1994–95, the voting positions of reform and opposition factions were sharply distinguished (and a very similar pattern may be observed again in 1996–97): the mean member of Russia's Choice was about as far from the mean for the entire chamber (normalized to equal zero) in the promarket, pro-Yeltsin direction as the mean communist deputy was in the opposite direction. This was the major axis on which factions were aligned in both Dumas and was the dominant dimension of policy conflict. On other voting dimensions, factions were aligned differently, but these were far weaker factors. For example, in

Table 7.4. Faction Ideological Positions, 1994–1995

Faction	Mean Faction Ideology Score	Standard Deviation	Number of Cases
CPRF	1.28	.38	46
Agrarian	.98	.55	51
LDPR	.80	.40	55
WOR	.59	.27	21
DPR	.24	.27	8
NRP	.15	.46	39
None	−.45	.86	65
Rossiia	−.24	.69	37
Stability	−.48	.73	37
PRES	−.88	.35	22
Yabloko	−.97	.29	27
Russia's Choice	−1.30	.13	54
$N = 462$			

$F = 101.9$. Significance of $F < .0000$

Abbreviations: CPRF: Communist Party of the Russian Federation; Agrarian: Agrarian Party of Russia; LDPR: Liberal Democratic Party of Russia; WOR: Women of Russia; DPR: Democratic Party of Russia; NRP: New Regional Policy; PRES: party of Russian Unity and Accord; Yabloko: the bloc Yavlinsky-Boldyrev-Lukin.

Note: The figures reported in this table reflect mean left-right scores for factions (membership taken as of 1995) for a set of votes that met a criterion for defining party-influenced votes: in a linear model predicting any given deputy's yea or nay vote, a set of dummy variables for deputy faction membership explains at least 50 percent of the variance in outcomes. This procedure eliminates about half of the electronically recorded votes in the Duma.

The mean score on this dimension is a measure of the location of the average member of each faction on the first principal component extracted from the matrix of recorded electronic votes in the 1994–95 Duma. This principal component is strongly associated with the dimension I refer to as the "communist vs. reformer" conflict. That is, the factor loads strongly on votes concerning property relations, fiscal stabilization, Yeltsin's power, and relations with the West.

The number of cases is greater than 450 because it includes deputies who were elected to fill positions vacated by departing members.

1996–97, Zhirinovsky's faction was distinct from all other factions on a second factor in the principal components analysis, but it is difficult to assign this dimension any substantive meaning. Notwithstanding the colorful rhetoric of nationalist opposition employed by Zhirinovsky, his faction's voting stance in parliament is inconsistent. On major issues dividing pro-Kremlin from opposition forces (such as the impeachment vote in May 1999; see table 7.12), he has often aligned his faction with the Kremlin, suggesting that considerations other than principle may explain his positions. In both the 1994–95 and 1996–99 Dumas, the only consistent policy dimension explaining variation in deputies' voting positions was the division between proreform, progovernment forces and the communist opposition. This was the axis along which factions defined their positions. For that reason, those factions with mean scores farthest from the center, such as the communists and Russia's Choice, on the first dimension also have the lowest standard deviations around that mean. Factions closer to the center have a more ideologically diverse membership.

This pattern reflects the fact that the so-called centrists are not so much centrists as they are a residual category: a heterogeneous group of independents sharing a common interest in obtaining the benefits of factional status. In many cases their policy outlook is pragmatic rather than doctrinal, and often their principal political loyalty is to the executive branch and whatever current "party of power" is affiliated with the executive branch. A good example is the formation of the deputy groups Russia (Rossiia) and Stability in spring 1995; these were progovernment deputies who were encouraged to break away from their existing factions and anticipated receiving support from the government in their reelection campaigns later in the year. Similarly, in late 1999, the Kremlin encouraged a group of deputies to form a new faction (called "People's Deputy") linked to the Unity electoral bloc, which would call upon government resources in helping its members' reelection campaigns. This group failed to win official recognition, however. As these examples indicate, office-related benefits have an electoral payoff, the value of which is higher for deputies as elections draw closer. Parliamentary factions' organizational resources—their telephones and fax machines, research and clerical staff, cars and drivers, offices and budgets—are crucially important to their members' electoral interests. Therefore, both for ideologically motivated and office-seeking parliamentary factions, factional status is a resource for future reelection.

It is scarcely surprising that the factions formed around ideological affinities show higher levels of cohesiveness in floor voting than do factions organized for more instrumental reasons. Of greater interest is the relatively high level of co-ordination in voting exhibited by both kinds of factions. To be sure, members vote with their feet: nearly one-quarter of faction members changed their affiliations over the 1994–95 period, and some did so more than once. Many simply left factions and failed to join new ones (or could not gather the requisite number of deputies needed to register a new group). By the end of 1995, more than fifty members of the first Duma were outside a faction or registered group;

Table 7.5. Factional Coordination of Legislative Work

1994 Deputy Survey ($N = 214$)

	CPRF	Agrarian	LDPR	Yabloko	RC	Dec. 12	PRES	NRP
Coordinate member's legislative work in committee (% responding "as a rule")	75.0	48.5	68.2	66.7	53.8	37.5	75.0	51.7
Guide member's position in committee discussion (% responding "as a rule")	62.5	36.4	50.0	50.0	41.0	37.5	37.5	41.4
Determining factional line on floor voting (% responding "as a rule")	71.9	51.5	77.3	27.8	56.4	75.0	25.0	37.9
Frequency of decision on disciplined voting (% responding "four times or more")	46.9	33.3	77.3	55.6	74.4	0	50.0	31.0

1996 Deputy Survey ($N = 175$)

	CPRF	Agrarian	LDPR	Yabloko	NDR	PP	RR
Coordinate member's legislative work in committee (% responding "as a rule")	57.6	47.6	69.2	50.0	58.6	52.9	45.0
Guide member's position in committee discussion (% responding "as a rule")	51.5	42.9	69.2	25.0	55.2	29.4	20.0

Table 7.5. (*Continued*)

1994 Deputy Survey (*N* = 214)

	CPRF	Agrarian	LDPR	Yabloko	NDR	PP	RR
Determining factional line on floor voting (% responding "as a rule")	63.6	47.6	76.9	57.1	55.2	29.4	45.0
Frequency of decision on disciplined voting (% responding "four times or more")	59.4	31.6	61.9	21.4	44.4	18.8	21.1

Abbreviations: CPRF: Communist Party of the Russian Federation; Agrarian: Agrarian Party of Russia; LDPR: Liberal Democratic Party of Russia; Yabloko: the bloc Yavlinsky-Boldyrev-Lukin; RC: Russia's Choice; Dec. 12: Liberal Democratic Group of December 12; PRES: Party of Russian Unity and Accord; NRP: New Regional Policy; NDR: Our Home Is Russia; PP: People's Power; RR: Russia's Regions.

as of May 1999, thirty members of the second Duma were unaffiliated. Faction leaders have very few levers for enforcing faction discipline; ideological affinity is the principal force for cohesion in faction behavior. If a faction chooses to expel a member, it cannot strip that member of a committee chairmanship acquired as a result of the interfactional power-sharing agreement, let alone deprive him of his seat.[20] In surveys taken in December 1994 and January 1995, and again in March-April 1996, deputies were asked questions about their experience with factional activity in committee work and floor voting.[21] The results, indicated in table 7.5, show that deputies in factions of the more ideologically oriented and electorally established parties, such as the communists, LDPR, Yabloko, and Russia's Choice, reported higher levels of factional involvement with their legislative work in committees, committee position-taking, and floor voting than did deputies belonging to independents' groups, such as the New Regional Policy, December 12, People's Power, and Russia's Regions groups.

The degree to which factions succeed in coordinating the policy positions of their members is low in comparison to European parliamentary democracies, but high in light of the extremely low levels of partisanship in mass electoral behavior in Russia and the fact that voting cohesion in parliament does not carry with it the responsibility for maintaining or challenging a governing coalition. Since governments are not formed from Duma majorities, no faction has the power to deprive a government of its mandate by withdrawing its support. The incentives for factionalism in the Duma are therefore based on the value of internal office-related resources for policy and electoral purposes and their members' shared outlooks on the dominant cleavage dividing supporters and opponents of market reform.

Many observers have been critical of the high level of Duma factionalism, believing that it has harmed the quality of legislation. A more detailed assessment of this point follows in the final section of this chapter, but it is worth noting here that factionalism has permitted the Council of the Duma to serve collectively as a center of agenda-setting power, replacing the heavily centralized system of chairman and Presidium that characterized Soviet and Russian parliaments before 1993. If members did not generally follow the lead of their factions in voting, leaders could not forge and deliver agreements able to win a stable majority of votes on the floor.

The 1995 Duma Elections

The cross-factional power-sharing agreement of January 1994 served as a precedent for the second Duma, which convened in January 1996. Once again, a package agreement solved the problem of organizing governance in an uncertain setting where no party or coalition commanded a majority. It gave party factions and factionlike groups just enough privileges to give each a stake in the parliament's operations without relinquishing majority control over outcomes. The fact that only four parties cleared the electoral threshold in the 1995 elections and entered the Duma with party factions may have eased the deputies' job of reaching a package agreement.

The first Duma succeeded in enacting a new law on parliamentary elections in time for the December 1995 elections.[22] Although it had been the object of an intense three-way contest among the Duma, Federation Council, and president, the new law in its final version differed little from the old one. It kept the half-and-half system of distributing seats with no compensatory seats, and kept as well the 5-percent threshold. It retained the single Russia-wide electoral district for the party-list ballot, although adding a vague requirement that electoral associations had to divide their candidate lists into a central portion consisting of no more than twelve candidates and one or more subnational lists to increase the representation of regional figures.[23] As before, the election in single-member districts would employ a single-round, plurality method and would be valid if as few as 25 percent of the eligible electorate participated.

Despite its authors' hope that the election law would lead to a consolidation of political forces in the country, an astonishing number of groups sought a place on the ballot. Sixty-nine organizations attempted to gather the necessary 200,000 signatures.[24] Forty-three succeeded. They included the parties that had competed in 1993 or their successors. The independents' groups in the Duma, Stability and Rossiia, became the nuclei of yet other parties. At President Yeltsin's behest, Prime Minister Chernomyrdin agreed to head a new electoral movement, called "Our Home Is Russia," which enjoyed the substantial advantages accruing to it as "the party of power."[25] As before, electoral associations that qualified enjoyed the benefits of free television time and state funds for their campaign and were allowed to raise more funds from private sources.

Many observers feared that with forty-three parties running, it might well turn out that none received at least 5 percent of the vote. In the event, nearly half of the party vote was wasted on parties that failed to clear the threshold, while the four winning parties each doubled the number of seats they would otherwise have received. By any standards, the election was dismaying for those who hoped that Russia's party system might be settling into a stable and consolidated instrument of political representation.

Under the circumstances, therefore, the degree of continuity in parliamentary representation yielded by the December 17 balloting is striking. Over one-third—157—of the newly elected deputies had served in the previous Duma; another 15 had served in the Council of the Federation. These deputies provided a foundation of legislative experience and leadership. For instance, 60 percent (17 of 28) of the chairmen in the new Duma had served in the previous Duma, and several had been chairs of the same committees (among them some of the most important committees—those on budget, security, public associations, labor and social welfare, and international affairs). Three of the 5 deputy chairmen of the new Duma had served in the previous Duma, as had 44 percent of the deputy chairmen of committees. Given the depth of the voters' dissatisfaction with the regime, this level of continuity among parliamentarians is striking.[26]

Since the four winning parties all had strong roots in the previous Duma, their success ensured substantial continuity in experience in the new Duma. The new CPRF, LDPR, and Yabloko factions inherited the leadership and organization of their predecessors. Russia's Choice was no longer a faction, but the new Our Home Is Russia faction inherited some of its assets, including some of its members, and close ties to the government, together with some of the members of other factions. Of the groups that formed, the agrarians were the direct successors of the Agrarian Party faction in the previous Duma (46 percent had been deputies before), while both the Russia's Regions (46 percent) and People's Power factions (36 percent) contained sizable shares of experienced members. The success of the communists meant that they gained a very large number of new deputies (only 22 percent of their faction's membership had been deputies in the previous Duma), but they were brought into a faction that was by far the most tightly organized and disciplined. Over half of the LDPR's members were previous Duma deputies. The continuity of members and factions helps explain the fact that the new Duma replicated the governing arrangements and lawmaking procedures of its predecessor.

The high level of continuity in factions enabled the new Duma to organize itself more quickly. As soon as it convened, deputies grouped into factions. This time, the communist faction had no objection to delegating members to friendly groups so as to bring them up to the thirty-five-member floor for registration. As before, SMD deputies allied by loose political affiliation, forming one group for those standing closer politically to the government (Russia's Regions) and another for those in opposition (People's Power). The third, the agrarian faction, resumed the role that the agrarian faction has played in each parliament we have examined—partly an interest-based lobby for the collective and state farm sector and partly an ideological ally of the communists. By the end of the first day of the proceedings of the new Duma, nearly all the members had affiliated with factions (see table 7.6). As in 1994, the great majority of deputies joined a faction, reflecting the party-oriented governance structure of the new Duma.

Once again, the election of a chairman of the chamber served as a rough test of factional strength. The victory of Gennadii Seleznev, from the Communist Party faction, proved that the alliance of the communists and other leftist factions could command a majority when its allies, the agrarians and People's Power factions, voted cohesively with it. Seleznev had been a deputy in the previous Duma and had become one of its deputy chairmen in January 1995.

Once the factions formed and the chairman was elected, faction leaders quickly worked out a package agreement for distributing leadership positions. First they decided to give each faction a deputy chairmanship of the chamber.[27] Then the committee chairmanships and deputy chairmanships were distributed in rough proportion to faction strength on the floor. The faction lead-

Table 7.6. Factional Membership in the State Duma, January 16, 1996

Faction	% of Vote Won in Party-List Ballot	Party-List Seats Received	Single-Member-District Deputies Affiliated	Total Seats	Share of Seats (%)
CPRF	22.7	95	54	149	33.1
LDPR	11.4	50	1	51	11.3
NDR	10.3	45	20	65	14.4
Yabloko	7.0	31	15	46	10.2
RR		0	41	41	9.1
Agrarian		2	33	35	7.8
PP		2	35	37	8.2
Unaffiliated		0	26	26	5.8

Abbreviations: CPRF: Communist Party of the Russian Federation; LDPR: Liberal Democratic Party of Russia; NDR: Our Home Is Russia; Yabloko: the bloc Yavlinsky-Boldyrev-Lukin; RR: Russia's Regions; Agrarian: Agrarian Party of Russia; PP: People's Power.

ers increased the number of committees from twenty-three to twenty-eight to accommodate demands by factions and individual members. As a result, some committee jurisdictions were overlapping. In all, around one-third of the members received leadership positions of some kind. The distribution of posts by faction is listed in table 7.7, indicating the number of positions in each category that each group was assigned and the percentage that share represented of all positions of that category. Note that the communists refrained from asserting majority control over the chamber, although they took advantage of the rules on group registration and Council of the Duma membership to multiply their points of leverage. They seconded enough members to the agrarian and People's Power groups to enable these potential allies of the CPRF to register as factions. Thus instead of one voice on the Council of the Duma, they now had their own plus two allied factions out of seven. But, as indicated in table 7.8, these factions were not always reliable allies of the communists in floor voting.

As in 1994, nonparty deputies objected strenuously to the package agreement on the grounds that it favored the interests of parties and party-list deputies over the interests of independents and deputies elected in single-member districts. The Russia's Regions group initially refused to accept the agreement and to delegate members to occupy the two committee chairmanships reserved for it. Several deputies considered sending an appeal to the Con-

Table 7.7. Leadership Positions by Faction in the State Duma, January 1996 (in absolute figures and percentages)

Faction	Chairman of Duma	Deputy Chairs of Duma	Committee Chairs	Deputy Committee Chairs
CPRF	1 (100)	1 (20)	9 (32.1)	17 (15.7)
LDPR		1 (20)	4 (14.3)	24 (22.2)
NDR		1[a] (20)	3 (10.7)	24 (22.2)
Yabloko			5 (17.9)	19 (17.6)
RR		1 (20)	3 (10.7)	8 (7.4)
Agrarian			2 (7.1)	8 (7.4)
PP		1 (20)	2 (7.1)	6 (5.6)
Unaffiliated				2 (1.9)
Total	1 (100)	5 (100)	28 (99.9)	108 (100)

Abbreviations: CPRF: Communist Party of the Russian Federation; LDPR: Liberal Democratic Party of Russia; NDR: Our Home Is Russia; Yabloko: the bloc Yavlinsky-Boldyrev-Lukin; RR: Russia's Regions; Agrarian: Agrarian Party of Russia; PP: People's Power.
[a]The NDR representative, Alexander Shokhin, was first deputy chairman of the Duma until September 1997, when he stepped down to assume the chairmanship of the faction and was replaced by another member of the NDR faction, Vladimir Ryzhkov.

stitutional Court that the distribution of committee chairmanships by agreement among faction leaders violated their constitutional rights.[28] After a day, however, when it was evident that the package agreement was unlikely to be overturned either by the Duma or by the Court, the Russia's Regions group withdrew its objections and named its two designated chairmen.[29]

The result of the interfactional power-sharing package deals is an institutional arrangement in the Duma that favors the collective interests of party factions at the expense of three categories of actors that had been relatively more powerful in the predecessor parliaments of the USSR and RSFSR: the chairman; nonparty and single-member-district deputies; and committees, particularly committee chairs. The latter, after all, had composed the steering unit in the previous parliaments.[30] It is important to recognize the limits on the power of factions and faction leaders, however. Most factions have relatively weak means to keep members in line. The factions preserved the rule of exclusive membership from the previous parliament, requiring that deputies could be members of no more than one faction, which had been a victory for faction leaders back in October 1991. Otherwise, the rights of individual deputies re-

Table 7.8. Faction Ideological Positions, 1996–1997

Faction	Mean Faction Ideology Score	Standard Deviation	Number of Cases
CPRF	.686	.829	147
Agrarian	.442	.389	36
PP	.093	.682	37
LDPR	.022	.572	51
RR	−.375	.591	44
Yabloko	−.447	.489	46
NDR	−.560	.550	66
None	−1.70	1.87	21

$F = 42.368$. Significance of $F < .0000$

Abbreviations: CPRF: Communist Party of the Russian Federation; Agrarian: Agrarian Party of Russia; PP: People's Power; LDPR: Liberal Democratic Party of Russia; RR: Russia's Regions; Yabloko: the bloc Yavlinsky-Boldyrev-Lukin; NDR: Our Home Is Russia.

Note: Scores represent the mean value of the members of Duma factions as of December 1996 on the first factor extracted through a principal components analysis of a set of 365 electronically recorded votes between January 1996 and May 1997. Included are all votes in "final passage," which comprise votes on bills in third reading, votes to override a veto by the Federation Council or president, and votes on the reports of agreement commissions. This factor loads strongly on issues where communists in the Duma clashed with the president and his supporters, among them votes on the human rights commissioner law, the Land Code, pensions bills, bills on military service, establishment of the continental shelf and others.

mained unaffected. Deputies continued to be free to join committees according to their own preferences (although in the more tightly organized factions, their choices were strongly influenced by their factional colleagues). Factions succeeded in depriving committee chairs of a vote on the Council of the Duma, but they have not greatly changed the freewheeling style of legislative procedure on the floor that was characteristic of the transitional union and RSFSR Supreme Soviets. Members were still able to frustrate decision making through high absenteeism and through frequent demands for votes on motions and amendments. The Duma is faction oriented, to be sure, but individual deputies have still not delegated faction leaders the degree of power over decisions that is found in parliaments with sharper divisions between majority and minority parties.

Internal Structures of the Duma

Faction leaders collectively control the chamber through the Council of the Duma, which has replaced the old Presidium as the steering body. The Duma chairman chairs the meetings of the Council of the Duma; the other members are the heads of each faction and recognized group. All sources agree that the factions are represented at the council's sessions by their highest-ranking leaders. These leaders do not have any other official duties in the parliament; they do not serve on committees or as leaders within the chamber. Their sole responsibility is to lead their parliamentary factions and represent them at the meetings of the Council of the Duma.

The Council of the Duma has inherited many of the duties that the Presidium once performed. One is to plan the agenda of the chamber through a set of longer- and shorter-term calendars. It also assigns all bills to committees. Occasionally it exercises this power in such a way as to favor one faction or coalition over another. An unusual case concerns the hotly contested legislation on production-sharing agreements. After a series of skirmishes and press conferences in June 1998, when the embattled chairman of the committee with jurisdiction over the legislation protested the actions of the opposition factions in blocking the bill, the Council of the Duma decided, over the objections of the Yabloko faction, to remove the legislation from the natural resource committee's jurisdiction and give it to another committee. But like all of its formal decisions, this had to be confirmed on the floor.[31]

Generally the powers of the Council of the Duma are comparable to those of the Presidium, but the Council of the Duma is far less subject to the chairman's influence than was the old Supreme Soviet Presidium. Most major decisions about procedure are made through consultation between the chairman and the factions and are subject to a vote on the floor. Members are willing to delegate power to their faction leaders to negotiate the political agreements needed to organize their proceedings and the shape of legislation, but these agreements must be worked out anew on every issue. The importance of the Council of the Duma as a steering mechanism for the Duma therefore lies in its ability to craft political bargains on legislation that will win a majority on the floor and yet still have a reasonable chance of being signed into law. It has been surprisingly successful at doing this. What had been an informal practice in the late Gorbachev-era Supreme Soviet—inviting leaders of the organized political factions to Presidium meetings and sounding them out about major issues of the day—and later a quasi-institutionalized form in the Khasbulatov Supreme Soviet had finally become the governing body of parliament itself.

Under Duma rules, each deputy must be a member of a committee, but of one committee only. Faction chairs and chamber leaders are not required to join committees and, in practice, do not. Deputies are largely free to choose their committee assignments, although interviews indicate that they do so in consultation with faction leaders. Committees vary in their factional composition. In only two cases, however, is there a pronounced disproportion between the committee makeup and the strength of factions overall. In the geopolitical affairs committee, which was created expressly to satisfy Zhirinovsky's demands for control of a committee dealing with defense or security issues, the LDPR has dominated the membership in both Dumas, giving it seven of its fourteen deputies in 1994, and eight of thirteen deputies in 1996. The agrarian faction has saturated the agricultural affairs committee even more strongly, constituting nineteen of its twenty-two members in 1994, and fifteen of its twenty-one members in 1996. With respect to other committees there tends to be a far less direct association between a committee and a particular faction.[32] A list of the committees in the Dumas of each convocation, their chairs, and the chairs' factional affiliations can be found in table 7.9.

BILL PROCEDURE IN THE STATE DUMA

Bill procedure was carried over from the older parliaments with very little change, suggesting that most participants considered existing practices to be politically neutral means of decision making. The deputies have made minor modifications to inherited rules but have not significantly changed the allocation of rights across individual members, committees, factions, or leadership. The net effect of the changes made is to provide more mechanisms for preventing poorly drafted or thinly supported items from reaching the floor, and to refine the methods for resolving disputes with the Federation Council and president. The Council of the Duma coordinates the process: it assigns bills to committee, schedules them for each step of the process, and decides on the composition of the agreement commission and special commissions created to resolve differences with the Council of the Federation and the president in case of a veto. Otherwise, the outlines of first, second, and third readings are remarkably similar to their analogues in the USSR and RSFSR Supreme Soviets. The first reading is intended to establish the basic outlines of a piece of legisla-

Table 7.9. Duma Committee Chairman as of Beginning of Convocation, 1994 and 1996

Committee	Chairman	Chairman's Factional Affiliation
1994		
Legislation and Judicial-Legal Reform	V. B. Isakov	Agrarian
Labor and Social Support	S. V. Kalashnikov	LDPR
Health Protection	B. A. Denisenko	Russia's Choice
Ecology	M. Ia. Lemeshev	LDPR
Education, Culture, and Science	L. P. Rozhkova	NRP
Affairs of Women, Family, and Youth	G. I. Klimatova	Women of Russia
Budget, Taxes, Banks, and Finance	M. M. Zadornov	Yabloko
Economic Policy	S. Iu. Glaz'ev	DPR
Property, Privatization, and Economic Activity	S. V. Burkov	NRP
Agrarian Issues	A. Z. Nazarchuk[a]	Agrarian
Industry, Construction, Transportation, and Energy	V. K. Gusev	LDPR
Natural Resources and Resource Use	N. P. Astaf'ev	LDPR
Defense	S. N. Iushenkov	Russia's Choice
Security	V. I. Iliukhin	CPRF
International Affairs	V. P. Lukin	Yabloko
CIS Affairs and Relations with Compatriots Abroad	K. F. Zatulin	PRES[b]
Nationality Affairs	B. B. Zhamsuev	NRP[c]
Federation Affairs and Regional Policy	S. A. Shapovalov	PRES
Issues of Local Self-Government	A. Ia. Sliva	PRES
Affairs of Public Associations and Religious Organizations	V. I. Zorkal'tsev	CPRF
Organization of the Work of the State Duma	V. A. Bauer	Russia's Choice[d]
Information Policy and Communications	M. N. Poltoranin	Russia's Choice[e]
Issues of Geopolitics	V. I. Ustinov	LDPR
Credentials Commission	V. I. Sevast'ianov	CPRF
1996		
Legislation and Judicial-Legal Reform	A. I. Luk'ianov	CPRF
Labor and Social Policy	S. V. Kalashnikov	LDPR
Veterans' Affairs	V. I. Varennikov	CPRF

Table 7.9. (*Continued*)

Committee	Chairman	Chairman's Factional Affiliation
1996		
Health Protection	N. F. Gerasimenko	Russia's Regions
Education and Science	I. I. Mel'nikov	CPRF
Affairs of Women, Family, and Youth	A. V. Aparina	CPRF
Budget, Taxes, Banks, and Finance	M. M. Zadornov	Yabloko
Economic Policy	Iu. D. Masliukov	CPRF
Property, Privatization, and Economic Activity	P. G. Bunich	NDR
Agrarian Issues	A. A. Chernyshev	Agrarian
Industry, Construction, Transportation, and Energy	V. K. Gusev	LDPR
Natural Resources and Resource Use	A. Iu. Mikhailov	Yabloko
Ecology	V. V. Zlotnikova	Yabloko
Defense	L. Ia. Rokhlin	NDR
Security	V. I. Iliukhin	CPRF
International Affairs	V. P. Lukin	Yabloko
CIS Affairs and Relations with Compatriots Abroad	G. I. Tikhonov	People's Power
Nationality Affairs	V. Iu. Zorin	NDR
Federation Affairs and Regional Policy	L. A. Ivanchenko	CPRF
Issues of Local Self-Government	A. A. Poliakov	NDR
Affairs of Public Associations and Religious Organizations	V. I. Zorkal'tsev	CPRF
The Standing Orders and Organization of the Work of the State Duma	D. F. Krasnikov	Agrarian
Information Policy and Communications	O. A. Fin'ko	LDPR
Issues of Geopolitics	A. V. Mitrofanov	LDPR
Conversion and Science-Intensive Technologies	G. V. Kostin	People's Power
Culture	S. S. Govorukhin	People's Power
Tourism and Sports	A. S. Sokolov	CPRF
Problems of the North	V. V. Goman	Russia's Regions
Credentials Commission	V. I. Sevast'ianov	CPRF

Abbreviations: Agrarian: Agrarian Party of Russia; LDPR: Liberal Democratic Party of Russia; NRP: New Regional Policy; Yabloko: the bloc Yavlinsky-Boldyrev-Lukin; DPR: Demo

continued

Table 7.9. (*Continued*)

cratic Party of Russia; CPRF: Communist Party of the Russian Federation; PRES: Party of Russian Unity and Accord; NDR: Our Home Is Russia.

[a]In January 1995, Nazarchuk was named minister of agriculture. He was replaced as chairman by A. A. Chernyshev, also from the agrarian faction.

[b]In November 1994, the PRES faction expelled Zatulin and attempted to recall him as committee chairman. The chamber, however, refused to strip him of his chairmanship.

[c]In 1995 Zhamsuev changed factional affiliations, quitting New Regional Policy to join the new Stability faction. He retained his committee chairmanship.

[d]In February 1995, the Russia's Choice faction accused Bauer of misusing his position as committee chairman and demanded his resignation from the faction and his chairmanship. He resigned from the faction but refused to step down as committee chairman. The faction's motion to remove him as chairman failed to receive a majority of votes in the chamber. Bauer continued to serve as chairman, meantime joining the New Regional Policy faction.

[e]Poltoranin resigned from Russia's Choice in June 1995 but retained his committee chairmanship.

tion—its concept, purpose, and means. As in the previous parliaments, first reading is designed to determine whether the members wish to proceed with action on the bill. And, as before, if more than one version of a piece of legislation is submitted, first reading is the point at which the chamber decides which is to be taken as the basis for proceeding. The 1998 rules add some new provisions on this point. As in other matters of legislative process, they limit the discretion of the standing committees. If alternative versions of a bill are introduced, the committee considers them and offers a recommendation as to which should be adopted and which rejected. A committee cannot on its own authority suppress an alternative draft that it dislikes: it must allow the floor to determine which to adopt.

Committees have discretion in developing their own procedures for considering bills, although the rules provide that they must adhere to the calendar set by the Council of the Duma. As in the past, committees can form working groups to draft or revise legislation and have freedom to draw up the membership of such groups. Typically, working groups are made up of both deputies and nondeputies. Among the latter, it is common for parliamentary staff, experts from research institutes, government officials, and members of the presidential administration to take part. Among deputies, members of other committees besides the lead committee are often included. The committee names one of its members to be the bill manager (*dokladchik*) and to coordinate the work of preparing the bill for the vote in first reading. That individual may have already taken the initiative in assembling a group of specialists or may be acting at the behest of outside interests who wish to see a particular piece of legislation passed. Interviews suggest that a committee member responsible for a measure has a good deal of discretion in assembling a working group to help in framing legislation, although resource constraints are sometimes a problem: a working group usually consists of Duma deputies and staff as well as outside experts. Often the latter expect to be compensated for their time, and the committee budget is limited. Deputies sometimes complain that they lack the means to form a group to draft a particular bill that they would like to submit. Staff resources are modest, so deputies generally depend on their committees or factions to develop legislation.[33] Overall, committees that are successful in achieving a sufficient degree of interfactional agreement on legislation in their domains are successful in winning passage for it in floor voting.[34]

Reaching Intercameral and Interbranch Agreement

After the Duma has passed a bill in third reading, it sends it to the Council of the Federation.[35] Bill procedures in the upper house are considerably simpler than those of the Duma.[36] The council votes (using a single reading) whether to approve the bill, but if it rejects a bill, it is sent back to the Duma, where the Council of the Duma refers it back to the original committee. The committee recommends either that the Duma override the Federation Council and pass the bill in the original wording, which requires a two-thirds vote, or that it kill the bill. Or, as is common, the two chambers decide to form an agreement commission (*soglasitel'naia komissiia*) to settle their differences. Any such decisions a commission makes must be approved concurrently by each chamber's delegation. The text of the bill presented by an agreement commission is not subject to amendment but is debated and put to a yes-or-no vote. If the Duma approves it, it goes on to the Federation Council. If the draft fails, the Duma can vote to pass the bill in the original wording, which requires a two-thirds majority. A bill that fails to pass either way dies. A bill that clears both chambers, or on which the Duma overrides the Federation Council, is then sent to the president for his signature.

The president has the right to sign or reject legislation passed by parliament. If he vetoes it, parliament can override his veto with a two-thirds vote in each chamber. A practice has developed (and been ruled constitutional by the Constitutional Court) by which the president may also choose simply to return it to the Duma or the Federation Council if he determines that it contains procedural, legal, or constitutional flaws. Returning it has essentially the same effect as vetoing it but avoids the confrontational gesture of rejecting the bill. It therefore allows parliament to make minor changes in the legislation by simple majority vote rather than choosing between capitulation to the president or gathering a two-thirds majority for an override.

Either way, the Duma has several options for responding. It can agree with the president's objections and, by simple majority, pass the bill in new language incorporating the president's recommendations (or if these are not specific, it can request that the president put his objections into the form of concrete amendments). But if any of the revisions proposed by the president are rejected, the bill must go back to the committee. If the president has recommended withdrawing the bill altogether, the Duma can vote to agree. The Duma may also insist on its original version of the legislation and vote to override the veto by a two-thirds majority. It can send the bill back to the first reading again. Or it can propose forming an agreement commission with the president's representatives to attempt reaching a compromise agreement. In this case, since the constitution does not explicitly provide for this mechanism, the rules call the commission a "special commission," but it operates in much the same way as other ad hoc bodies set up to overcome disagreements in the legislative process. Apart from the logical requirement that each side's delegation must concur with the decisions of the commission, the creation of such commissions appears to be guided by the leadership's judgment of the nature and severity of the disagreement. As with intercameral and intercommittee agreement commissions, no specific rules govern the formation and composition of such bodies. The Duma's delegation reports to the floor on the work of the commission (and is required to submit a report on what proposals were made to overcome specific disagreements), and the revised text is voted up or down.

If both chambers vote to override the president's veto, he must sign it. An April 1998 decision of the Constitutional Court makes this requirement clear. If both chambers have voted by a two-thirds majority to pass the bill over the president's objections, he does not have the right to withhold his signature.[37]

This is the standard bill process. Variations on these procedures exist for particular types of vote. For instance, the budget process uses a fourth reading in the Duma. The rules specify particular methods for handling constitutional amendments, presidential impeachment, and votes of confidence and no confidence.

Table 7.10. Representation of Territorial Subjects in the Federation Council

Type of Territorial Unit	Number of Units	Seats per Unit	Total
Oblast	49	2	98
Krai	6	2	12
City[a]	2	2	4
Republic	21	2	42
Autonomous oblast	1	2	2
Autonomous okrug	10	2	20
Total	89		178

[a]Moscow and St. Petersburg gained the status of federal subjects with the 1992 Federation Treaty.

THE FEDERATION COUNCIL

Yeltsin's last-minute change of heart about the composition of the Federation Council led him to decree that elections to the upper chamber would be held on a one-time basis only and for a two-year term for the first cohort of Federation Council members. Of the 497 candidates who ran, 172 were elected; another 5 deputies were elected in spring 1994 in regions where elections had not been held and or had been declared invalid due to insufficient competition or other reasons.[38] Each federal subject was treated as a two-member district.[39] After the new law on the composition of the Federation Council took effect in December 1995, the members of the Council of the Federation were to be the heads of the executive and representative bodies of state power in each federal subject.[40] As elections were held for chief executives in the regions in the course of 1996 and 1997 and for their representative bodies, the Council of the Federation renewed its membership substantially.[41] Table 7.10 indicates the makeup of the Federation Council by type of territorial subject.

For the most part, the 1993 elections to the Council of the Federation were conducted without reference to party. Only twenty-eight of the winners declared a party affiliation (twelve with the communists, eight each with Russia's Choice and Democratic Party of Russia). Instead, the elections tested the electoral clout of local notables. Presidents and prime ministers of republics, and the heads of administration of ordinary regions, ran for seats in sixty-six territories, and almost 90 percent won seats.[42] Another twenty-three winners occupied other leading executive positions in their home regions. In all, around three-quarters of the members of the Federation Council were ranking officials from the regional executive or legislative branches, came from the federal level executive, or had recently been senior executive officials. Another twenty-three members were the directors of enterprises. The great majority of notables kept their jobs, serving in the Federation Council on a part-time basis. Only around forty of the deputies worked full time in the chamber. Overall, sixty-five (37 percent) of the new deputies had served in the post-1989 Russian or USSR parliaments.

Structuring the Federation Council

Mitiukov's commission debated whether to employ a party principle in the governance of the Federation Council and decided against it. There was no place for organized party factions in their draft rules or for a presidium, for that matter. They envisioned a much simpler steering mechanism—a chairman and deputy chairmen. The 1993 elections of members of the Council of the Federation were not organized by party, for the most part, and the new deputies chose not to create factions or to give them any recognition under the rules. Informally, some deputies had clear political affiliations; around forty-five of the new members could be considered supporters of the reform cause, and about thirty were close to the left opposition camp. Around thirty were considered "centrists."[43] In mid-1994 a loose opposition group formed, called "Constructive Cooperation," and a Primary Party Organization (PPO) of members of the Communist Party in the chamber formed in February 1995 (the communists in the Duma also created a Primary Party Organization).[44] But factions did not form in the Federation Council, then or since. A proposal by the chamber's own Rules and Procedures Commission to amend the Standing Orders to allow for the formation of voluntary deputy groups with no fewer than twelve members failed to win a majority on July 13, 1994.[45] The next day the Constructive Cooperation group formed, conceiving its role as a counterweight to the informal grouping of regional governors that had its own association, the League of Governors, and direct access to the president. The group had little influence, however, being very diverse ideologically, and it did not spur the formation of any other groups. In the Council of the Federation that convened in January 1996, as the two-year terms of the first, elected, group of members expired and they were replaced by the heads of legislative and executive branches in each federal subject, members again voted not to structure the chamber by faction.

More important than the division between communist-leaning and reform-oriented members in influencing the structure of the Federation Council was the division between full-time and part-time deputies. The transition provisions added to the constitution by Yeltsin's team envisioned that the first cohort of Federation Council members would only serve part time, but soon the rules allowed for the possibility that members would be allowed to be employed by the chamber full time. Only around forty members of the first cohort were full-time parliamentarians, but they made up the leadership of the chamber; the chairman and deputy chairmen of the Federation Council; and the chairmen, deputy chairmen, and core members of its committees.[46] Between them and the part-timers, understandably, there was some tension. The full-time deputies wished to make the chamber more influential in federal lawmaking— a chamber of "senators," as some put it, rather than a chamber of "governors" (and still less a "House of Lords," as one quipped). Frustrated by the chronic problem of assembling a quorum, they pushed for legislation that would make the future Federation Council entirely elective and full time, and they sought ways of making such an electoral law compatible with the constitutional requirement that the chamber be composed of representatives of the executive and legislative branches of each region. Ultimately their efforts were defeated, however, and the law on formation of the Council of the Federation passed at the end of 1995 provided for a chamber made up on an ex officio basis of the heads of each subject's legislative and executive branches, while stipulating that these individuals were to be elected to those positions. The electoral rules on the recruitment of members of the Federation Council have probably been the most important influence on the structure and political role of the chamber.

With no steering committee and no factions, the Council of the Federation leaves a great deal of discretion in governance of the chamber to its elected chairman. The first chairman was Vladimir Shumeiko, a Yeltsin ally who had served most immediately as first deputy chairman of the government. Voting revealed a closely divided chamber: Shumeiko received the required majority over a communist rival only on the third ballot. Along with Shumeiko, the chamber elected three deputy chairmen, who worked out a loose division of labor among themselves. On an informal basis, Chairman Shumeiko consulted regularly with committee chairs about their legislative priorities. In April the council discussed whether to modify the Standing Rules so as to create a presidium made up of the committee chairmen, the deputy chamber chairs, and Shumeiko, but the motion was defeated. It was defeated when it came up again in May.[47] Clearly a majority of members preferred a simpler governing process, based on informal consultations between the chairman and the committees and personal relations between individual members and the chairman. Each proposal to alter this system has been defeated.

Shumeiko worked successfully to strengthen the powers of the chairman over bill referral, agenda, and management of the staff. The fact that most of the members of the chamber were not working full time as deputies made it simpler for Shumeiko to establish a larger role for chairman than in the State Duma. The rules of procedure were simpler, as well. The Council of the Federation would only consider legislation that had been passed by the Duma, although members had the right to participate in the Duma's legislative process by submitting bills and participating in working groups. But the lighter workload and part-time nature of most of the members (and of all of them after January 1996) meant that the chamber needed fewer committees—only eleven were created in 1994 plus three commissions—and no subcommittees. Initially the chamber adopted a rule requiring that each committee must have at least ten members, but this had to be lowered in July to a minimum of seven.

The part-time nature of the chamber has also contributed to a larger role for its staff than in the Duma. This is reflected in the Federation Council's larger staff structure. As of late 1995, the Federation Council had 935 staff positions, organized into functional divisions serving the chamber, departments corresponding to the standing committees and commissions, and the secretariats of the chairman and deputy chairs. This works out to a ratio of about 5 staff members per seat in the chamber.[48] The Duma at the same time had 1,490 staff positions, 125 serving the factions and groups, 415 serving the committees, and 1 for each deputy. This is equivalent to about 3.3 staff members to each deputy.[49] The larger staff, smaller number of committees, simpler committee structure, and, above all, absence of a formal steering committee combine to give the Federation Council's chairman considerably more discretion than his Duma counterpart in determining the order of proceedings, the timing and method of voting, committee jurisdiction, and other procedural matters. For example, absenteeism at sessions of the Federation Council was and remains a problem; often there are not many more deputies than the quorum. In July 1995, the chamber changed the Standing Rules to lower the quorum from two-thirds to one-half and stipulated that if there were too few members present to reach a decision, the vote could be postponed. Shumeiko made use of this rule to judge whether an issue could pass on the floor. If he judged that an item he wanted to have passed had insufficient support, he would postpone the vote and instead hold a vote by mail ballot, which avoided a floor debate and allowed him to structure the issue. Likewise when sessions were coming up, Shumeiko telephoned members whose support he deemed crucial for the passage of particular items and urged them to be sure to attend the session.

Shumeiko publicly called for constitutional amendments that would further expand the chamber's power, such as prolonging the term of the current deputies, making the chamber's members full time, and giving the chamber power to pass laws over Duma opposition. None of these won the support of the president or the members of either chamber. Nonetheless, Shumeiko's broad procedural powers gave him more personal influence over the Federation Council than Rybkin had in the Duma.

The Federation Council after 1996

The mandates of the first members expired on January 15, 1996. The new members were individuals who had been elected chief executive (typically governors in ordinary regions and presidents in republics) and heads of the legislative bodies of the territorial subjects of the federation. When the new Council of the Federation convened on January 23, many members had kept their seats: sixty-four of the new members had served in the 1994–95 council. In contrast with the 1994–95 period, however, all the new members kept their regular positions in the regions, visiting Moscow twice a month for the brief sessions of the council.[50]

The new members who took office in January 1996 resolved their organizational questions quickly. They retained the inherited Standing Rules in virtually all respects. They did add one new feature, however: the rules permitted a member to give his proxy to the other member from the same region on all but secret votes.[51] Egor Stroev, governor of Orel oblast, was elected chairman without opposition and decided to serve without relinquishing his governorship. The next day the members voted to confirm a slate of deputy chairs, balancing them between legislative and executive branch leaders and between regular regions and ethnic republics. They, too, served without giving up their regional positions. The members elected chairs of the standing committees, keeping the same structure of eleven committees and two commissions inherited from the previous body. As before, deputies were free to join committees according to their interests. The chamber's standing committees are listed in table 7.11. In all, the members agreed to almost every organizational proposal that the chairman and the preparatory commission put before them.[52]

Proceedings of the Federation Council in the 1996–99 period settled into a routine. On those weeks when the Federation Council convened (usually two weeks out of a month), committee chairs met with the chamber's chairman on

Table 7.11. Committees and Commissions of the Federation Council, 1996

Constitutional Legislation and Judicial-Legal Questions
Issues of Security and Defense
Budget, Tax Policy, Financial, Currency, and Customs Regulation
Issues of Social Policy
Issues of Economic Policy
International Affairs
Commonwealth of Independent States (CIS) Affairs
Agrarian Policy
Science, Culture, Education, Health Protection, and Ecology
Federation Affairs, the Federal Treaty, and Regional Policy
Affairs of the North and Nonpopulous Peoples
Commission on the Standing Orders and Parliamentary Procedures
Credentials Commission

Tuesday morning to discuss the agenda for the week. Committee meetings were held on Tuesday, and at the end of the day the committee chairs met again with the chamber chairman to report on the committees' decisions. Wednesday and Thursday were devoted to plenary sessions. The chamber tended to dispose of its business rather quickly, relying on committee reports and staff advice to determine whether an item could be approved or rejected and sent to an agreement commission.[53] The relatively simple procedures used reflected the greater influence of chairman, committees, and staff than in the Duma. By the same token, however, the Federation Council surrounded its proceedings with considerably secrecy. For instance, records of member-by-member voting on particular issues are not kept, so that it is impossible to analyze voting alignments except on the very small number of items for which roll-call votes are taken.

CONSTITUTION AND COMMITMENT

The violence of October 1993 left both president and parliament acutely aware of the fragility of the new constitutional order in January 1994. As a result, the two sides proceeded cautiously in their dealings with one another. The new constitution resolved a number of unresolved issues in the balance of presidential-parliamentary power, but many issues remained to be settled, and it was unclear to each side how seriously committed the other was to abiding by the new rules of the game. Yeltsin suspected the communists of harboring designs to restore Soviet rule, and the communists viewed Yeltsin as an unscrupulous dictator, who happened at the moment to have the support of the army and the West, ruling over a corrupt regime. Neither, however, was willing to press its case too far: the army's support for Yeltsin had been granted reluctantly, and the communists were aware that that they could be arrested. Neither side wished to trigger a civil war. For the time, therefore, both Yeltsin and his opposition were willing to abide by the rules of the constitutional game put in place in December 1993.

Accordingly, with constitutional change a distant prospect, parliament and president have expended a surprising amount of effort since January 1994 at settling their differences through negotiation and persuasion. In the first months of 1994, when the new constitutional arrangements were still untested, the president's representatives and parliament's leadership worked to prevent another disastrous collision. The president's advisers devised ways to develop a cooperative relationship with the parliament's leadership.[54] They met frequently with faction and committee leaders to discuss the legislative agenda and formed a joint executive-legislative commission on the legislative agenda. The president's team deliberately proposed bills on which they anticipated agreement could be found with the parliament. They held conferences and seminars, organized parliamentary clubs, and invited parliamentary leaders to social events and holiday weekends at government sanatoria. They held a showy signing ceremony for an "agreement on civic accord" as a way of pressuring a variety of political groups to commit themselves publicly to the new constitutional rules of the game. They worked to establish close working relations with the chairman of the Duma, Ivan Rybkin. They appointed a respected legal scholar, Alexander M. Yakovlev, as the president's representative to the parliament. When the Duma amnestied those jailed for participating in the August 1991 and October 1993 coup attempts, the president reacted angrily, but he was persuaded to accept the Duma's action. Yeltsin also signed several bills he disliked, such as the law on the status of deputies, on the strength of the argument that it was important to demonstrate good will toward parliament and reinforce its commitment to the new constitution. In turn, the new leadership of parliament generally responded favorably to the president's overtures. Chairman Rybkin, in particular, in his public statements strongly emphasized the importance of the parliament's contribution to social stabilization after the traumatic crises of the previous years; he did not publicly criticize the president's actions or complain about the fact that the reconciliation he was working for was on the president's terms.[55]

With time, the president and government developed much more extensive staffs devoted to legislative liaison. In January 1996 the president appointed representatives to both chambers, each working closely with the government's liaison office. In addition, in each government ministry a first deputy minister with the rank of "state secretary" is charged with shepherding legislation important to the ministry through the legislative process. The government liaison seeks to coordinate this work and to ensure that all the government's representatives are following a common set of priorities. In turn, the president's representatives coordinate the work of all government representatives as well as the officials in the presidential administration who work with parliament, parties, factions, and individual deputies. The president's representative also tracks all legislation that moves through the Duma, reporting to the presidential administration on the status of each bill and assessing its implications for the president and for government policies. In all, by summer 1998, there were nearly one hundred executive branch officials whose primary responsibility was working to advance the executive's interests in parliament.[56]

Over the 1996–99 period, President Yeltsin and the Duma remained deeply divided on many issues, of course, notwithstanding the extensive use of liaison officials and working groups to resolve differences through bargaining. Twice the Duma voted no confidence in the government. Especially in the 1996–99 Duma, when the communist camp was stronger than in 1994–95, the opposition worked to remove Yeltsin through impeachment and to demand constitutional reform. Yet these efforts were made entirely by constitutional means.

Confidence Votes

The constitution gives the Duma two forms of no-confidence votes:[57] a vote on *confidence* in the government on a motion brought by the government, and a vote on a motion of *no confidence* put by the Duma. The Duma amended its rules on these procedures to give itself room for maneuver. It did this in response to an episode that exposed its vulnerability to presidential blackmail. In spring 1995, the Duma passed a motion of no confidence in the government. Most deputies evidently expected that they would be able to use the full three-month interval provided in the constitution between the first and second votes to pressure the government to be more responsive to their demands. Instead, Prime Minister Chernomyrdin unexpectedly demanded that they vote immediately on a vote of confidence. This demand put the deputies before a difficult choice. If the confidence motion failed, the president would have the right to dissolve the Duma and call new elections, and the deputies would lose their privileges (free transportation, communications, and access to the media; their

Moscow apartments; the Duma premises; and so on). But if the motion passed, they would be justifiably accused of selling out their principles for the sake of political expediency. Deputies responded to Chernomyrdin's maneuver with outrage and distress.

The government and Duma leadership then began to seek a compromise that would avert parliamentary dissolution while saving the Duma's collective face. The president and prime minister consulted with faction leaders on their demands to dismiss some ministers they held responsible for the government's handling of the war in Chechnia. The government agreed to a procedural device for avoiding a direct confidence vote. Instead of voting on a confidence motion, the Duma would vote on a no-confidence motion again. If it failed, the government would agree to withdraw its demand for a confidence vote. The faction leaders in turn counted votes carefully to ensure that a sufficient number of deputies would fail to support the motion, either by not voting in favor of it or by simply being absent from the chamber at the time of the vote. The device succeeded, and the crisis was averted.

After this unpleasant episode, the Duma looked for a way to avoid being threatened with dissolution by the government again over a confidence vote motion. Clearly the Duma deputies would much prefer allowing a no-confidence motion to fail than a confidence motion to pass. Accordingly, in November 1995 they amended the rules so that if the government demands a vote on a confidence motion, the Council of the Duma must immediately respond by organizing an expert evaluation of the legal and substantive basis for the demand. Meantime, if it should happen that "during the period" when the government proposes a confidence vote, the Duma itself decides to consider a vote of no confidence, the confidence vote is postponed until the no-confidence vote is held. If the no-confidence vote passes, the confidence vote demanded by the government is put off for three months. Moreover, if a confidence vote is held and fails to pass, the Duma then votes on no confidence. If that vote fails, then the entire matter is dropped. In short, the Duma has effectively protected itself against the government's constitutional right to demand a vote of confidence.

Impeachment

In spring 1998 the Duma took the impeachment process further than it had previously gone. The opposition finally succeeded in placing impeachment on the agenda. In June 1998 the deputies agreed to form a commission to consider five charges against Yeltsin: that he had committed treason by signing the

Belovezh agreement in December 1991 to dissolve the Soviet Union; that he had illegally dissolved the Russian congress and Supreme Soviet in 1993; that he had illegally initiated the war in Chechnia in 1994; that he had destroyed Russia's defense capacity; and that he had committed genocide against the Russian people by the effects of the economic policies of his government since 1992. In March 1999 the commission approved all five charges and submitted them to the full chamber for its consideration.

The Duma began debate on impeachment on May 13, 1999, and on May 15 voted on the five charges. Although the third charge came close, none gained the required 300 votes (see table 7.12).[58] The anticlimactic nature of the impeachment vote was reinforced by the fact that, although the president had chosen the eve of the debate—May 12—to dismiss the government yet again, the Duma went along with Sergei Stepashin's nomination as Primakov's successor and approved Stepashin's appointment by 301 votes to 55.[59]

Constitutional Reform

Over the 1996–99 period, the opposition also drafted a number of proposals for constitutional reform aimed at strengthening the Duma's control of government and weakening presidential power. Many Duma deputies, in particular the communists, were strongly dissatisfied with the current constitutional arrangements. In July 1998, the communist chairman of the legislation committee (Anatolii Luk'ianov, erstwhile chairman of the USSR Supreme Soviet and a determined opponent of Yeltsin) introduced a package of constitutional amendments for consideration by the Duma. These proposed amendments shed light on the constitutional changes the left opposition would make given an opportunity. One amendment would make it easier to remove the president, dropping any mention of specific grounds for impeachment and eliminating the Supreme Court's concurrence from the sequence of required steps. Another would grant parliament the power of approving the appointment of deputy chairmen of the government and the heads of the power ministries (internal affairs, state security, defense, and foreign affairs). Another would empower the Duma to vote no confidence in particular members of government, forcing their removal without allowing the president to choose between removing the minister and dissolving the Duma. Still other amendments would alter the balance between Duma and Federation Council, in the Duma's favor. The Duma, not the council, would have the right to vote on confirmation of the procurator general and the judges on the highest courts, and the Federation Council would lose its power to prevent parliament from overriding a presidential veto.[60]

Table 7.12. Factional Support for Impeachment of President Yeltsin, May 15, 1999, by Percentage of Affirmative Votes

Charge	CPFR	Agrarian	PP	LDPR	Yabloko	RR	NDR	Independent	Total Yea Votes
Bolovezh accord	98.4	100	91.5	2.0	10.9	45.5	1.7	30	241
Dissolved parliament	99.2	100	91.5	4.1	52.2	50	0	30	263
Chechen war	99.2	100	89.4	2.0	80.4	63.6	1.7	40	284
Destroyed army	98.4	100	91.5	4.1	6.5	45.5	3.3	30	241
Genocide	98.4	100	91.5	4.1	0	43.2	3.3	30	237

Abbreviations: CPRF: Communist Party of the Russian Federation; Agrarian: Agrarian Party of Russia; PP: People's Power; LDPR: Liberal Democratic Party of Russia; Yabloko: the bloc Yavlinsky-Boldyrev-Lukin; RR: Russia's Regions; NDR: Our Home Is Russia.

The Duma also tried to enact constitutional change through ordinary legislation, passing a law on presidential elections that would have replaced direct popular election of the president with election by an electoral college consisting of members of the Federal Assembly and representatives of the regions. Not surprisingly, President Yeltsin vetoed the law on the grounds that it was unconstitutional.[61]

A particularly telling episode occurred in August 1998. As Russia's financial system collapsed and Yeltsin sought to recall Chernomyrdin to head the government, Chernomyrdin discussed the possibility of a constitutional "pact" with the opposition. Under its terms, which were widely reported in the press, Yeltsin would refrain from dissolving the Duma for the remainder of its term in return for the Duma's support of Chernomyrdin and its agreement not to proceed with impeachment; would agree not to interfere in government policy making; and, most significantly, would agree to allow the Duma to vote on confirmation or removal of all ministers except for those heading the "power ministries." On August 31, the communist faction leader, Gennadii Ziuganov, declared that his faction would refuse to go along with any such agreement on the grounds that it was unenforceable. Nonetheless, the outlines of the agreement suggested that a bargain was possible, which would have altered the constitutional balance between president and parliament.

Such a pact, or the communists' proposed amendments, would return to a constitutional arrangement something like that of mid-1991. So far, however, the partitioning of decision-making authority that Yeltsin built into the constitution has made it unlikely that the communists can persuade either the regional leaderships or the president to alter the present arrangements. As I have argued, the constitution separates the plane of left-right conflict from that of center-regional competition. To overturn it, the communists would need either to give up power to the president to win his agreement or to the regions to win them over on a redistribution of power from the president. But the regional leaders are hardly likely to give up power to the federal center to make the communists stronger, and a president is unlikely to give up his powers for the sake of a stronger federal center. In effect, Yeltsin's constitution gave veto rights over constitutional revision to each of the three sides in this triangle of relations.

Amending the constitution, moreover, is extremely difficult. Amendments to the portions of the constitution dealing with political institutions require approval by a two-thirds vote in the Duma and a three-quarters vote in the Federation Council, as well as approval by the legislative bodies of two-thirds of the subjects of the federation. Success would require that one political camp hold a sizable majority in both chambers of parliament and in two-thirds of the constituent territories of the federation. More probable than a constitutional amendment reducing presidential power, therefore, is the limitation of presidential power through the accumulation of precedent and decisions by the Constitutional Court. The fact that Yeltsin retreated in the face of adamant parliamentary opposition to his decision to bring back Chernomyrdin to head the government in September 1998, and instead chose a figure with wide support in the Duma, may serve as a kind of precedent about the relative strength of president and parliament when parliament takes a cohesive stance in opposition to the president.

Over the period from 1994 to 1999, then, both president and parliament behaved as if they were willing to abide by the terms of the new constitution so long as the other side did so as well. To a large extent, as a result, much conflict between the president and the communist forces in parliament took the form of bargaining over legislation. This leads to the question of whether this new institutional framework has managed the legislative process any more successfully than its predecessors.

THE LEGISLATIVE RECORD

The organization of the Federal Assembly is in part a reflection of the constitutional choices made by Yeltsin and other players in the political arena and the election rules used in 1993 and later. But it is also the product of agreements among parliamentary leaders and rank-and-file deputies on ways of sharing power in an environment where no one camp controlled a majority. Some of the institutional choices that parliament made were intensely controversial, whereas others, especially the rules on lawmaking, were carried over from previous parliamentary models with relatively little change. The standing committee system, the three readings procedure, the use of working groups to draft legislation and agreement commissions to reconcile disagreements, the absence of restrictive rules for particular pieces or classes of legislation, the procedures for floor debate including the daily agenda debate: in all these formal respects parliamentary institutions in the Federal Assembly closely resemble their predecessors. Evidently the opposing camps saw little point in altering them significantly. But in structuring leadership and governance, and in distributing jurisdictional rights, the Federal Assembly differs substantially from the Soviet-era legislatures by virtue of the collective control exercised by political factions in the Duma and the separation of parliament into two distinct chambers with different electoral bases and constitutional powers. Bicameralism and factionalism are the great institutional innovations in the new legislative structure. What difference have they made in practice?

Some observers believe that factionalism has turned the Duma into a circus, where deadlock, wasted effort and political posturing have replaced serious lawmaking. In Joel Ostrow's opinion, the party-dominated governing structure has failed at conflict management. Duma procedure is "complete chaos," a "mess," and "incapable of effecting major policy change. . . . The Duma as a result is a legislature of 450 split personalities, and outcomes are highly unstable and unpredictable."[62]

Against this, of course, it might be argued that unlike its predecessors, the Duma has twice managed to serve out its full constitutional term, and it has done so without abdicating its legislative responsibilities by delegating emergency decree powers to the president. How does it compare with them, however, in its ability to reach coherent decisions on major legislation? How often are bills stymied by deadlock within the Duma, between the chambers, or between the branches? We need a way to assess the effectiveness of parliamentary decision making, given the parliament's reduced status in the constitutional setting in place since 1993. Beyond this, even if we had some agreed standard for comparing parliament's effectiveness in lawmaking or in conflict management in the larger society with its predecessors, to what degree are the changes in institutional arrangements responsible?

Assessing Parliament's Effectiveness

I have argued that Yeltsin traded off representational rights to party factions and regional leaders in separate chambers of parliament in return for their acceptance of a constitution giving him wide powers, including the constitutional power to introduce bills and veto laws and to make law by decree. How do these arrangements affect the parliament's ability to pass laws and reach agreements with the president, and, correspondingly, the president's willingness to negotiate with parliament over new legislation? We can restate these questions as follows: First, does Duma lawmaking regularly end in chaos and deadlock? Second, how does the parliament's capacity to make decisions affect the president's calculations about whether or not to seek negotiated agreements with it over legislation?

Let us consider evidence on these two issues. To judge the willingness of the president to rely on decrees to rule, let us examine the record of presidential laws and decrees in the light of an alternative hypothesis—that the new constitution frees the president of the pressure to compromise with parliament to achieve his policy objectives because he can rule by decree. To determine how effective parliament is at passing laws, let us examine the record of legislative outcomes for different types of measures that are introduced into parliament. Let us compare how many and what kinds of bills clear the successive hurdles to passage through the Duma, the Council of the Federation, and the president's signature. What is the success rate for bills proposed by the parliament and government, as opposed to bills introduced by the Duma's own deputies, in the Duma and when they reach the president's desk? There are two sources of variation here in success rates for bills: category of sponsor (parliament or executive), and stages in the legislative process (first, second, third reading in the Duma, Federation Council consideration, presidential consideration).

We would expect that if the Duma were controlled by a stable partisan majority hostile to the president, relatively few bills would be defeated after first reading but many would be vetoed by the president. In a multiparty parliament, however, where no party or coalition held a stable majority, the search for cross-party support to pass legislation would require a good deal of bargaining and mutual accommodation among factions over individual items, either ending in deadlock within the Duma or modifying the content of bills sufficiently so as to reduce the distance between bills passed in final reading and the president's own position. In the latter case we would expect many bills to be defeated in first and second readings, and the president to sign a high proportion of those that reached his desk. The ratio of bills signed to bills passed in third reading would be greater than the ratio of bills passed in third reading to bills introduced.[63] Therefore we should compare the rates of success and failure at successive stages of the legislative process.

The question of lawmaking and decree making can be examined on the basis of the record of laws and decrees over time and by policy area. If the president saw little reason to seek compromise with parliament over legislation, we would expect to see the largest number and most important policy decisions being enacted by decree. But if the parliament is an important player, we should see a different pattern of presidential behavior: the president would seek to win passage of his desired policies in the form of laws. This would be the case regardless of whether a friendly or opposition majority prevailed in parliament. Parliament's institutional power would require him to work with it to attain his objectives.

Conflict and Compromise in the Legislative
Process: Empirical Measures

We have four questions, then. First, how do bills fare at successive stages of leg-islative consideration? Second, how does the success rate of executive-initiated bills compare with that of deputy-sponsored bills? Third, how does the presi-dent's lawmaking activity compare with his use of his decree power? Finally, how is the president's relation with the Duma affected by a change in its politi-cal composition?

The data for testing these propositions come from several sources. Steven S. Smith, Moshe Haspel, and I have analyzed patterns of lawmaking and decree making in the 1994–97 period across different areas of policy. In addition, the Duma's own internal analytical staff publishes reports of the activity of the Duma, which add valuable detail, as do press reports and articles and speeches by parliamentary leaders.

Concerning the first question, the second Duma considered 1,693 pieces of legislation over the entire 1996–99 term ("considered" here means that the Duma took at least one vote on the bill); of these, it adopted—that is, passed in third reading—1,036 (or 61.2 percent); and of these, 771 (74.4 percent) were signed by the president and have come into force (see table 7.13). Thus the ratio of bills signed to bills passed is in fact higher than the ratio of bills passed to bills considered. This supports the premise that when the Duma's internal bar-gaining processes succeed in winning passage for a bill, the odds are good that the president will sign it.

Moreover, the Duma passes executive-sponsored legislation at a higher rate than deputy-sponsored bills. Figures on the fate of bills by different categories of initiators for the period from January 1996 through December 1999 are pre-sented in table 7.14. Percentages read horizontally across the table, so that of all items initiated by a particular category of sponsor, the table indicates what pro-portion of them were actually taken up by the Duma, what proportion were passed by the Duma, and what proportion were signed by the president. Note that the success rates at each of these stages of the process were higher for items sponsored by the president or government than for items sponsored by dep-uties or other sponsors. Table 7.15 indicates the sponsors of the bills that the Duma accepted for consideration over this period.

With respect to the third question, the volume of lawmaking and decree making in the 1994–95 period is compared in table 7.16 with that in the first two years of the new Duma's existence. The numbers suggest that the rate at

Table 7.13. Success Rates of Legislation by Stage of Consideration,
January 1, 1996–December 31, 1999

Stage of Consideration	Absolute Number of Bills	Percentage
All bills accepted for consideration	3,303	100.0
All bills that the Duma considered (i.e., at least voted on them in first reading)	1,693	100.0
Passed in third reading	1,036	61.2
Of bills passed by Duma in third reading	1,036	100.0
Rejected by Federation Council or president	445	43
Of which were:		
rejected by Federation Council	238	23
rejected by president	207	20
Bills signed by president (of those passed by Duma over this period)	771	74.4

Source: Federal'noe Sobranie—parlament Rossiiskoi Federatsii. Gosudarstvennaia Duma.
Analiticheskoe upravlenie, vyp. 3. *Statisticheskie kharakteristiki zakonodatel'noi deiatel'nosti Gosudarstvennoi Dumy vtorgo sozyva (1996–1999)* (Moscow, 2000), pp.6–8.
Note: Bills signed by president included 210 treaty ratifications.

which the Duma passes laws and the president issues decrees is comparable. Published normative presidential *ukazy* (thus leaving unpublished decrees aside, as well as all decrees classified as purely executive, or nonpolicy making) and laws that have cleared the Duma in third reading are counted in the table. There is no great quantitative disproportion in the laws and decrees. Let us look more closely at this question.

Decrees have been strongly affected by the immediate political and policy goals of the president. Although the rate of decree making was fairly steady in 1994 and 1995 (201 in 1994 and 240 in 1995), it expanded significantly in 1996 (458 decrees) and fell back to 190 in 1997. There were two peaks of decree activity in 1996: one, associated with Yeltsin's springtime reelection campaign in 1996, when he used decrees to win the support of particular regions, industries, and social groups, and the other when he used decrees to carry out a substantial reorganization of the presidential administration in late 1996 after the victorious Yeltsin appointed Anatolii Chubais as head of the presidential office. In 1997 the scale of decree activity fell back substantially. It remained at the same level in 1998 and declined further in 1999.[65] The great majority of decrees in 1998 and 1999 concerned executive reorganization and many simply rescinded

Table 7.14. Success of Legislation, by Category of Sponsor, January 1996–
December 1999 (in absolute figures and as percentage of preceding column)

Sponsor	Bills Taken Up for Consideration	Actually Considered	Passed in Third Reading	Signed by President
President	165 (100)	126 (76.4)	106 (84.1)	100 (94.3)
Government	661 (100)	532 (80.5)	367 (69.0)	332 (90.5)
Duma deputies	1,629 (100)	784 (48.1)	488 (62.2)	292 (59.8)
Federation Council	297 (100)	117 (39.4)	27 (23.1)	16 (59.3)
Regions	528 (100)	116 (22.0)	33 (28.4)	20 (60.6)

Source: Federal'noe Sobranie—parlament Rossiiskoi Federatsii. Gosudarstvennaia Duma. Analiticheskoe upravlenie, Analiticheskii vestnik, vyp. 3. *Statisticheskie kharakteristiki zakonodatel'noi deiatel'nosti Gosudarstvennoi Dumy vtorogo sozyva (1996–1999)* (Moscow, 2000), pp. 6–8.

earlier decrees that contradicted subsequent laws and decrees. Thus in comparison with the 1991–92 period, when Yeltsin enacted most of his major policy and constitutional reforms by decree, decree making has settled into a much more routine activity. The expansion of policy areas regulated by legislation has restricted the president's ability to fill gaps in existing law through the use of decrees.[66]

The fourth question had to do with the effects of the shift in the Duma's political composition after the 1995 election. At this time the communists increased their seat share significantly and, with their allies, came close to controlling a majority. Did this increase the veto rate? An overview of presidential decisions about bills that passed the Duma in third reading broken down by category of initiator, for the 1994–95 and 1996–99 periods is provided in table 7.17. Yeltsin signed around three-quarters of the bills passed by the Duma.[67]

Not surprisingly, as shown in table 7.17, many more of the bills initiated by the president or government are signed than are those initiated by the Duma or by other sponsors. Council of Federation members have a lower success rate, and lowest of all is the rate for bills submitted by the legislative bodies of the regions.

Let us look more closely at the legislative process in the Duma to see how well the Duma is able to dispose of its legislative workload. In the spring 1999 session, the Duma considered 218 bills (meaning the Duma took at least one vote on the item in a first or subsequent reading); for all of 1998 it considered 443 bills; and for the entire period from January 1996 through December 1999

Table 7.15. Bill Sponsorship in State Duma, by Category of Sponsor, January 1996–December 1999

	Absolute Number	Percentage of Total
All bills accepted for consideration	3,303	100
President	165	4.9
Government	661	20.0
Duma deputies	1,629	49.3
Federation Council	297	8.9
Regional assemblies	528	15.9
High courts	23	69

it considered 1,693.[68] But the Duma is forever falling behind its own legislative program. At the start of the spring 1999 session, the Duma had 502 bills on its calendar for spring, and over the course of the spring session, this number more than doubled.[69] More than half of the bills that are placed on the calendar fail to be considered in the scheduled time period. By far the most severe hurdle for bills introduced into the Duma, therefore, is simply to be brought up for a vote. The fact that the executive branch's bills are considered at a higher rate than deputies' own bills and that, once considered, they are more frequently passed, indicates that the Duma responds to the executive branch's legislative priorities.

The data support the hypothesis that the political disagreements within the Duma are, generally speaking, wider than the disagreements between the Duma and the president. As a result, when the Duma is able to work out agreements on legislation among its own factions, the laws it passes stand a good chance of being signed into law. President- and government-sponsored bills stand a much higher chance of actually being taken up by the Duma than do bills submitted by Duma deputies; they also have a better chance of being passed by the Duma and a better chance of being signed into law.

Legislation and Political Conflict: Selected Issues

Ideally these aggregate assessments would be complemented with a more refined examination based on the number and nature of major legislative acts that were passed and signed or instances where the three sides deadlocked. In the absence of hard data, let us consider some examples of major issues where parliament and president succeeded in reaching agreement and several where they remained too far apart to overcome their differences.

Table 7.16. Number of Presidential
Decrees and Duma-Passed Laws,
1994–1997

Year	Decrees	Laws
1994–95	441	464
1996–97	648	473
Total	1,098	937

Laws on the annual budget for each year have been passed, some before the year began, others only afterward. A number of vital laws on the judicial system have passed, including a constitutional law bringing all courts of general jurisdiction under the system of federal courts; a new federal criminal code; parts 1 and 2 of the new Civil Code (considered by virtually every expert observer to be an extremely important step toward reform and often cited as the single most important act of the 1994–95 Duma); a constitutional law on the commercial courts, which has enabled this new branch of the judiciary to confirm the legal validity of countless acts of privatization. A series of major electoral laws has passed: laws on elections to the Duma, presidential elections, referenda, the formation of the Federation Council, and electoral rights of citizens throughout the country (providing the grounds for the Constitutional Court to strike down some restrictions on the franchise imposed in some of the ethnic republics and other regions). The Duma has passed and the president signed a constitutional law defining the rights and structure of the government; this law required years of interbranch negotiation. A law defining the procedures for the privatization of state enterprises has been passed and signed by the president, under which the branches agreed that the Duma must approve the list of enterprises to be privatized each year. The branches have passed the first part of a revised new tax code, setting out the general principles of taxation and thus limiting the freedom of regional and republic governments to impose other taxes. After years of disputes, the two chambers passed a law on mortgage loans over the veto of the president. The law authorizes property-secured debt so long as agricultural land is not used as security.

The branches remain deadlocked over the issue of private ownership of land. The president's unwillingness to sign any legislation on land ownership that does not allow farmers the right to buy and sell farmland has resulted in an impasse over several major legislative acts, including the Land Code, regulating

Table 7.17. Rate of Presidential Signing of Bills Passing Duma in Third Reading, by Category of Sponsor (in absolute figures and percentage)

Sponsor	1994–95	1996–99
President or government	179 (97.2)	432 (91.3)
Duma	259 (64.1)	292 (59.8)
Other	26 (53.8)	47 (62.6)
Total	464 (76.3)	771 (74.4)

Source: For 1994–95, Thomas F. Remington, Steven S. Smith, and Moshe Haspel, "Decrees, Laws, and Inter-Branch Relations in the Russian Federation," *Post-Soviet Affairs* 14, no. 4 (1998): 287– 322; for 1996–99, Federal'noe Sobranie—parlament Rossiiskoi Federatsii. Gosudarstvennaia Duma. Analiticheskoe upravlenie, Analiticheskii vestnik, vyp. 3 *Statisticheskie kharakeristiki zakonodatel'noi deiatel'nosti Gosudarstvennoi Dumy vtorog sozyva (1996– 1999)* (Moscow, 2000), pp. 6–8.

land relations generally. There have been several attempts to settle their differences through conciliation commissions and "big four" consultations involving the president, prime minister, and chairmen of the Duma and Federation Council. Sometimes there are reports that the sides have reached a compromise, but by the end of the second Duma's term, none had materialized. Deep disagreements also remain over social spending, tax legislation, and regulation of foreign loans and investments. The Duma has refused to pass most of the government's bills aimed at replacing universal entitlements with a system of targeted benefits, while the president has vetoed opposition-sponsored bills that would have greatly expanded social benefits without increasing revenues commensurately. The president has also vetoed opposition-sponsored bills that would restrict political rights, such as the bill that would have established a "Supreme Council for Protecting Morality in Television and Radio Broadcasting" and a bill that would have reestablished the volunteer citizens' militias (*narodnye druzhinniki*) that were used by the Soviet authorities in the 1960s and 1970s to enforce public order and social control. Many issues thus continue to divide reformers from the opposition.

Legislation on many issues is shaped by the three-way relations among Duma, Council of the Federation, and president. Many laws passed by the Duma are blocked by the upper house either on the grounds that regional leaders object to losing prerogatives or because they oppose the expansion of federal fiscal authority. In some cases, when the Duma and upper house modify a bill so that it is acceptable to both, the president vetoes it on the grounds that it puts unacceptable limits on his power. A case in point is legislation delineating the powers of the federal government and of the constituent territories. Not surprisingly, this has been an extremely controversial piece of legislation. The Council of the Federation rejected the Duma's bill three times. Finally the chambers were able to resolve their differences and to pass the bill in a form that would allow the Council of the Federation (rather than the Duma) the right to ratify bilateral treaties between the federal government and individual regions. In its original form, the Duma had reserved that right to itself, but the Council of the Federation had objected. But even the Duma's concession of this power to the upper house was too great a restriction on the president's freedom to sign such agreements, and he initially vetoed the bill. After further bargaining, however, he signed it in June 1999. In other cases, the president and Duma agree on a bill that the Council of the Federation opposes, passing it either after a Duma override of the Council of the Federation or, more commonly, after intense lobbying by the executive branch to win over the Council of the Federation.

Legislative Effectiveness and Deputy Efficacy: Survey Data

These indicators of the Federal Assembly's capacity to produce laws can be complemented with testimony from its members. The data come from surveys conducted by Steven Smith and me among the deputies of the State Duma in December 1994-January 1995 and March-April 1996.[70] We found that most deputies in both Dumas participated actively in lawmaking: of five possible forms of activity (speaking on the floor of the chamber, sponsoring a bill, sponsoring an amendment, joining a working group to draft or revise a bill, and joining an agreement commission), few deputies had done two or fewer of them, and more than half had done at least four of them.

Substantial percentages of deputies, moreover, were satisfied with the level of influence they had as legislators. Forty-five percent of the 1994 contingent and 53 percent of the 1996 cohort described themselves as "satisfied" or "mostly satisfied" with their level of influence over lawmaking. Among the 1994 deputies, satisfaction with influence was positively correlated with participation: the more forms of legislative activity deputies had engaged in, the likelier they were to feel satisfied with their level of influence. Interestingly enough, however, this was not the case for the 1996 group. Among them, level of participation in legislative activity had no significant impact on level of satisfaction with influence. Participation was modestly correlated with a different measure of satisfaction ("how satisfied are you with your work in the State Duma in 1996"); but although the relationship was significant, it was not strong (r = .10). Rather, for the 1996 deputies, political ideology was a stronger predictor of a deputy's sense of efficacy than was level of engagement. The more leftist a deputy was in political ideology (as measured by a first dimension factor score), the more satisfied he was likely to be with his level of influence (r = .29); and members of the communist faction were distinctly more satisfied than other deputies with their legislative impact. In 1994, there had been no discernible relation between political ideology and the sense of efficacy. Clearly the communists had asserted their dominant, if not majority, position in the chamber. The survey data thus show that in the new State Duma, deputies in both the class of 1994 and class of 1996 were actively involved in lawmaking, and although opportunities to participate made the 1994 deputies somewhat more satisfied with their ability to influence the outcomes of lawmaking, the 1996 deputies were no less active but were not satisfied with their efficacy unless they were part of the leftist camp.

Over the 1989–99 decade, the bargains struck between leaders and deputies had replaced the hierarchical, centralized structure of parliament with the collective control of an all-factions steering committee. In the two interim parliaments, legislative factionalism was essential to the political strategy of the democratic activists elected in 1989 and 1990. Through their political factions, they had challenged the bureaucracy's control over parliament's structure and agenda in order to make parliament an instrument for transforming Russia into a democracy. They therefore willingly cooperated with opposing factions and the leadership in progressively expanding factional rights to participate in parliamentary activity. Their pursuit of this larger political agenda thus explains both their interest in winning rights for factions to participate in parliamentary activity and their interest in making political careers. So, just as the intention to run for reelection was correlated with membership in a radical democratic faction among Russian deputies in Colton's 1991 survey (see chapter 5, note 12), today the members of the Duma nearly all seek reelection: 90 percent of the members of the outgoing 1995 Duma ran for reelection. But, while the faction-dominated structure of the new State Duma has given deputies wider opportunities to use parliament for their political ends, it has also created a new set of obstacles to efficacy for deputies who do not belong to the dominant camp.

Parliamentary Productivity

Is it possible in any meaningful sense to compare the Federal Assembly to its transitional predecessors with respect to its effectiveness in lawmaking? Certainly contextual differences between periods render any such comparison doubtful. On one hand, to compare levels of raw output of legislation over time gives only the most imperfect indication of the ability of the parliament to cope with its workload, either in qualitative or quantitative terms, because we do not have complete data on the scale or number of items submitted to the parliaments at each point. On the other hand, it can be argued that the task of putting major policy decisions into legislative form began with Gorbachev and that output figures are some indication of the parliament's capacity to produce agreements at various times under the pressure of a workload that did not decrease with time. So, despite the crudeness of the data, it is of some interest to examine parliamentary decisions in raw output terms (see table 7.18).

Overall, the processing capacity of parliament has risen in each phase and has increased over the long term. Of some interest is the fact that the number of decrees has declined. To the extent that decrees, petitions, declarations, and other political gestures are an alternative to the more labor-intensive work that goes into passing legislation, the fact that the parliament spends less time on them and more on lawmaking is an indication of greater effectiveness. Moreover, there are no more decrees, edicts and orders of the Presidium and chairman. These used to account for hundreds of decisions per year, many of them opportunities for the leadership to distribute particularistic benefits.[71] One major consequence of the more horizontal governing structure of the Duma and of the separation of the two chambers is the internalization of decision-making responsibility by parliament: all decisions must be passed by parliament. Nonetheless, the parliament has found ways to aggregate its members' demands for legislative decisions without relying on a presidium. The record is consistent with the argument that as parliament's capacity to process legislation has grown, the use of presidential decree making and other nonlegislative instruments of policy making has declined. In any case, the record does not support the argument that the faction-dominated governance structure of the Duma has reduced parliament's capacity for legislative decision making. Rather, at least for the time being, it seems to have provided the major organized political forces in Russia with incentives to follow the rules of the constitutional game in seeking agreement on legislative issues.

The Federal Assembly in Perspective

The evidence presented here gives little support to the conventional wisdom about the Federal Assembly and its relation to the president. Contrary to popular impression, the great majority of laws passed by parliament are signed into

Table 7.18. Legislative Output of Russian Parliaments, 1937 to present

Time Period	Number of Sessions (*sessii*)	Number of Laws Passed	Number of Decrees (*postanovleniia*) Passed	Mean Number of Laws per Session (approx.)
Stalin era, 1937–1954				
Nov. 1937–Feb. 1946	12	64	33	13
Feb. 1946–Mar. 1950	5	30	30	6
Mar. 1950–Mar. 1954	5	26	15	5
Post-Stalin era, 1954– 1966				
Mar. 1954–Mar. 1958	9	51	70	6
Mar. 1958– Mar. 1962	7	72	59	10
Mar. 1962– June 1966	7	51	60	7
Gorbachev era, 1989–91				
June 1989– Nov. 1990	4	62	274	15.5
Jan. 1991–July 1991	1	50	*n.a.*	50
RSFSR, 1990–93				
June 1990–July 1991	3	69	252	23
Apr. 1992– Nov. 1992	2	53	268	26
Jan. 1993– July 1993	1	98	104	100
State Duma 1994–99[a]				
Jan. 1994–Dec. 1995	4	464	*n.a.*[b]	116
Jan. 1996– July 1996	1	145	156	145
Jan.–Dec. 1998	2	287	435	143
Jan. 1996– Dec. 1999	8	1,036	*n.a.*	129

Sources: For pre-Gorbachev period: M. Saifullin, ed., *The Soviet Parliament: A Refernce Book* (Moscow: Progress Publishers, 1967) 15–16. For 1989–91: *Narodnyi deputat*, no. 1 (1991): 15. For 1990–93: *Rossiiskaia gazeta,* November 14, 1992; July 24, 1993; August 10, 1993. For Duma, 1994: "Informatsiia o rabote Gosudarstvennoi Dumy v 1994 godu (s 11 ianvaria po 23 dekabria)," report of Department of Organizational Support of Sessions of the State Duma, distributed to deputies on January 12, 1995. For Duma, 1996–99: Federal'noe sobranie— parlament Rossiiskoi Federatsii Gosudarstvennaia Duma. Analiticheskoe upravlenie, *Gosudarstvennaia Duma vtorogo sozyva v vesenniuiu sessiiu 1996 goda. Informatsionno-analiticheskii biulleten',* no. 6 (Moscow, 1999), p. 15; Federal'noe Sobrainie—parlament Rossiiskoi Federatsii. Gosudarstvennaia Duma. Analiticheskoe upravlenie, *Gosudarstvennaia Duma vtorogo sozyva v vesenniuiu sessiiu 1999 goda. informatsionno-analiticheskii biulleten',* no. 6 (Moscow, 1999), p. 4; Federal noe Sobranie—parlament Rossiiskoi Federatsii. Gosudarstvennaia Duma. Analiticheskoe upravlenie, *Gosudarstvennaia Duma vtorogo sozyva v*

continued

Table 7.18. (*Continued*)

---

vesenniuiu sessiiu 1999 goda. Informatsionno-analiticheskii biulleten', no. 5 (April 21–May 18, 1999) (Moscow, 1999), pp. 89–90; Federal'noe Sobranie—parlament Rossiiskoi Federatsii. Godsudarstvennaia Duma. Analiticheskoe upravlenie, Analiticheskii vestnik, vyp. 3 *Statisticheskie kharakeristiki zakonodatel'noi deiatel'nostii Gosudarstvennoi Dumy vtorogo sozyva (1996–1999)* (Moscow, 2000), pp. 6–8.

[a]Figures refer to all federal and constitutional laws passed in third reading by the State Duma.

[b]The Duma adopted 41 decrees in 1994, the first time since Stalin's death that Russia's parliament passed more laws than decrees.

law; the president does not rule by decree but actively works with parliament to ensure passage of the legislation he wants and needs to have passed, and he devotes substantial resources to this effort; presidential and government bills enjoy higher priority in parliament than do the bills of its own members; and an all-parties governing arrangement provides a measure of stability by finding compromise solutions for divisive political issues. Below the surface turbulence in Russian politics there is a steady stream of normal legislative politics within the Duma, between the two chambers, and between parliament and president. For this reason, parliament's ability to contain and manage political conflict through the Duma's all-parties representational system and the separation of a federal chamber has had a stabilizing influence on Russia's postcommunist politics.

The sequence of institutional evolution helps explain the establishment of these features. The Federal Assembly took over and adapted institutional arrangements developed in the two preceding transition parliaments. Many features of its organization are the product of decisions outside its control, such as the president's use of force to win the adoption of a constitution to his liking and the adoption of a law on elections that was the product of extensive discussion among political leaders. Once they convened, however, the new deputies quickly found a stable set of governing arrangements to enable them to meet their needs. Each chamber of parliament devised a governing arrangement that gained the stable support of a majority of its members. The new structure adapted old mechanisms, such as the Council of Factions, to new needs; abolished some institutions that most deputies considered undesirable; and left intact many others that the deputies were satisfied with. In turn, the new arrangement enabled parliament to face the powerful presidency of Boris Yeltsin with a capacity for decision making that its predecessors never developed. Both the USSR and RSFSR transitional parliaments, faced with mounting economic and social crisis, relinquished their constitutional responsibilities to decide national policy and delegated sweeping emergency powers to the president of the day. The Federal Assembly, however powerless it has been to stem the effects of a failed economic reform strategy, at least managed to force the president to take seriously his own constitution.

Chapter 8: Does Parliament Matter?

> We went on a little further, and I looked to the right again, and
> said, in rather a doubtful tone of voice, "Why, there are the
> Houses of Parliament! Do you still use them?"
>
> He burst out laughing, and was some time before he could
> control himself; then he clapped me on the back and said:
>
> "I take you, neighbor; you may well wonder at our keeping
> them standing, and I know something about that, and my old
> kinsman has given me books to read about the strange game
> that they played there. Use them! Well, yes, they are used for a
> sort of subsidiary market, and a storage place for manure, and
> they are handy for that, being on the water-side."
> —William Morris, *News from Nowhere*

At the end of the 1990s, Russia's parliament is an altogether different creature from its transitional predecessors, let alone the Stalinist
Supreme Soviet that they were based on. It is structurally flatter—less
centralized—and politically far more important than they were. Party
leaders and regional officials have gained formal rights of representation at the expense of the former centralized structures of Presidium,
staff, and chairman. Deputies are confronted with a heavier burden of

choice than their predecessors, but they also have more effective means for autonomous participation in the legislative process, for generating and weighing alternatives, and for forming majorities. Gone are the amateur deputies of the soviet era; in their stead are full-time politicians faced with the usual challenges democratically elected parliamentarians deal with, of juggling competing electoral, policy, and party pressures.[1] The Federal Assembly grapples, with varying degrees of success, with most of the major policy issues facing the country. New constitutional, electoral, and procedural rules are responsible for these changes in parliament's role. Above all, two new forms of institutional representation— political factions and a federal upper house—have replaced the old centralized parliament, which served the party-state as its lawmaking arm. Effective exercise of their powers as elected representatives in a pluralized parliament required the deputies to find new ways of aggregating their preferences and of reaching majority agreement for legislation, but to do so without restoring the old transmission belts of chairman, Presidium, and apparat.

Yet, as this account of the period has emphasized, a good deal of continuity links institutional forms over the decade. The Federal Assembly carried over many of the rules of lawmaking nearly intact from earlier models. Its most notable innovations, the party-dominated organization of the lower chamber and the separation of the two chambers in their electoral bases, jurisdictions, terms, and governance, were modifications of earlier arrangements, which arose as improvised solutions to leaders' and deputies' political needs. The complementary interests of leaders and deputies allowed them to agree to incorporating these new arrangements into parliamentary and electoral rules. At each stage, the bargain between leaders and deputies trading off expanded rights of participation for factions for support of a leader represented a new equilibrium among competing political forces. In turn, it made a similar deal in the next round more likely.

I have argued that as a result of this path of evolution, Russia's parliament has expanded its capacity to represent a diverse range of political interests, to enact legislation, and to manage its conflict with the president. Unlike the USSR and RSFSR transitional legislatures, the Federal Assembly has not been blackmailed into relinquishing its constitutional powers. Therefore, although it is constitutionally weaker than its predecessor parliaments, which were considered constitutionally to hold supreme power in the state, the Federal Assembly has used the limited powers it has to consider a good deal of significant legislation. More than he had anticipated, President Yeltsin had to accept the Federal Assembly as a legitimate counterweight in the political arena. Opposition groups, regional leaders, and president have been willing to settle their differences through constitutional means rather than by ignoring or tearing down the constitution. It is highly likely, therefore, that the relative stability that has prevailed at the level of high politics has to do with the fact that parliament has given the opposing sides a stake in preserving the current arrangements.

If this is true, it flies in the face of the everyday impressions that Russians and outside observers form of parliament. Such unforgettable spectacles as fistfights on the floor, hair-raising motions passed nearly unanimously, outrageous ethnic slurs, and fantastic flights of paranoia have contributed to the widespread view that the Duma is not only constitutionally weak, but it has made itself irrelevant by politicizing all issues that come to it and turning them into occasions for venting steam or, at most, turning political office into lucrative opportunities to sell votes to powerful interests. Senior staff officials in the Duma frequently bemoan the constant intrusion of party politics into the Duma's life, unfavorably contrasting the Duma with the calmer and more orderly proceedings under Luk'ianov and Khasbulatov. Observers are horrified by stories that wealthy and corrupt individuals pay fabulous sums to buy themselves a spot on a party list or to win the favor of the voters of a single-member district in order to win a seat and thereby gain full legal immunity from all criminal prosecution.

But the record of legislative accomplishment suggests that, offstage, a great deal of serious work gets done; the theatrics obscure the fact that parliament and president are continually engaged in discussions and negotiations over the agenda and outcome of parliamentary decision making. It is my contention that parliament's ability to be taken seriously derives from the fact that it has an independent capacity to aggregate preferences and form a collective will, based on the partisan organization of the lower chamber and the upper chamber's function as veto player protecting the collective interests of the regional power establishments. The result is to diffuse conflict, making decision making messy and often inconclusive (although not more so than under the previous arrangements) as well as having the significant advantage of giving more players a stake in preserving the rules of the game. If that is so, then it is of some historical, as well as theoretical, interest to know where these new governing arrangements came from. They were not the product of a grand constitutional agreement or pact among political rivals who sat down to negotiate a new constitutional system in the expectation that a rule-governed process of power competition and policy making would make all better off. Nor were they designed as an institutional solution to the problem of lowering transaction costs to let competitors capture gains from trade. Rather, they were improvised outcomes of power struggles, in which players traded off rights in one arena for power in another. But as a result of these side deals, the capacity of parliament to represent and aggregate diverse interests was increased, with stabilizing effects for the larger political system.

This is an account that envisions adaptive evolution as the product of joint choices by competing political actors resulting in relatively stable equilibria; outcomes that are off the equilibrium path are likely to be unstable (as when major players simply ignore the institutions they have created in pursuing their political aims). Institutional effectiveness did not arise as a trial-and-error process of variations and choice through natural selection, with the functional fitness of institutions progressively improved through time. Rather, the choice of new institutions in the stream of tinkering and catastrophe over this period was largely a matter of the strong dictating to the weak the terms of new arrangements *but* providing enough in the way of compensatory side payments to induce their commitment to participation in the new arrangements. These institutional side payments made what had been informal practices into formal features of the new arrangements. The new features benefited a range of organized interests, doing so, in particular, by enabling them to overcome their own difficulties in acting collectively.

We have treated the evolution of parliamentary arrangements as a sequence of linked choices over constitutional, electoral, and legislative rules: the consequences of choices made at a previous time become constraints on the actors at a subsequent time. The outcomes of prior choices influence subsequent events by providing actors with information, shaping their immediate objectives, and defining the set of relevant participants in the process. Outcomes at any one point can only be fully explained by specifying the rules chosen as the outcome of prior choices, and so on back through an endless regression of historical events. I chose to begin my account with Gorbachev's constitutional reforms, but these were modifications of a set of arrangements put into place at the height of Stalin's power. Stalin's constitution gave institutional form to a revolution. Stalin's model of a Supreme Soviet reflected the contempt in which he and the Bolsheviks held "bourgeois parliamentarianism": rather than being a "talking shop," as Lenin dismissively called democratic parliaments, the Soviet parliament would embody the solidarity of Soviet society. In it there was no room for party competition. The extreme centralization of political power was accompanied by mass participation in voting and service in soviets: throughout the country, some two million people served as people's deputies by the end of the Soviet regime. But such mass participation not only did not render Soviet parliaments representative, it also necessitated centralized control to ensure stable and consistent decisions.

Only in 1989 did the constitutional environment change sufficiently to render the Stalinist model a problem for the leadership. We saw that Gorbachev had a largely free hand in designing the modifications of Stalin's Supreme Soviet model in such a way as to serve his own political strategy of gradual democratization. At that point, with the election of a large body of new deputies, some of then keen to use these institutional means as a way of replacing communist rule itself with something else, parliamentary rules and procedures became the object of a heated contest by new political actors.

To explain subsequent modifications of these arrangements, we needed to know more than simply the goals and constraints influencing Gorbachev: we needed to be able to characterize the distribution of outlooks among the broader body of elected deputies, since many of the developments in the way the congress-Supreme Soviet structure worked were influenced by the actions of the newly elected deputies. The huge assembly of deputies who met for the first time in May 1989 had virtually no means of aggregating preferences and reaching decisions except those which the leadership—Gorbachev and his coterie of advisers, backed by a large, experienced, well-organized, inherited staff structure—chose to give them. As Gorbachev scrambled to reinforce his own political power, he railroaded the deputies into creating a new presidency, and later into delegating emergency decree powers over social and economic policy to the president. A year later, Yeltsin persuaded the Russian congress to do much the same thing, first creating a presidency to strengthen the Russian Republic's position vis-à-vis the union center, and later endowing it with emergency decree powers. But in both cases, these moves ended in stalemate. Not only did many deputies simply exit the new institutions (as when the Baltic delegations stopped attending USSR Supreme Soviet sessions and when two hundred or so of the RSFSR deputies went to work in the executive branch), but some chose to conspire against them. In fact, in both cases, these were not a few disgruntled rank-and-file members; the parliamentary leadership itself conspired to overthrow the system. As president, Gorbachev found himself a commander with no army to command and at the same time unable to use the congress or Supreme Soviet as a means of crafting a new constitutional settlement. Likewise Yeltsin could not use his powers as president to win the congress's consent to the constitutional plan he wanted. Parliamentary leadership and president had enough power to frustrate one another's objectives, but not enough to impose their own solutions by constitutional means.

Before their demise, however, both of these transitional parliaments created some new forms of organization. The open electoral mobilization in 1989 prompted self-conscious legislative caucuses with policy goals to form in the congress. For the first time since the Bolshevik Revolution, competitive parliamentary politics took shape. This fact in turn led to consequences that Gorbachev and Luk'ianov probably did not foresee and certainly could not control.

Recognition of the rights of groups progressively expanded over the terms of the USSR and RSFSR parliaments. These developments resulted from the deals offered by parliamentary leaders to the leaders of groups and factions, each side pursuing its own political advantage. Parliamentary leaders wanted to reinforce their political base in the legislature and were willing to trade off organizing rights to factions for wider support. Factions, especially faction leaders, benefited from the opportunity to develop followings, act collectively, stake out jurisdictions, and build political reputations. This process came about as leaders adapted existing institutional forms, old rules and new informal practices, to accommodate new tasks. For example, when the new USSR congress convened in May 1989, the only groups recognized were territorial delegations, which served traditionally as mechanisms for communication and control by higher communist party authorities. Soon, though, informal interest-based caucuses formed at the congress, beginning with the agrarian group. Immediately afterward the Inter-Regionals formed a group that gained official recognition: it was a nonterritorial, and non-interest-specific group, but it was given analogous rights to those enjoyed by territorial and interest groups, including the right to initiate proposals and voice collective demands. The establishment of the Inter-Regional Group led to the adoption of a rule that politically based groups, not just interest-based or territorial groups, were permitted to exist. Next, political groups were not merely tolerated, but gained semi-official recognition as representing the major currents of opinion among the deputies. Affiliation with organized political groups became an informal criterion for evaluating the level of balance of committees and of the Supreme Soviet, and spokesmen of political groups were regularly invited to inform the Presidium about their groups' views on matters of current policy. These steps were all deliberate grants of rights by the chairman and Presidium of the Supreme Soviet of the USSR that consolidated his own control over the institution, by allowing him to balance more competing centers of power and to inform himself of the demands and interests of deputies. The grant of rights to political groups was an exchange of rights for policy control.

When the RSFSR Congress and Supreme Soviet system formed, political groups were recognized at the outset but were given no precedence over other groups. This changed in fall 1991 when political factions gained preferential rights and deputies were prohibited from belonging to more than one such faction. Once again, the chairman granted political groups expanded rights in return for the support given his leadership by the Council of Factions, representing the faction leaders' interests in faction rights. Khasbulatov's effort to create greater room for maneuver for himself in this way failed, however, as he became hostage to the opposition majority in the Congress. The opposition was able to block the legislative initiatives of the president, many of which required two-thirds votes because they concerned constitutional amendment. But it was unable to win control over the executive, having created a powerful presidency, ceded extensive decree power to it, and blocked the president's efforts to put a constitutional solution to the impasse to popular referendum. The result was the bloody crisis of September-October 1993.

This account shows the close link between changes in the forms of executive power and the succession of exchanges of rights that result in the expansion of rights for parliamentary parties. Consider this sequence of events:

- In February-March 1990 Gorbachev finally agreed to modify Article 6 and legalize the principle of a multiparty political system, packaging this reform with the creation of a new, executive presidency;
- Yeltsin was elected chairman of the Supreme Soviet of the RSFSR in June 1990. Immediately upon being elected, he encouraged the free formation of political groups, met with the newly formed groups, and promised to consult with them regularly;
- When the RSFSR congress deadlocked over the election of a chairman to replace Yeltsin at the end of October 1991, informal consultation among faction leaders produced a deal breaking the impasse and enabling Ruslan Khasbulatov to be elected to the chairmanship of the Supreme Soviet. Yeltsin was granted sweeping emergency powers to make policy by decree; the congress adopted a rules change that elevated political factions to privileged status; and Khasbulatov formed the Council of Factions, all at the same time. It is reasonable to suppose that a kind of grand package agreement was constructed involving the faction leaders, Khasbulatov, and Yeltsin, giving each side what it wanted in exchange for agreeing to the deal. Faction leaders gained leverage

through the rule that a deputy could be a member of only one faction, and Khasbulatov won the support of the faction leaders in his bid for the chairmanship. The Council of Factions again supported Khasbulatov in late 1992 at a moment when the communist opposition wanted to vote no confidence in the reformist Gaidar government and the democratic forces wanted to vote out Khasbulatov as chairman of the Supreme Soviet. The council worked out a package agreement under which parliamentary support for Gaidar was traded off against support for Khasbulatov.

- Finally, once Yeltsin ultimately dissolved parliament and established his own preferred constitutional model, Yeltsin's representatives (Mitiukov as head of the Rules Commission drafting rules of procedure for the new Duma) devised a governing formula for the new Duma that put power to regulate the chamber in the hands of a council of factions formed on a parity basis. The rules further strengthened the leverage of faction leaders by providing that a deputy could only be a member of one faction *or* group. Party leaders coordinated on a steering body for the Duma—the Council of Factions—that enabled them to discard the presidium form and run the parliament under their collective control.

If factionalism was one of the great innovations in this institutional evolution, bicameralism was the other. Once again, institutional evolution occurred by adapting informal institutions and making them part of the formal fabric of structural arrangements. In the old, pre-Gorbachev system, bicameralism was purely nominal (in the USSR Supreme Soviet, that is; the RSFSR Supreme Soviet did not even use bicameralism, although the Russian Republic was formally federal). Well into the 1989–91 and 1990–93 periods, the division of the Supreme Soviet into two chambers was largely ceremonial. Despite the stock, repeated complaints by virtually all the participants to the effect that parliament would work better if the two chambers had more clearly distinct profiles and powers, it was never in anyone's interest really to separate them. The Presidium and the chairmen of the standing committees (who made up most of the membership of the Presidium) had no interest at all in relinquishing control over parliamentary proceedings and agendas to the chambers. Bicameralism remained a dead letter so long as the old Presidium-Supreme Soviet structure remained in place.

Nonetheless, the principle of bicameralism as an instrument of meaningful federalism enjoyed wide support among the political elite. In the constitutional debates of 1991–93, most proposals envisioned creating directly elected chambers with separate bases of representation. Informally, both Gorbachev and Yeltsin began experimenting with advisory bodies made up of equal numbers of representatives from each territorial subject, and usually their leaders. Gorbachev negotiated the "9 + 1" treaty with the heads of state of the union republics, as if that group already had some formal constitutional status. The model of such a chamber was widely familiar. Whether such a federal upper chamber should be directly or indirectly elected, however, was much more contentious. The outcome of that dispute depended on the power balance between Yeltsin and the regional leaders in late 1993.

My account seeks to answer the question of where the supply of new institutions came from by assessing the political calculations of the actors who fought over them and treating the creation of institutions as the outcome of collective choice processes. A low-cost solution to the problem of supply was to employ familiar informal practices and use them for exchanges of jurisdictional rights: an executive leader expanded his base of support and freedom of maneuver by granting representative rights to other collective actors, which in turn solved collective dilemmas for them.

To explain how and why the actors did or did not reach constitutional-level agreements about the shape of a new legislature, one needs an understanding of how the political conflict was structured. A spatial model helps to explain the relation between the two major dimensions of conflict. Certainly the struggle between the communist forces and liberal democrats was a constant throughout the period and has remained a powerful organizing principle for political conflict. Yet over this same period, both before and after the breakup of the union, both camps divided over the issue of how much power the central level of government should have as opposed to subcentral levels of government. These axes of conflict, I argued, could be represented as orthogonal to one another.

If there were only one great axis of division, the player's positions could be represented as locations along a one-dimensional axis. In such settings, subject as well to the requirement that each actor be able to rank his or her preferences transitively, social choice theory has demonstrated, the option preferred by a majority will have certain properties: it will be that option that the actor whose position is closest to the median point in the distribution prefers. No majority can form that does not include the actor at or nearest to the median point. This theorem means that groups in such cases are able to form a collective will even if they are free to consider as many alternatives as any of them wish to propose. But in the absence of such conditions, a group of actors is likely to find itself unable to aggregate the preferences of its individual members unless someone who can control the nature or order of the alternatives they consider restricts the range of alternatives over which they exercise a collective choice. As theory shows, as the number of dimensions over which the members hold preferences increases, the probability that they can find one alternative that commands a stable majority decreases sharply.

This problem bears directly on the Russian case. In the Russian congresses, any proposal for constitutional reform affected the interests of deputies in both the economic reform and central-regional power dimensions because any change over the status quo would have clear and predictable consequences for power and policy. On a number of occasions, Yeltsin could win narrow majorities in the congresses on particular issues, but no one was able to command a two-thirds majority in support of a new constitution. When he put the issue to the electorate in a straight yes-or-no vote, however, his plan carried. Did he succeed solely because of the implicit threat of chaos and the explicit use of force in October 1993 to suppress his opposition? I have argued that, in fact, the constitution resulted from a long process of intraelite debates that had begun in 1990 when the Russian congress first convened. Yeltsin, I argued, made just enough concessions to the other players that they preferred to participate in the new constitutional arena rather than to mobilize to overturn it.

As it happened, these constitutional innovations corresponded to the two features of parliamentary evolution that I identified. Factionalism in the State Duma grew out of the organization of party factions elected under the mixed, half party-list, half-SMD election law that Yeltsin put in place for the December 1993. Bicameralism grew from the agreement to give direct representation to regions on an equal basis that was Yeltsin's concession to regional leaders in his struggle with his parliamentary opposition in 1992 and 1993. Each feature provided the other participants with instruments for representation and collective action. Each was therefore the product of a deal, implicit or explicit, over an institution. Each institutional choice, in turn, has proven to be self-perpetuating. The Duma retained its initial set of rules and procedures following the 1995 elections and retained the principle of the mixed, half-and-half electoral system that made collective factional control an agreed principle of governance in the Duma. The Federation Council preserved its streamlined, senatorial system of rules even after the law on the composition of the chamber was changed and a new membership entered.

These institutional developments had an impact on parliament's effectiveness. Broad allowance must be made for the rapid change in contextual circumstances over this period. Yet all the quantitative indicators suggest that although the Federal Assembly is highly inefficient—only succeeding in actually taking up fewer than half of the items it places on its agenda—it nonetheless has passed more legislation than did any of its predecessors; has passed a higher share of executive-sponsored legislation than deputy-sponsored measures; and has found agreement with the president on the enactment of around three-fourths of the laws it has passed. Similarly, we found that the president works intensively with parliament to reach agreement on legislation, fielding a sizable staff of presidential and governmental liaison officials and making less use of his decree power to make major policy decisions as time passes. These effects may well have been unexpected for both Yeltsin and his opposition. The commitment of future presidents and future oppositions to abide by the rules of the new game may continue for some while to be contingent on each side's judgment of the other's commitment to do so. The constitution could readily fail at any time. That these arrangements have had a longer shelf life than anyone predicted, outlasting both Yeltsin and the first two Dumas, is testament to the axiom that the consequences of institutional choices may outlive the circumstances of their creation.

Where did the new representative institutions of the Russian parliament come from? A sizable body of scholarship shows that social institutions do not arise simply or naturally in response to their environments. As products of choice, they are often the objects of negotiation and struggle by self-interested actors forced to take one another's differing preferences into account. Like such fundamental economic arrangements as property rights, representative political institutions form a particularly important class because they can allocate advantage and disadvantage to opposing interests. Unlike economic institutions, however, the effects of representative institutions on their environments are harder to assess. As a result, explaining their adoption as a social choice is frequently difficult. We can agree with William Riker that if a particular outcome forms an equilibrium for a group of rational decision makers, such that none has an incentive to depart from his or her choice given the strategies of the others, then the existence of the equilibrium itself is the explanation for their actions. That is because the equilibrium is the set of foreseen consequences of the actors' choices that are both necessary and sufficient conditions for those choices.[2] What goals do political actors seek to attain in creating new representative institutions? Models of distributional conflict posit that institutions are constructed to fix actors' claims on private goods. Models of efficient institutions, however, allow for the possibility that some arrangements may make all participants better off; this possibility, I argued, may be an emergent property of side arrangements negotiated or accepted as part of distributional games in cases where they confer advantages in other domains, such as electoral chances and office- or career-related benefits. Moreover, such side deals may improve the aggregate efficiency of the new arrangements, as well as their attractiveness for competing political actors, if they enable some collective actors to overcome their organizational dilemmas. The existence of multiple domains over which actors may have interests and preferences expands the scope for efficiency-improving outcomes of institutional choices, even as products of distributionally motivated competition.

Moreover, some public goods commonly considered to be products of representative institutions benefit members, but members may be unable or unwilling to provide them on their own at the expense of their own private benefits. These include the classic normative ideals of clear and decisive electoral choice over government policy, inclusiveness and representativeness of the representative bodies, and good public policy. Although there is general agreement in the literature that these cannot all be maximized simultaneously, so that any given set of arrangements tends to favor one set at the expense of another, it is fair to say that there is an ideal frontier, set by the constitution and its own rules of procedure, beyond which a legislature cannot be more representative or more powerful in policy making. There is also a considerable zone below it where through parliament's own inefficiency, it fails to realize its potential for policy influence and the representation of diverse interests. Its effectiveness, therefore, is a product of the ability of its institutional arrangements to enable it to aggregate its members' preferences and to form a collective will.

But politicians do not necessarily seek efficient representative institutions because of the multiplicity of goals for which they may be efficient and because politicians have goals in multiple domains. How then can we explain the choice of institutions? That is, to say that the existence of an equilibrium institution for a set of actors is both the necessary and sufficient condition to bring about their choice of that institution leaves open the possibility that the equilibrium properties of the institution were themselves unintended outcomes rather than the goals motivating the actors' choices.

In a setting where actors are uncertain about basic constitutional stability, the equilibrium characteristics of a legislative institution directly influence its policy-making effectiveness: if actors are unwilling to commit themselves to adhere to the constitutional powers and procedures of the legislature, its capacity to influence policy or check executive power will vanish. What would make one set of arrangements more or less likely to win the acceptance of a set of deeply divided actors, each interested in structuring the rules to its own political advantage? With respect to the Russian case, I have argued that a distributional conflict could yield institutional innovations that were sufficiently efficiency-improving for all sides to induce their commitment to the new arrangements. This was because each side gained enough of what it preferred so that the benefit of abiding by the arrangements outweighed the disadvantages. For ambitious party leaders, a lower house run by and for a cartel of parliamentary party factions gave them leverage over followers and rights useful for serving other interests, including electoral resources and privileges of office. For regional bosses, an upper chamber with reserved seats that was independent of the lower chamber provided a collective veto over federal policy; simple majority rule enables them to pool their collective power even in the absence of partisanship and well-defined committee jurisdictions. Ex officio membership in the chamber created a new representative right for the regional leaders. For his part, Yeltsin got most of what he wanted: decree power with no parliamentary override or confirmation, veto power, and control of the government. The ability of these arrangements to satisfy several domains of interest at once may perhaps help to explain the constitution's ability to survive the country's social and economic crises. Moreover, the existence of legislative institutions capable of aggregating the diverse preferences of its members raised the costs for Yeltsin of defying parliament's will too frequently and gave the country's premier representative institution, its parliament, an unexpected capacity for political influence.

Notes

PREFACE

1. Thane Gustafson, *Capitalism Russian-Style* (Cambridge: Cambridge University Press, 1999).
2. David Collier and Steven Levitsky, "Democracy with Adjectives: Conceptual Innovation in Comparative Research," *World Politics* 49, no. 3 (1997): 30–451.

CHAPTER 1. POLITICAL REPRESENTATION AND PARLIAMENTARY POWER

1. Michael McFaul, *Russia's 1996 Presidential Election: The End of Polarized Politics* (Stanford, Calif.: Hoover Institution Press, 1997).
2. Stephen White, Richard Rose, and Ian McAllister, *How Russia Votes* (Chatham, N.J.: Chatham House, 1997), 270.
3. Guillermo O'Donnell and Philippe C. Schmitter, *Transitions from Authoritarian Rule: Tentative Conclusions about Uncertain Democracies* (Baltimore: Johns Hopkins University Press, 1986), 26.
4. Kenneth A. Shepsle, "Studying Institutions: Some Lessons from the Rational Choice Approach," *Journal of Theoretical Politics* 1, no. 2 (1989): 131–47.
5. William Mishler and Richard Rose, "Public Support for Legislatures and Regimes in Central and Eastern Europe," in *Working Papers on Comparative*

Legislative Studies, ed. Lawrence D. Longley, (Appleton, Wis.: Research Committee of Legislative Specialists, International Political Science Association, 1994), 67.

6. Gerhard Loewenberg and Samuel C. Patterson, *Comparing Legislatures* (Boston: Little, Brown, 1979).

7. Robert A. Dahl, *After the Revolution? Authority in a Good Society,* rev. ed. (New Haven: Yale University Press, 1990), 30–42.

8. The first problem occurs when no alternative to the status quo can win the support of an affirmative majority of the voters. The second problem—when any given majority decision can be defeated by a different alternative supported by a different majority—is called cycling. Cycling refers to a dilemma of collective choice that arises when a group of individuals who must choose one of a set of alternative actions are unable to settle on any single alternative and instead cycle through a number of alternatives, each of which can command a majority in its favor but which in turn can be defeated by a majority for another outcome.

Either dilemma renders decision making under majority rule unstable. Political scientists have given a considerable amount of attention to decision-making rules (institutions) that enable groups to avoid such a dilemma and to the properties of those institutions that themselves succeed in escaping being subject to such instability. A thorough introduction to the problem is provided in William H. Riker, *Liberalism against Populism* (Prospect Heights, Ill.: Waveland Press, 1982). There is now a substantial literature that discusses how various alternative arrangements for solving such collective choice dilemmas in legislature arise and what their consequences are for decision making. Recent examples are John Aldrich, "A Model of Legislature with Two Parties and a Committee System," *Legislative Studies Quarterly* 19 (1994): 313–39; Rick K. Wilson, "Transitional Governance in the United States: Lessons from the First Federal Congress," *Legislative Studies Quarterly* 24, no. 3 (1999): 543–68; and Jo Andrews, *When Majorities Fail: The Implications of Disequilibrium in Transitional Legislatures* (Cambridge: Cambridge University Pres, 2000).

9. John M. Carey, Frantisek Formanek, and Ewa Karpowicz, "Legislative Autonomy in New Regimes: The Czech and Polish Cases," *Legislative Studies Quarterly* 24, no. 4 (1999): 577.

10. A useful analogy is the "guns vs. butter" production possibilities curve that economists use to model the production of two commodities by an economy. At any given level of productive capacity, the society can turn out more of one good, such as guns, and less of another, such as butter. Because of diminishing returns from the increasing use of resources to produce more of one good at the expense of the other, the line linking the points defining the maximum production of the combination of the two goods is not straight but forms a convex (outward-bulging) curve. By investing in greater productive capacity, the economy can expand its ability to produce both commodities, but at any *particular* level of capacity, it can put out more of one good only by producing less of the other. And of course, it can produce less of both than the maximum defined by its productive potential if it uses its resources inefficiently.

In like fashion, for any given constitutional setting, a legislature can be more representative or more efficient at producing decisions, but it cannot increase both representativeness and decision-making efficiency simultaneously. We might even go so far in applying this analogy as to say that, as in an economy, where the opportunity costs of diverting resources from the production of one good to the other bring about diminishing returns, so the legislature faces a point where additional gains in efficiency or representativeness are more and more costly in terms of the other good. As in a production possibilities model, we can suppose that a legislature can increase its overall ability to produce both goods—pushing the frontier outward—by acquiring more rights and resources. Similarly, we can suppose that a legislature that falls short of its potential to produce decisions given a certain level of heterogeneity of interests represented is less influential vis-à-vis other actors in the political system than it could potentially be.

11. Bingham Powell, *Contemporary Democracies: Participation, Stability and Violence* (Cambridge: Harvard University Press, 1982); Arend Lijphart, *Democracies: Patterns of Majoritarian and Consensus Government in Twenty-one Countries* (New Haven: Yale University Press, 1984); Arend Lijphart, "Democracies: Forms, Performance, and Constitutional Engineering," *European Journal of Political Research* 25 (1994): 1–17; Kenneth A. Shepsle, "Representation and Governance: The Great Legislative Trade-Off," *Political Science Quarterly* 103, no. 3 (1988): 461–84; Richard Rose and William Mishler, "Representation and Leadership in Post-Communist Political Systems," *Journal of Communist Studies and Transition Politics* 12, no. 2 (June 1996): 224–47; Stephan Haggard and Robert R. Kaufman, *The Political Economy of Democratic Transitions* (Princeton: Princeton University Press, 1995).

12. Matthew Sobert Shugart and John M. Carey, *Presidents and Assemblies: Constitutional Design and Electoral Dynamics* (Cambridge: Cambridge University Press, 1992).

13. Kaare Strom, *Minority Government and Majority Rule* (Cambridge: Cambridge University Press, 1990).

14. Giuseppe Di Palma, *Surviving without Governing: The Italian Parties in Parliament* (Berkeley: University of California Press, 1977).

15. John D. Huber, *Rationalizing Parliament: Legislative Institutions and Party Politics in France* (Cambridge: Cambridge University Press, 1996).

16. Ezra N. Suleiman, "Presidentialism and Political Stability in France," in *The Failure of Presidential Democracy: Comparative Perspectives,* ed. Juan J. Linz and Arturo Valenzuela (Baltimore: Johns Hopkins University Press, 1994), 137–62.

17. Gary W. Copeland and Samuel C. Patterson, eds., *Parliaments in the Modern World: Changing Institutions* (Ann Arbor: University of Michigan Press, 1994); Arend Lijphart, ed., *Parliamentary versus Presidential Government* (Oxford: Oxford University Press, 1992); Donald L. Horowitz, *Ethnic Groups in Conflict* (Berkeley: University of California Press, 1985); Arend Lijphart and Carlos H. Waisman, eds., *Institutional Design in New Democracies: Eastern Europe and Latin America* (Boulder: Westview, 1996); Jon Elster, Claus Offe, and Ulrich K. Preuss, *Institutional Design in Post-Communist Societies: Rebuilding the Ship at Sea* (Cambridge: Cambridge University Press, 1998); Carey, Formanek, and Karpowicz, "Legislative Autonomy," 569–604.

18. Alfred Stepan and Cindy Skach, "Constitutional Frameworks and Democratic Consolidation: Parliamentarism versus Presidentialism," *World Politics* 46 (1993): 1–22.

19. Juan Linz, "Presidential or Parliamentary Democracy: Does It Make a Difference?" in

The Failure of Presidential Democracy: Comparative Perspectives, ed. Juan J. Linz and Arturo Valenzuela (Baltimore: Johns Hopkins University Press, 1994), 3–90.

20. Lijphart, "Democracies," 1–17.

21. R. Kent Weaver and Bert A. Rockman, eds., *Do Institutions Matter: Government Capabilities in the United States and Abroad* (Washington, D.C.: Brookings Institution Press, 1993).

22. Shugart and Carey, *Presidents and Assemblies.*

23. Adam Przeworski, *Democracy and the Market* (Cambridge: Cambridge University Press, 1991); Giuseppe Di Palma, *To Craft Democracies: An Essay on Democratic Transitions* (Berkeley: University of California Press, 1990); Arend Lijphart, *Democracy in Plural Societies: A Comparative Exploration* (New Haven: Yale University Press, 1977); Guillermo O'Donnell and Philippe Schmitter, eds., *Transitions from Authoritarian Rule: Prospects for Democracy* (Baltimore: Johns Hopkins University Press, 1986).

24. Douglass C. North and Barry R. Weingast, "Constitutions and Commitment: The Evolution of Institutions Governing Public Choice in Seventeenth-Century England," *Journal of Economic History* 44 (1989): 803–32; Douglass C. North, "Institutions and Credible Commitment," *Journal of Institutional and Theoretical Economics* 149 (1993): 11–23; David L. Weimer, ed., *The Political Economy of Property Rights: Institutional Change and Credibility in the Reform of Centrally Planned Economies* (Cambridge: Cambridge University Press, 1997); Avner Greif, Paul Milgrom, and Barry R. Weingast, "Coordination, Commitment and Enforcement: The Case of the Merchant Guild," in *Explaining Social Institutions,* ed. Jack Knight and Itai Sened (Ann Arbor: University of Michigan Press, 1995), 27–56.

25. Philippe Schmitter and Terry Lynn Karl, "What Democracy Is and Is Not," *Journal of Democracy* 2, no. 2 (1991): 75–88.

26. Hugh Heclo, "Ideas, Interests, and Institutions," in *The Dynamics of American Politics: Approaches and Interpretations,* ed. Lawrence C. Dodd and Calvin Jillson (Boulder: Westview, 1994), 366–92.; Nelson W. Polsby, "The Institutionalization of the U.S. House of Representatives," *American Political Science Review* 62 (1968): 144–68.

27. Samuel P. Huntington, *Political Order in Changing Societies* (New Haven: Yale University Press, 1968); Samuel C. Patterson and Gary W. Copeland, "Parliaments in the Twenty-first Century," in *Parliaments in the Modern World,* ed. Patterson and Copeland, 1–11.

28. Douglass C. North, *Institutions, Institutional Change and Economic Performance* (Cambridge: Cambridge University Press, 1990); Robert D. Putnam, *Making Democracy Work: Civic Traditions in Modern Italy* (Princeton: Princeton University Press, 1993).

29. Elinor Ostrom, *Governing the Commons: The Evolution of Institutions for Collective Action* (Cambridge: Cambridge University Press, 1990), 42.

30. Jack Knight, "Models, Interpretations, and Theories: Constructing Explanations of Institutional Emergence and Change," in *Explaining Social Conflict,* ed. Jack Knight and Itai Sened (Ann Arbor: University of Michigan Press, 1995), 95–120.

31. Jack Knight, *Institutions and Social Conflict* (Cambridge: Cambridge University Press, 1992).

32. Przeworski, *Democracy and the Market.* A good example of the application of this argu-

ment to constitution making in former communist states is provided by Timothy Frye. See Timothy Frye, "A Politics of Institutional Choice: Post-Communist Presidencies," *Comparative Political Studies* 30, no. 5 (October 1997): 523–52.

33. White, Rose, and McAllister, *How Russia Votes.*

34. Elster, Offe, and Preuss, *Institutional Design in Post-Communist Societies;* Juan Linz and Alfred Stepan, *Problems of Democratic Transition and Consolidation: Southern Europe, South America, and Post-Communist Europe* (Baltimore: Johns Hopkins University Press, 1996); Lijphart and Waisman, eds., *Institutional Design.*

35. M. Steven Fish, *Democracy from Scratch: Opposition and Regime Change in the New Russian Revolution* (Princeton: Princeton University Press, 1995).

36. Richard Pipes, *Russia under the Old Regime* (New York: Scribner's, 1974); and Reinhard Bendix, *Work and Authority in Industry: Ideologies of Management in the Course of Industrialization* (Berkeley: University of California Press, 1974). On the contending interpretations of Russian political culture and its implications for structural change, see Harry Eckstein, Frederic Fleron, and Erik P. Hoffmann, eds., *Can Democracy Take Root in Post-Communist Russia? Explorations in State-Society Relations* (New York: Rowman and Littlefield, 1998).

37. Linz and Stepan, *Problems of Democratic Transition and Consolidation.*

CHAPTER 2. GORBACHEV'S CONSTITUTIONAL REFORMS

1. On Gorbachev's reforms, see Stephen White, *Gorbachev and After* (Cambridge: Cambridge University Press, 1992); Archie Brown, *The Gorbachev Factor* (Oxford: Oxford University Press, 1996); Richard Sakwa, *Gorbachev and His Reforms, 1985–1990* (New York: Prentice-Hall, 1990; Jerry F. Hough, *Democratization and Revolution in the USSR* (Washington, D.C.: Brookings Institution, 1997). A comparative treatment of regime collapse and state collapse in the Soviet Union and other communist states is Valerie Bunce, *Subversive Institutions: The Design and the Destruction of Socialism and the State* (Cambridge: Cambridge University Press, 1999).

2. In his memoirs, Gorbachev often employs the language of gamesmanship to describe his institutional reforms, revealing the tactical or strategic intent behind a particular move. Although he is sometimes being disingenuous, supplying rationality ex post facto to a particular decision or passing over crucial events in silence, he does provide some useful insights into his thinking at key moments. Mikhail Gorbachev, *Memoirs* (New York: Doubleday, 1995).

3. Gorbachev comes close to saying as much in his memoirs when he acknowledges that his longer-term economic reform plans needed to be "shielded" by a controlled shift of power from party to soviets. Gorbachev, *Memoirs,* 315.

4. Examples are Marshall Goldman, *What Went Wrong with Perestroika* (New York: W. W. Norton, 1991); and Minxin Pei, *From Reform to Revolution: The Demise of Communism in China and the Soviet Union* (Cambridge: Harvard University Press, 1994); see also the collection of essays edited by Gilbert Rozman, with Seizaburo Sato and Gerald Segal, *Dismantling Communism: Common Causes and Regional Variations* (Washington, D.C., and Baltimore: Woodrow Wilson Center Press and Johns Hopkins University Press, 1992).

5. Liberalization is understood here as the expansion of rights for political expression and the articulation of demands. Liberalization is therefore distinguished from participation. Robert A. Dahl, *Polyarchy: Participation and Opposition* (New Haven: Yale University Press, 1971); Guillermo O'Donnell and Philippe C. Schmitter, eds. *Transitions from Authoritarian Rule: Tentative Conclusions About Uncertain Democracies* (Baltimore: Johns Hopkins University Press, 1986).

6. Thomas F. Remington, *The Truth of Authority: Ideology and Communication in the Soviet Union* (Pittsburgh: University of Pittsburgh Press, 1988); idem, "A Socialist Pluralism of Opinions: Glasnost' and Policy-Making under Gorbachev," *Russian Review* 48, no. 3 (1989): 271–304.

7. M. Stephen Fish, *Democracy from Scratch: Opposition and Regime in the New Russian Revolution* (Princeton: Princeton University Press, 1995), 122–23; John B. Dunlop, *The Rise of Russia and the Fall of the Soviet Empire* (Princeton: Princeton University Press, 1993).

8. Remington, "Socialist Pluralism of Opinions."

9. Overviews of Gorbachev's political reforms may be found in Brown, *Gorbachev Factor,* 155–211; Sakwa, *Gorbachev and His Reforms,* 126–99; White, *Gorbachev and After,* 28–75.

10. On the process through which the plan was developed, see Michael E. Urban, *More Power to the Soviets* (Brookfield, Vt.: Edward Elgar), 1990.

11. Sakwa, *Gorbachev and His Reforms,* 129.

12. In his memoirs, Gorbachev describes the reform of the soviets in exactly these terms, saying that the activation of popular participation was a "maneuver" designed to put pressure on the conservative bureaucracy, and that he coupled it with the elimination of some of the most hard-line conservative opponents from power. Gorbachev, *Memoirs,* 278.

13. A party or government official could choose not to run for deputy, of course, but the party leadership signaled that it expected lower leaders to face this test or resign. Gorbachev, however, avoided facing an open electoral contest himself. Instead, he ensured that he was among the 100 candidates nominated by the Communist Party of the Soviet Union for the 100 seats reserved for it in the new congress. Similarly, a year later, when he created the new post of the president of the USSR, he decided against requiring that the post be filled by direct popular election. Instead, he had himself elected to the position by the congress. His shyness in the face of popular elections stood in dramatic contract to Yeltsin's extraordinary success in election campaigns. Gorbachev did eventually run for public office in a direct popular election when he ran president of Russia in 1996, but he took only half of 1 percent of the vote.

14. V. A. Kolosov, N. V. Petrov, and L. V. Smirniagin, eds., *Geografiia i anatomiia parlamentskikh vyborov* (Moscow: Progress Publishers, 1990).

15. Fish, *Democracy from Scratch;* Darrell Slider, "The Soviet Union," *Electoral Studies* 9, no. 4 (1990): 295–302; Brendan Kiernan, *The End of Soviet Politics: Elections, Legislatures and the Demise of the Communist Party* (Boulder: Westview, 1993); Brendan Kiernan and Joseph Aistrup, "The 1989 Elections to the Congress of People's Deputies in Moscow," *Soviet Studies* 43 (1991): 1049–64.

16. Jerry F. Hough, "Gorbachev's Endgame," *World Policy Journal* (fall 1990): 656.

17. Gorbachev, *Memoirs,* 319.

18. Seweryn Bialer, "The Yeltsin Affair: The Dilemma of the Left in Gorbachev's Revolution," in *Politics, Society and Nationality: Inside Gorbachev's Russia,* ed. Seweryn Bialer (Boulder: Westview, 1989), 91–120.

19. Chiesa, Giulietto, with Douglas Taylor Northrop, *Transition to Democracy: Political Change in the Soviet Union, 1987–1991* (Hanover, N.H.: Dartmouth College Press, published by University Press of New England, 1993), 70–71.

20. White, *Gorbachev and After,* 56; Martha Merritt, "If Checks Won't Balance: Parliamentary Review of Ministerial Appointments," in *Elites and Leadership in Russian Politics,* ed. Graeme Gill (New York: St. Martin's, 1998), 7–23.

21. Kiernan, *End of Soviet Politics,* 77.

22. Hough, *Democratization and Revolution,* 378.

23. Chiesa, *Transition,* 131.

24. Below I argue that at the First Congress of Russian Deputies in May-June 1990, equivalent lines of conflict dominated constitutional conflict as well. Among the Russian republic deputies, however, the democratic wing tended to cluster around both radical promarket and anticentralist sentiments, whereas the conservatives divided between prounionists and "bureaucratic nationalists." See chap. 3.

25. Chiesa, *Transition,* 134–35.

26. See Brown, *Gorbachev Factor,* 194, for evidence on this point.

27. Brown, *Gorbachev Factor,* 193; Chiesa, *Transition,* 132–34; White, *Gorbachev and After,* 64–65.

28. Gorbachev observes in his memoirs that they were "organically" linked, not simply combined into a single package of reforms for tactical reasons. Gorbachev, *Memoirs,* 318.

29. Brown, *Gorbachev Factor;* Chiesa, *Transition,* 180.

30. Anatoly Sobchak, *For a New Russia* (New York, Free Press, 1992), chap. 9; Chiesa, *Transition,* 180–82.

31. Chiesa, *Transition,* 185.

32. *Vedomosti S"ezda Narodnykh Deputatov SSSR i Verkhovnogo Soveta SSSR,* no. 12, (March 21, 1990), item 189, pp. 230–32.

33. Gorbachev, *Memoirs,* 320, 323–24.

34. Ed A. Hewett, "The New Soviet Plan," in *The Soviet System in Crisis: A Reader of Western and Soviet Views,* ed. Alexander Dallin and Gail W. Lapidus (Boulder: Westview, 1991), 384.

35. *Vedomosti,* no. 40, (October 3, 1990), item 802, pp. 977–78.

36. *Vedomosti,* no. 1, (January 2, 1991), item 3, pp. 10–11.

37. Stephen White, Graeme Gill, and Darrell Slider, *The Politics of Transition: Shaping a Post-Soviet Future* (Cambridge: Cambridge University Press, 1993), 134–37.

38. Brown, *Gorbachev Factor,* 275.

39. Stephen Foye, "The Case for a Coup: Gorbachev or the Generals?" *RFE/RL Report on the USSR* 3, no. 2 (January 11, 1991).

40. I attended a huge rally on Manezh Square (next to Red Square) on March 10, 1991, where at least half a million people demonstrated against Gorbachev and for Yeltsin.

The most popular slogans called for Gorbachev's resignation and supported for Yeltsin. Organizers from Democratic Russia, the coalition of radical and reform forces, told me the next day that they believed that between eight hundred thousand and one million people had turned out for the rally.

41. *Kommersant,* no. 17, 1991.

42. White, *Gorbachev and After,* 181.

43. Yuri Shchekochikhin, "Mikhail Gorbachev: The Last Days of the Presidency," *Demokratizatsiya* 1, no. 1 (summer 1992): 11.

44. Jailed until December 1992, he was amnestied along with the other conspirators in February 1994 by the newly elected State Duma. He was elected to the Duma both in 1993 and in 1995. In the second Duma, he served as the chairman of the Committee on Legislation and Judicial-Legal Reform, where by all accounts he conducted himself in an exemplary and thoroughly professional way. He was also a senior leader of the communist faction in the Duma.

45. Mikhail Gorbachev, "'Andropov ne poshel by daleko v reformirovanii obshchestva,'" *Nezavisimaia Gazeta,* November 11, 1992.

CHAPTER 3. ORGANIZING THE NEW USSR PARLIAMENT

1. Employing a simple index of left-right voting (explained below), we can compare the three categories of members. We might expect that the mean "liberalism" score of the deputies elected in the TIOs would be higher than for the other categories of deputies because these districts had the most electoral competition. We would expect deputies elected from public organizations to be the most conservative, on average, because the party apparatus had the largest influence in selecting candidates for these seats. Deputies from national-territorial districts included both the very liberal Baltic delegations as well as the very conservative Central Asian delegations, so the mean score should be in between those of the other two categories of mandates. Analysis confirmed this expectation. The mean score for TIO members was 3.17, for members from public organizations, 2.63, and for NTIO members, 2.99. See the appendix to this chapter for detail on construction of this index.

2. A detailed and pioneering analysis of the regional differences in the nature and outcomes of the 1989 election is found in V. A. Kolosov, N. V. Petrov, and L. V. Smirniagin, eds. *Vesna 89: Geografiia i anatomiia parlamentskikh vyborov* (Moscow: Progress Publishers, 1990).

3. *Vedomosti Verkhovnogo Soveta Soiuza Sovetskikh Sotsialisticheskikh Respublik* (hereafter *VVS SSSR*), no. 49, (December 7, 1988), item 813, pp. 816–17.

4. Ibid., pp. 819–20.

5. The pre-Gorbachev Supreme Soviet had also had two chambers, a Council of the Union and a Council of Nationalities, and was also formed with exacting attention to the quotas for representation. The Council of the Union was made up of deputies elected in single-member territorial districts (1 deputy per 300,000 inhabitants). The Council of Nationalities consisted of 750 deputies elected in multimember national-territorial dis-

tricts, with 32 deputies elected from each union republic; 11 from each autonomous republic; 5 from each autonomous oblast; and 1 from each national okrug. M. Saifulin,
The Soviet Parliament (Moscow: Progress Publishers, 1967), 23–24.

6. Theodore H. Friedgut, *Political Participation in the USSR* (Princeton: Princeton University Press, 1979); Jeffrey W. Hahn, *Soviet Grassroots: Citizen Participation in Local Soviet Government* (Princeton: Princeton University Press, 1988).

7. *Narodnyi deputat*, no. 1 (1991): 15.

8. Legislative committees of the Supreme Soviet were: planning and budget (51 members);
industry, transport, and communications (41 members); construction and construction
materials industry (31 members); agriculture (41 members); public health and social security (31 members); public education, science and culture (31 members); trade and public amenities (31 members); legislative proposals (31 members); foreign affairs (31 mem-
bers); and credentials (31 members).

9. See Luk'ianov's comments on Moscow television, as cited in FBIS-SOV-89–106-S, June
5, 1989, p. 53.

10. For the Council of the Union, Luk'ianov proposed commissions on: planning, budget
and finance; industrial development; transportation and communications; labor, prices
and social policy. For the Council on Nationalities, he proposed commissions on: interethnic relations; social and economic development of the union and autonomous republics, autonomous oblasts and okrugs (equivalent, he explained, to the planning and
budget commission of the other chamber); consumer goods, retail trade, everyday mu-
nicipal and other services of the population; development of culture, language, ethnic,
and interethnic traditions and protection of historical monuments. The fourteen committees would be composed by the two chambers on the principle of parity, consisting
of committees on: international affairs; defense and state security; legislation, legality,
and legal order; work of soviets, development of government, and self-government
(Luk'ianov was at pains to note that the formation of this committee was based on the
recommendations of many deputies); economic reform; agrarian issues and food (this
was urged by the Council of Elders); construction and architecture (another idea proposed by deputies); science, public education, culture, and upbringing; public health
protection; affairs of women, protection of the family, motherhood, and childhood; affairs of veterans and invalids; youth affairs; issues of ecology and rational use of natural
resources; issues of glasnost', rights, and appeals of citizens.

11. See pp. 80–81 of FBIS-SOV-89–111-S, June 12, 1989, from Moscow television coverage
on June 10.

12. *Biulleten' Verkhovnogo Soveta SSSR*, no. 32, April 2, 1991.

13. Timothy J. Colton, "Professional Engagement and Role Definition among Post-Soviet
Legislators," in *Parliaments in Transition: The New Legislative Politics in the Former
USSR and Eastern Europe*, ed. Thomas F. Remington (Boulder: Westview, 1994), 62.

14. Ibid., 61.

15. This was rather unusual. Most bills passed once amendments had been voted on in the
course of voting on each section and article of the bill during the second reading stage.
However, a third reading was sometimes required if certain important provisions could

not pass during the second reading. In that case, Luk'ianov generally convened a reconciliation commission comprising key committee chairs and interested deputies, charging them with reaching a compromise.

16. An interesting and historically based explication of the concepts of *zakon* and *ukaz* is provided by G. N. Seleznev (chairman of the State Duma following the December 1995 elections), in his book *Vsia vlast'—zakonu!* (Moscow: Gruppa Segodnia, 1997), 35–64.

17. Peter Vanneman, *The Supreme Soviet: Politics and the Legislative Process in the Soviet Political System* (Durham: Duke University Press, 1977), 182. Vanneman explains that Stalin explicitly rejected granting the Presidium the power to make law. But its power to issue edicts was an indirect form of lawmaking power.

18. See John M. Carey and Matthew Soberg Shugart, eds., *Executive Decree Authority* (Cambridge: Cambridge University Press), 1988.

19. Saifulin, *Soviet Parliament*, 78–79.

20. Article 17 of the "Reglament Verkhovnogo Soveta Soiuza Sovetskikh Sotsialisticheskikh Respublik," *VVS SSSR*, no. 17, April 25, 1979, p. 299.

21. Specifically, the rules assigned the Presidium the following duties: (1) to examine and decide on matters pertaining to amendment of existing legislation; to form and abolish government ministries and state committees; to interpret laws; to award state orders, medals, and titles; to grant amnesty and pardon; to grant and deprive persons of citizenship; (2) to form permanent and ad hoc commissions to consider matters under its purview; (3) to present its decrees to the Supreme Soviet for confirmation; (4) to prepare legislative and other items for Supreme Soviet sessions and plans the order of proceedings for floor deliberation; (5) to draft a proposed agenda for the Supreme Soviet for its approval; (6) to provide deputies with all necessary documentary materials pertaining to the Supreme Soviet sessions; (7) to ensure that Supreme Soviet decisions are published; (8) to coordinate the work of the permanent commissions of the Supreme Soviet; (9) to hear the reports of deputies about their meetings with constituent and assigns deputies tasks concerning the oversight of state bodies and organizations in areas where the Supreme Soviet has an oversight mandate; (10) to oversee the consideration by state and public organizations of comments made by deputies as part of their oversight responsibility; (11) to provide deputies with copies of reference materials and official publications of the Supreme Soviet and inform deputies of measures taken in response to their interpellations and suggestions; and (12) to assist deputies in exchanging information about their work in their constituencies.

Note that the Russian Republic Supreme Soviet's Standing Rules described the duties of the Presidium of its unicameral Supreme Soviet in nearly identical terms; the rules differed from the union-level rules only in providing that within the republic, the Presidium was to supervise lower soviets.

These formal powers gave the Presidium substantial influence over lawmaking. We must bear in mind that the process of drafting laws, particularly in the Brezhnev period, was a slow and ponderous exercise. Numerous affected party and state organizations proposed revisions and criticisms to a draft decision. A few policy decisions in this period took the form of laws after being circulated widely by the Supreme Soviet staff officials to government ministries, party departments, union republic governments, and official public associations. A somewhat idealized portrait of this activity is provided in Anatoly Agranovsky, "Soviet Parliament: A Working Body," *World Marxist Review* 14, no. 5 (May 1971): 77–85.

22. A good illustration of the first point is the published resolution (*postanovlenie*) of the Presidium of the RSFSR Supreme Soviet in July 1978, which enumerated the legislative acts that had to be drafted and passed to bring current legislation into accord with the new constitution of the RSFSR. The order took the form of a *plan* of legislation to be drafted, in two lists. The first enumerated new laws that were required, the second alterations to existing legislation. The new laws included a law on elections to the Supreme Soviet of Russia; a law on local soviet elections; a new set of Standing Rules; a new law on the Council of Ministers; a new law on oblast- and krai-level soviets; a law on referenda; and various laws on housing, forestry, the legal system and other matters. For each item that required legislative action, a deadline for the preparation of the initial draft was specified and a body responsible for preparing the initial draft was assigned. For example, the laws on elections to the Supreme Soviet and to local soviets were to be prepared by the Presidium of the Supeme Soviet with the participation of the Council of Ministers. The law on the Council of Ministers was to be prepared by the Council of Ministers, as were the laws on defense of the animal kingdom and on atmospheric protection. The law on recall of judges was to be drafted by the Ministry of Justice jointly with the Supreme Court, and the deadline set was February 1981. The items listed for revision of existing legislation were assigned to responsible organizations, but specific deadlines were not set. Instead, a general deadline of 1978–80 was named with the notation that bills were to be presented according to their state of readiness.

23. *Vtoroi S'ezd Narodnykh Deputatov SSSR,* Biulleten' no. 13, December 20, 1989.

24. Saifulin, *Soviet Parliament,* 78.

25. Luk'ianov, after all, had had extensive experience running the staff machinery of the Supreme Soviet and presumably knew exactly how centralized staff control of legislative decision making worked. He had been working in the apparat of the Supreme Soviet since 1961, becoming head of the Secretariat in 1977, and then moved over into the party Central Committee apparat in 1983. See Jerry F. Hough, *Democratization and Revolution in the USSR, 1985–1991* (Washington, D.C.: Brookings Institution Press, 1997), 156.

26. Luk'ianov alludes to this triangle in an interview in *Nezavisimaia gazeta,* September 18, 1992.

27. Arkadii Murashev, "Mezhregional'naia deputatskaia gruppa: Khronika minuvshego goda," *Ogonek,* no. 32, (August 1990): 6–9.

28. On the Moscow elections of 1989, see Giulietto Chiesa, with Douglas Taylor Northrop, *Transition to Democracy: Political Change in the Soviet Union, 1987–1991.* (Hanover, N.H.: Dartmouth College Press, published by University Press of New England, 1993).

29. Cited in Murashev, "Mezhregional'naia deputatskaia gruppa," 8.

30. Colton, "Professional Engagement," 63–64.

CHAPTER 4. THE POWER GAME IN RUSSIA

1. Gail Warshofsky Lapidus, "Ethnonationalism and Political Stability: The Soviet Case," *World Politics* 36, no. 4 (1984): 355–80; Teresa Rakowska-Harmstone, "The Dialectics of

Nationalism in the USSR," *Problems of Communism* 23, no. 3 (1974): 1–22; Victor Za-slavsky, "Success and Collapse: Traditional Soviet Nationality Policy," in *Nations and Politics in the Soviet Successor States,* ed. Ian Bremmer and Ray Taras (Cambridge: Cambridge University Press, 1993), 29–42; Grey Hodnett, "The Debate over Soviet Federalism," in *The Soviet Nationality Reader,* ed. Rachel Denber (Boulder: Westview, 1992 [1967]), 121–46; Philip G. Roeder, "Soviet Federalism and Ethnic Mobilization," *World Politics* 23, no. 2 (1991): 196–233.

2. James Critchlow, *Nationalism in Uzbekistan: A Soviet Republic's Road to Sovereignty* (Boulder: Westview, 1991), 14–15; Martha Brill Olcott, "Central Asia: The Reformers Challenge a Traditional Society," in *The Nationalities Factor in Soviet Politics and Society,* ed. Lubomyr Hajda and Mark Beissinger (Boulder: Westview, 1990), 253–80.

3. Valuable accounts may be found in Ronald Grigor Suny, *The Revenge of the Past: Nationalism, Revolution, and the Collapse of the Soviet Union* (Stanford: Stanford University Press, 1993); David D. Laitin, *Identity in Formation: The Russian-Speaking Populations in the Near Abroad* (Ithaca: Cornell University Press, 1998).

4. Richard Pipes, *Russia under the Old Regime* (New York: Scribner's, 1974); Reinhard Bendix, *Work and Authority in Industry* (Berkeley: University of California Press, 1974).

5. Stephen White, Graeme Gill, and Darrell Slider, *The Politics of Transition: Shaping a Post-Soviet Future* (Cambridge: Cambridge University Press, 1993), 85.

6. A typical example of this thinking was an article in *Literaturnaia Rossiia,* in which the author argued that Russia was the primary victim of the capricious rule of the union center. He compared Russia to the eldest sister in a family who has scrimped and saved and sacrificed her life to raise her younger sisters, only to see them turn against her in resentment and ingratitude. Vladimir V'iunitskii, "Rossiia I 'tsentr' . . . ," *Literaturnaia Rossiia,* no. 49 (1990): 10–11. The deputy chairman's figures were presented in *Sovetskaia Rossiia,* April 8, 1990.

7. A recent article by Anatolii Shabad, a prominent member of the Democratic Russia camp, makes a similar argument about the political motives of conservative supporters of the Declaration on Sovereignty. See Anatolii Shabad, "Kak rozhdalas' nezavisimost'," *Segodnia,* June 11, 1999.

8. Brendan Kiernan, *The End of Soviet Politics* (Boulder: Westview, 1993), 60. The figure refers to races in territorial and national-territorial electoral districts.

9. Sobyanin, A., and D. Yur'ev, *S"ezd Narodnykh Deputatov RSFSR v zerkale poimennykh golosovanii: rasstanovka sil i dinamika razvitiia politicheskogo protivostoianiia* (Moscow: Informatsionno-Analiticheskaia Gruppa, 1991).

10. Jerry F. Hough, *Democratization and Revolution in the USSR, 1985–1991* (Washington, D.C.: Brookings Institution, 1997), 307; Joan Barth Urban and Valerii D. Solovei, *Russia's Communists at the Crossroads* (Boulder: Westview, 1997), 38–39.

11. The near unanimity in voting for the sovereignty declaration should not be taken to indicate an absence of controversy over it. As Jerry Hough shows, an extended and difficult discussion took place over the language of the declaration. The margin of support for the final wording of the most important article of the declaration was very close: only 540 votes were cast in favor, with 302 voting against and 217 not voting, or only 10 votes to spare. Taking the distribution of votes on this question and two others that were

direct tests of opposition to Communist Party rule, Hough cross-tabulated support for the radical position on Russian sovereignty with support for banning the Communist Party's cells in the military. He found that the radical democrats voted cohesively both for Russian sovereignty and for the ban on party organs in the military. But the conservatives were divided. Almost 200 deputies opposed the ban on the CPSU's branches but favored Russian sovereignty: these are the "bureaucratic nationalists" whose support, I surmised, was critical for Yeltsin's election as chairman. For example, the republic's head of government called at the congress for "full-fledged economic and political sovereignty" for Russia, and Vitalii Vorotnikov, at the time a member of the CPSU Politburo, demanded sovereignty for Russia and criticized the central leadership for having restricted Russia's demands in the past. There were also more than 100 deputies who supported the ban on party activity but opposed the radical position on sovereignty. Thus the voting alignments show that these two axes of conflict, pro- versus anti-CPSU power and prounionist versus pro-Russian sovereignty, are cross-cutting. Some radical democrats were prounionist, and a larger number favored Russian sovereignty. Conservatives were more evenly divided over the issue of Russian sovereignty, so that a skillful leader with agenda control could win over a majority of deputies by appealing to all the democrats and some conservatives on an issue pitting Russian Republic prerogatives against the power of the central union government. See Hough, *Democratization and Revolution,* 386, 389, 390–91. Also see Radio Liberty Daily Reports for May 21, May 23, and June 13, 1990.

12. This is the general argument of Hough's *Democratization and Revolution,* which portrays Gorbachev as a more principled but politically less skillful politician than Yeltsin.

13. Sobyanin and Yur'ev, *S"ezd Narodnykh Deputatov,* 9; Thomas F. Remington, Steven S. Smith, D. Roderick Kiewiet, and Moshe Haspel, "Transitional Institutions and Parliamentary Alignments in Russia," in *Parliaments in Transition: The New Legislative Politics in the Former USSR and Eastern Europe,* ed. Thomas F. Remington (Boulder: Westview, 1994), 166.

14. Hough, *Democratization and Revolution,* 339, 407.

15. The question put to the voters was: "Do you consider it necessary to preserve the Union of Soviet Socialist Republics as a renewed federation of equal sovereign republics in which the rights and freedoms of all nationalities will be fully guaranteed?" The vague wording suggests that the issue was intended to give Gorbachev a broad popular endorsement both to hold the union together and to seek its restructuring in any way he saw fit. The question on the Russian presidency was straightforward: "Do you consider it necessary to introduce the post of RSFSR president, who would be elected by a republicwide popular vote?"

16. Stephen White, Richard Rose, and Ian McAllister, *How Russia Votes* (Chatham, N.J.: Chatham House, 1996), 75–77.

17. Sobyanin and Yur'ev, *S"ezd Narodnykh Deputatov,* 18.

18. Hough, *Democratization and Revolution,* 410–15.

19. *Vedomosti S"ezda Narodnykh Deputatov i Verkhovnogo Soveta RSFSR* (hereafter *Vedomosti SND & VS RSFSR*), no. 15 (April 11, 1991), item 495, pp. 405–6; Urban and Solovei, *Russia's Communists,* 41–42; Hough, *Democratization and Revolution,* 408.

20. See, for instance, the interview Yeltsin gave to Russian Radio on April 13, 1991, one week after the Third Congress had ended: British Broadcast Company, *Summary of World Broadcasts*, pt. 1, the USSR; B. Internal Affairs; SU/1047/B/ 1, April 16, 1991.

21. The text of the law as published in *Sovetskaia Rossiia* is in FBIS-SOV-91–084, May 1, 1991, pp. 57–58.

22. For example, Jerry Hough has suggested that as part of the negotiations over the new union treaty which was to redefine the terms of the union between Soviet republics and the USSR central government, Gorbachev agreed to support Yeltsin's demand to create a presidency and suspended his strategy of weakening Yeltsin through encouragement for the separatist aspirations of ethnic republics within Russia in return for Yeltsin's backing of the new treaty of union and Yeltsin's agreement to relinquish the Russian Republic's claim to the right to nullify union legislation on Russian territory. Hough, *Democratization and Revolution,* 416–17.

23. White, Rose, and McAllister, *How Russia Votes,* 38–39.

24. On the coup and its consequences, see John B. Dunlop, *The Rise of Russia and the Fall of the Soviet Empire* (Princeton: Princeton University Press, 1993), chap. 5.

25. Thomas F. Remington, "Menage a Trois: The End of Soviet Parliamentarism," in *Democratization in Russia: The Development of Legislative Institutions,* ed. Jeffrey W. Hahn (Armonk, N.Y.: M. E. Sharpe, 1996), 106–39.

26. Alexander Sobyanin, "Political Cleavages among the Russian Deputies," in *Parliaments in Transition,* ed. Remington, 185.

27. Factor analysis reveals that the alignment pitting radical democrats versus communists explained far less of the variance in voting patterns than a dimension pitting Democratic Russia, Agrarians, Industrial Union, and Union of Workers against Radical Democrats, Rossiia (a hard-line nationalist faction), and some communists. Strange bedfellows indeed!

28. *Vedomosti SND & VS RSFSR,* no. 44 (October 31, 1991), item 1455, p. 1722.

29. Ibid., item 1456, p. 1723; Scott Parrish, "Presidential Decree Authority in Russia," in *Executive Decree Authority,* ed. John M. Carey and Matthew Soberg Shugart (Cambridge: Cambridge University Press, 1998), 71–72.

30. Parrish, "Presidential Decree Authority in Russia," 68–69.

31. Sobyanin, "Political Cleavages," 188; Urban and Solovei, *Russia's Communists,* 47.

32. Parrish, "Presidential Decree Authority in Russia," 72.

33. Matthew Soberg Shugart and John M. Carey, *Presidents and Assemblies: Constitutional Design and Electoral Dynamics* (Cambridge: Cambridge University Press, 1992); Carey and Shugart, eds., *Executive Decree Authority.*

34. Khasbulatov remained outside any faction. His deputy chairs spanned the spectrum of left, right, and center. Sergei Alexandrovich Filatov, who was elected first deputy chairman, was affiliated with the Democratic Russia faction. Filatov had been proposed for chairman of the Supreme Soviet but had demurred, supporting Khasbulatov instead. His elevation to the position of first deputy chairman must have been a gesture of accommodation by Khasbulatov to the democratic wing. At the same time, balancing Filatov politically was Yuri Voronin, a leading member of the Communists of Russia, who became an ordinary deputy chairman. Rounding out the slate as deputy chairs were

Vladimir Shumeiko and Yuri Yarov, who were centrists, Shumeiko having been affiliated with the Industrial Union faction and Yarov for a time with the Left Center. The group bears all the earmarks of a carefully constructed collective agreement in which each major political tendency was represented among the governing officials, and factions gained formal access to the machinery of parliament.

35. On the Sixth Congress, see A. A. Sobyanin, ed., *Shestoi S"ezd Narodnykh Deputatov Rossii: Politicheskie itogi i perspektivy. Analiticheskii otchet* (Moscow: Ekspertnaia infor-matsionno-analiticheskaia gruppa pri Organizatsionnom otdele Prezidiuma Verkhov-nogo Soveta Rossiiskoi Federatsii, 1992); Remington et al., "Transitional Institutions," and the Daily Reports put out by Radio Free Europe/Radio Liberty.

36. White, Rose, McAllister, *How Russia Votes,* 82.

37. Dunlop, *Rise of Russia,* 299; editorial, *Economist* 49 (October 9, 1993): 56.

38. Urban and Solovei, *Russia's Communists,* 83.

CHAPTER 5. DEPUTIES AND LAWMAKING IN THE RSFSR SUPREME SOVIET

1. *Vedomosti Verkhovnogo Soveta RSFSR* (hereafter *VVS RSFSR*), no. 44 (November 2, 1989), item 1303, pp. 865–66.

2. There was a difference in the preelection procedures between the 1989 USSR deputy elections and the 1990 RSFSR elections. In the latter, the election rules did not call for district election meetings, which had been a device used in 1989 to reduce the number of candidates eligible to run by requiring that those candidates nominated through resi-dential districts needed to have the support of a majority of participants at an open meeting of the district. These meetings lent themselves to manipulation and abuses by the authorities, so they were dropped in the RSFSR election system. As a result, al-though the process was more open, there were relatively more registered candidates run-ning for each seat, and correspondingly fewer races decided in the first round when a candidate required an absolute majority of the votes cast to win. After the second round, when a plurality sufficed to win but there had to be at least two candidates running, forty seats still remained open. Even by the end of the second week of the First Con-gress, twenty-eight seats were vacant.

3. The other eighty-four NTIO districts were distributed throughout the nonethnic ad-ministrative-territorial units of the Russian Republic, consisting of forty-nine oblasts, six kraia, and two large cities of equivalent status. These districts were apportioned in rough proportion to population, such that that each unit had at least one such NTIO and that no NTIO crossed their boundaries. As indicated in table 5.1, the number of na-tional-territorial districts assigned to administrative units varied according to the hierar-chical status of the unit. Autonomous republics were considered the highest-level terri-tories and were generally the most populous. Therefore they received a larger number of electoral districts. (Today all the autonomous republics and all but one of the au-tonomous oblasts are designated simply "republics" of the Russian Federation, and one of the former autonomous republics has split into two republics.) The reason for this system was to give more representation to smaller ethnic national groups, at least those with their own territorial homelands.

4. Note that this built a considerable imbalance into the structure of the parliament: the pool of deputies eligible to sit in the Council of Nationalities barely exceeded the number of seats—168 NTIO deputies for 126 seats—while the 900 deputies elected in ordinary territorial districts would have to compete for the 126 Council of the Republic seats. The authors of this elaborate system feared the consequences of underrepresenting Russia's ethnic minority territories, so they built a considerable overrepresentation into the structure. The inequity between the two streams of deputies into the Supreme Soviet, and more generally the view that the two-tiered system was a device used by the party-state leadership to dilute and weaken democratic representation, led democratically oriented deputies to propose a motion at the First Congress to amend the constitution by dropping the two-tier system and turning the entire congress into the Supreme Soviet. The motion gained a large majority (603 votes in favor, 317 opposed, and 46 abstaining), but it did not carry the two-thirds needed to amend the constitution.

5. The Russian Constitutional amendments can be found in *VVS RSFSR,* no. 44 (November 2, 1989), item 1303, p. 872.

6. *Vedomosti S"ezda Narodnykh Deputatov RSFSR i Verkhovnogo Soveta RSFSR* (hereafter *Vedomosti SND & VS RSFSR*), no. 45 (November 7, 1991), p. 1769.

7. *Reglament Verkhovnogo Soveta RSFSR* (Moscow: Verkhovnyi Sovet RSFSR, 1991) (hereafter *Reglament*), Article 17, par. 2, p. 13.

8. *Biulleten' Verkhovnogo Soveta RSFSR,* Zasedaniie Soveta Natsional'nostei, no. 6 (October 23, 1991). The *Biulleten'* is the stenographic report of the proceedings of the congresses of people's deputies, the Supreme Soviet, and its separate chambers, the Council of Nationalities and the Council of the Republic. Hereafter cited as *Biulleten'* and the abbreviation of the appropriate body—the CPD, SS, CN, or CR—along with the issue number and date.

9. S. Filatov, "Trudnye problemy parlamenta Rossii," *Narodnyi deputat,* no. 17 (1991): 10.

10. *Vedomosti SND & VS RSFSR,* no. 46, (November 14, 1991), pp. 1829–31.

11. *Vedomosti SND & VS RSFSR,* no. 26 (June 27, 1991), pp. 1013–24.
    As of June 1991, a full-time deputy received a salary of 800 rubles per month, a subcommittee chairman 1,000 rubles; a deputy committee chairman, 1,200 rubles; a committee chairman or deputy chairman of chamber, 1,600 rubles; and a chairman of chamber, 1,900 rubles.

12. Timothy J. Colton, "Professional Engagement and Role Definition among Post-Soviet Legislators," in *Parliaments in Transition: The New Legislative Politics in the Former USSR and Eastern Europe,* ed. Thomas F. Remington (Boulder: Westview, 1994), 62–63.

13. Filatov, "Trudnye problemy," 9.

14. Thomas F. Remington, "Ménage à Trois: The End of Soviet Parliamentarism," in *Democratization in Russia: The Development of Legislative Institutions,* ed. Jeffrey W. Hahn (Armonk, N.Y.: M. E. Sharpe, 1996), 119, based on my tabulations of data provided by the Supreme Soviet data center and reports of the Sobyanin Information-Analytic Group.

15. *Nezavisimaia gazeta,* July 14, 1993, and July 24, 1993.

16. The absolute majority rule applied not only to laws, but also to amendments and legislative resolutions. Only a narrow class of procedural questions was exempted from the

majority threshold rule; they could pass by a simple majority of those present and voting. *Reglament,* Article 114, p. 73; *Vedomosti SND & VS RSFSR,* no. 44 (November 2, 1989), p. 869; *Reglament,* chap. 8, pp. 48–56.

17. *Biulleten'* CN, no. 10 (December 4, 1991), p. 53.

18. Note that in Russian, each sitting or session of the Supreme Soviet, usually lasting several months at a time, was called a *sessiia* A *sessiia* was that bloc of the Supreme Soviet's continuous meetings that occurs between two Congresses of People's Deputies. "Convocation" (*sozyv*) was the bloc of sessions occurring between elections of a new body of deputies. The term *zasedanie* was used for a day's proceedings as well as for the meetings of committees and chambers.

In the post-1993 Federal Assembly, a *sessiia* refers to the bloc of continuous work between winter and summer recesses; thus there are usually two "sessions" per year, spring and fall. A convocation (*sozyv*) is the body of deputies elected to hold mandates following elections to the Duma. A *zasedanie* refers to the sitting or proceedings of the parliament on a given day, and can be used for the meetings of committees.

19. Article 110 of the constitution stipulated that: "The right of legislative initiative at the Congress of People's Deputies of the RSFSR and in the Supreme Soviet of the RSFSR belongs to people's deputies of the RSFSR, the Soviet of the Republic, the Soviet of Nationalities, the Presidium of the Supreme Soviet of the RSFSR, the chairman of the Supreme Soviet of the RSFSR, the Committee of Constitutional Supervision of the RSFSR, the Council of Ministers of the RSFSR, autonomous republics in the person of their supreme organs of state power, to krais, oblasts, autonomous oblasts, and autonomous okrugs in the person of their Soviet of People's Deputies, to standing commissions of the chambers and the committees of the Supreme Soviet of the RSFSR, to the Committee of People's Control of the RSFSR, to the Supreme Court of the RSFSR, the Procurator of the RSFSR, the Chief State Arbitrator of the RSFSR.

"The right of legislative initiative is also possessed by public organizations in the person of their republican organs, and in the case of their absence, by unionwide organs."

Note that some public organizations lacking a Russian-level, republican organ (such as regional associations) considered this provision unfair in that it denied them the right of legislative initiative simply because they lack a republic-level governing body. Nevertheless, as deputies pointed out in interviews, it is not clear that mere possession of this right was decisive because regardless of whether an organization could introduce a bill directly or not, it still needed a substantial base of support in parliament in order to secure its passage. An organization seeking to propose a law was allowed under the rules and encouraged by good sense to find deputies to sponsor it. As a result, the right of legislative initiative, in a formal sense, was rarely controversial, although the initiator of a bill probably had some advantage over his rivals in shaping the basic conception of the bill. *Vedomosti SND & VS RSFSR,* no. 44 (November 2, 1989), p. 869.

20. Recall that each chamber had four standing commissions, and that there were another twenty standing committees under the joint jurisdiction of the Supreme Soviet as a whole. I call both bodies "committees."

21. *Reglament,* Article 64, pp. 42–43.

22. Filatov, "Trudnye problemy," 11.

23. It happened sometimes that different bills with opposing policy objectives were developed on the same subject by the government and the Supreme Soviet, although this was rare. In such a case the committee sometimes held hearings to try to air the differences and determine where a compromise could be found. In the end, of course, it was the vote on the floor that decided which draft bill was to be taken as a basis for further consideration; amendments to that draft were then discussed in committees and, ultimately, on the floor at the time of the second reading.

24. In at least one case that I was told about, a particular committee with relevant jurisdiction was excluded from the deliberations on a particular bill, although whether through sloppy organization or malicious intent it is hard to know. When the bill was presented to the floor for consideration, the committee objected, and the bill was sent back to committee. The case was treated as a rare and exceptional instance illustrating the misuse of agenda-setting power by the Presidium.

25. *Rossiiskaia gazeta,* November 14, 1992, and July 24, 1993.

26. The deputy chairmen of the Supreme Soviet divided up administrative responsibilities among themselves, at least until Khasbulatov changed the arrangement in August 1992. The first deputy chairman oversaw the apparat and the budget and managed the processing of legislative business. Another deputy chairman was responsible for maintaining liaison with the non-full-time deputies, and another managed liaison with the government. In addition, each deputy chairman supervised a particular set of committees. *Biulleten'* CN, no. 6 (October 23, 1991); interview with a senior staff supervisor, Moscow, June 1992.

27. *Biulleten'* CN, no. 6 (October 23, 1991), pp. 19–20.

28. from *Biulleten'* CR, no. 3 (October 2, 1991), pp. 28ff.

29. *Kommersant,* no. 13 (March 23–30, 1992).

30. Interview with a committee chairman, June 1992.

31. *Rossiiskaia gazeta,* November 14, 1992.

32. Thomas F. Remington, Steven S. Smith, D. Roderick Kiewiet, and Moshe Haspel, "Transitional Institutions and Parliamentary Alignments," in *Parliaments in Transition: The New Legislative Politics in the Former USSR and Eastern Europe,* ed. Thomas F. Remington (Boulder: Westview, 1994), 159–80.

33. Remington et al., "Transitional Institutions," 163–70; A. Sobyanin and D. Yur'ev, *S"ezd narodnykh deputatov RSFSR v zerkale poimennykh golosovanii: rasstanovka sil i dinamika razvitiia politicheskogo protivostoiiania* (Moscow: Informatsionno-Analiticheskaia Gruppa, 1991); Jerry F. Hough, *Democratization and Revolution in the USSR, 1985–1991* (Washington, D.C.: Brookings Institution, 1997), 298–304.

34. Sobyanin and Yur'ev, *S"ezd narodnykh deputatov RSFSR,* 7.

35. For simplicity's sake, I will refer to the standing commissions of the separate chambers of the Supreme Soviet as well as to the standing joint committees of the Supreme Soviet as "committees."

36. Brendan Kiernan, *The End of Soviet Politics* (Boulder: Westview, 1993), 200–201.

37. V. Novikov (interview), "Fraktsii na s"ezde i v parlamente: ili Kakov rasklad politicheskikh sil," *Narodnyi deputat,* no. 18 (1992): 20.

38. All four candidates for the first deputy chairman post were from the Communists of

Russia group, whereas three candidates from Democratic Russia were nominated for one of the second secretary positions; the commission behaved as if it had decided to ensure that there was an alternation of factional affiliations in the leadership posts of the parliament such that if the chairman was to be a democrat, the next-ranking official should be a communist, and so on.

39. Kiernan, *End of Soviet Politics,* 200.

40. Sobyanin and Yur'ev, *S"ezd,* 7; Remington, "Ménage à Trois," 123.

41. Figures from V. Pribylovskii, *Politicheskie fraktsii i deputatskie gruppy rossiiskogo parlamenta* (Moscow: Panorama, 1992), 3.

42. *Narodnyi deputat,* no. 1 (1991): 15.

43. Novikov, "Fraktsii," 20–21.

44. "Parlamentskie fraktsii i bloki," supplement to weekly publication, *Parlamentskaia nedelia* ("Parliamentary Week"), published by the Press-Center of the Supreme Soviet, March 26, 1993 (Moscow: Izvestiia, 1993), p. 28. Note that the group Radical Democrats was omitted from this list, although it had probably formed by this time as well.

45. *Vedomosti SND & VS RSFSR,* no. 44 (October 31, 1991), Postanovlenie Verkhovnogo soveta RSFSR, "O vnesenii izmenenii vo Vremennyi reglament S"ezda narodnykh deputatov RSFSR," p. 1710.

46. If the former, then each faction would send a single representative, regardless of the number of members. If proportional, then each faction was to delegate an equal number of representatives for every fifty members.

47. *Vedomosti SND & VS RSFSR,* no. 44 (October 31, 1991), pp. 1710–12.

48. Blocs were to be made up of at least three factions and factions could not join more than one bloc. To register, a group, faction, or bloc was required to lay out its tasks, size, members, leaders, with signatures of each member. At least two coordinators of factions had to sign the list of factions forming a bloc. Groups, factions, and blocs were not to share the same name. They had to reregister each year.

49. At that point there was no formal mechanism to force the government to resign by voting no confidence in it. A no-confidence vote would have had serious political ramifications, however. At the Sixth Congress, Gaidar and the entire government had scored a political victory by submitting their resignations in the face of harsh criticism from the deputies. The resignation put pressure on the congress to find some acceptable compromise that would allow the government to withdraw its resignation and continue to function. Constitutionally, the government was supposed to be subordinate to the congress, but this provision had been temporarily superseded by the emergency decree powers the Fifth Congress had given Yeltsin, which included the right to form the government on his own authority. Yeltsin took advantage of this constitutional privilege to make Gaidar acting prime minister without submitting the nomination to the Supreme Soviet for confirmation. Therefore a vote of no confidence would have had political impact but would not have forced Yeltsin to dissolve the government.

50. Novikov, "Fraktsii," 19.

51. *Smena,* in Russian, refers to a a turnover or shift change, as at a factory; in this case the reference was to a change of generations.

52. Faction membership figures are taken from "Parlamentskie fraktsii i bloki," March 26, 1993.

Ideological position scores are computed as follows. The scores reported are the mean values and standard deviations on the first factor extracted by a principal components analysis from the electronically recorded roll-call votes for all contested votes (defined here as votes where no more than 75 percent of the deputies voted the same way) across the Seventh, Eighth, and Ninth Congresses, for factions as of the Eighth Congress. These congresses took place in an extremely polarized political atmosphere, where Yeltsin's opposition rallied to block his plans to institute a new constitution giving him wide powers to implement radical reform. Thus the environment contributed to high political polarization between Yeltsin's supporters and his opponents and thus clarify the interpretation of this factor. At the Eighth Congress, this first dimension accounts for about 35 percent of the variance in voting alignments. Negative scores indicate positions that are strongly opposed to Yeltsin and his policies, while positive scores reflect pro-Yeltsin, proreform positions. The difference of group means for ideology is strong and significant at the .00001 level.

53. Colton, "Professional Engagement," 64.

54. Ibid., 64.

55. Boris Yel'tsin, *Zapiski prezidenta* (Moscow: Ogonek, 1994), 303.

CHAPTER 6. FRAMING A NEW CONSTITUTION

1. Articles dealing with these dimensions of constitutional conflict include: Michael Urban, "December 1993 as a Replication of Late-Soviet Electoral Practices," *Post-Soviet Affairs* 10, no. 2 (April/June 1994): 127–58; Joel Hellman, "Winners Take All: The Politics of Partial Reform in Postcommunist Transitions," *World Politics* 50, no. 2 (1998): 203–34; Philip G. Roeder, "Varieties of Post-Soviet Authoritarian Regimes," *Post-Soviet Affairs* 10 (1994): 61–101; Scott D. Parrish, "Presidential Decree Power in the Second Russian Republic, 1993–96 and Beyond" in *Executive Decree Authority*, ed. John M. Carey and Matthew Soberg Shugart (Cambridge: Cambridge University Press, 1998); Timothy Frye, "A Politics of Institutional Choice: Post-Communist Presidencies," *Comparative Political Studies* 30, no. 5 (1997): 523–52; Gerald M. Easter, "Preference for Presidentialism: Postcommunist Regime Change in Russia and the NIS," *World Politics* 49, no. 2 (1997): 184–211; Steven L. Solnick, "The Political Economy of Russian Federalism: A Framework for Analysis," *Problems of Post-Communism* 43, no. 6 (1996): 13–25; Steven L. Solnick, "Federal Bargaining in Russia," *East European Constitutional Review* 4, no. 4 (1995): 52–58.

2. Cf. Robert Sharlet, "The Prospects for Federalism in Russian Constitutional Politics," *Publius* 24, no. 2 (spring 1994): 122.

3. Of course, in the policy space of Gorbachev's USSR, Yeltsin defended Russia's sovereignty *against* the central government, a good instance of the contingency of policy positions on the institutional setting.

4. We will suppose that each actor cares equally about both policy dimensions, so that the same units of distance for the two dimensions refer to equal degrees of preference. This assumption yields perfectly circular indifference curves, rather than ellipses, making the

alignments of actors easier to visualize. See Melvin J. Hinich and Michael C. Munger, *Analytical Politics* (Cambridge: Cambridge University Press, 1997).

5. Josephine Andrews, *When Majorities Fail: The Implications of Disequilibrium in Transitional Legislatures* (Cambridge: Cambridge University Press, 2000).

6. In several works, Kenneth Shepsle addresses the question of when and how institutional arrangements are subject to instability in the light of distributional conflicts over their consequences for actors' preferred outcomes. Cf. Kenneth A. Shepsle, "Studying Institutions: Some Lessons from the Rational Choice Approach," *Journal of Theoretical Politics* 1, no. 2 (1989): 131–47.

7. George Tsebelis and Jeannette Money, *Bicameralism* (Cambridge: Cambridge University Press, 1997). Other models also illustrate the use of an institutional mechanism to partition cross-cutting dimensions of policy in order to devise a stable equilibrium solution to the problem of forming a government in multiparty parliamentary systems. See, e.g., Michael Laver and Kenneth A. Shepsle, *Making and Breaking Governments: Cabinets and Legislatures in Parliamentary Democracies.* (Cambridge: Cambridge University Press, 1996); Kenneth A. Shepsle and Barry R. Weingast, "The Institutional Foundations of Committee Power," *American Political Science Review* 81 (1987): 85–104; Barry R. Weingast and William J. Marshall, "The Industrial Organization of Congress; or, Why Legislatures, Like Firms, Are Not Organized as Markets." *Journal of Political Economy* 96, no. 1 (1988): 132–63; Gary W. Cox and Mathew D. McCubbins, *Legislative Leviathan: Party Government in the House* (Berkeley: University of California Press, 1993).

8. A fundamental theorem of spatial theory is that in institutional settings where decision makers' preferences are distributed along one, common dimension of policy, and where each member most prefers one particular alternative and can rank other alternatives transitively, there will be one alternative that can command a majority of support. That alternative is the one closest to the preference of the median member. Melvin J. Hinich and Michael C. Munger, *Analytical Politics* (Cambridge: Cambridge University Press, 1997); William H. Riker, *Liberalism against Populism: A Confrontation between the Theory of Democracy and the Theory of Social Choice* (San Francisco: W. H. Freeman, 1982).

9. It did not harm the chances of his constitution being approved that he put intense pressure on the governors to ensure high turnout in the voting. Yeltsin was far more concerned about whether the turnout threshold would be met than about whether the constitution would be approved or not: he was confident that a majority of voters would approve it because there was effectively no alternative; but it was not at all clear that 50 percent of the voters would bother to take part. As it was, there is considerable reason to doubt whether the 50-percent threshold was in fact met. See note 16, below.

10. This assertion and others of a similar nature about the breadth and level of support for or opposition to constitutional forms are deliberately couched in very general terms and do not pretend to much precision or confidence. They are judgments based on a variety of sources, including press discussions, texts of the draft constitutions circulated by many parties and groups, and interviews with a great many participants and observers.

11. Vera Tolz, "Drafting the New Russian Constitution," Radio Free Europe/Radio Liberty (RFE/RL) Research Reports, July 16, 1993.

12. Edward W. Walker, "The New Russian Constitution and the Future of the Russian Federation," *Harriman Institute Forum* 5, no. 10 (June 1992): 2.

13. The draft was published in a special issue *Argumenty i Fakty*, no. 47 (November 1990). Its ideological orientation was democratic, noncommunist, and non-Soviet. It eliminated references to the USSR and to communism although it did allow for a possibility that Russia might voluntarily join into a "Union (or Commonwealth) of Sovereign States." It called for two chambers, a popular chamber and a "Federal Council," and a president and prime minister.

14. An exchange at a meeting in Washington, D.C., that I attended in January 1993 illustrates this thinking. A small delegation of Russian parliamentary deputies visited the United States to learn more about the American political system. While in Washington, they participated in a day of briefings given by staff experts of the Congressional Research Service about Congress and the separation of powers system in the United States. One of the issues discussed was how the Congress of the United States exercises legislative oversight over the executive branch. At one point, one of the Russian parliamentarians, a radical democrat, declared that for him and his allies, the task was not to increase the Russian parliament's power vis-à-vis the president, but to reduce it as much as possible. Their interlocutor from the CRS, a distinguished specialist on interbranch relations in the United States, replied that he would predict that in a few years, the same deputy would be coming back to Washington to learn how to reclaim the power that the parliament had given up to the president.

15. Darrell Slider, "Federalism, Discord and Accommodation: Intergovernmental Relations in Post-Soviet Russia," *Local Power and Post-Soviet Politics*, ed. Theodore H. Friedgut and Jeffrey W. Hahn (Armonk, N.Y.: M. E. Sharpe, 1994), 247–48.

16. The Tatar and Chechen leaders refused to sign the treaty, and three other republics did so only after concluding special agreements with the Yeltsin government granting them additional special rights.

17. "Draft Constitution of the Russian Federation," *Argumenty i Fakty*, no. 12 (March 1992), pp. 1–8; from FBIS-SOV-92–063-S, April 1, 1992.

18. Tolz, "Drafting."

19. In a television interview soon after the draft was published, Alekseev denied that his committee had written the constitution specifically to serve Yeltsin ("pod El'tsina"). Asked whether he was at all worried that someone with dangerously antidemocratic tendencies might become president in the future and abuse the powers they had conferred on the president, he declared straight-facedly that they were not at all concerned about this.

20. Konstitutsiia (Osnovnoi zakon) Rossiiskoi Federatsii: Proekt (Moscow: n.p., 1993), Article 74.

21. Tolz, "Drafting."

22. Konstitutsiia (Osnovnoi zakon) Rossiiskoi Federatsii: Proekt.

23. Tolz, "Drafting."

24. Ibid.

25. Konstitutsiia Rossiiskoi Federatsii: Proekt. typescript. (Moscow: Kreml', July 12, 1993).

26. Technically, his edict, "On the gradual constitutional reform in the Russian Federa-

tion," ("O poetapnoi konstitutsionnoi reforme v Rossiiskoi Federatsii") ended the existence of the parliament and put into effect a regulation (a *polozhenie*) entitled "Polozhenie on federal organs of power for the transition period," which replaced those sections of the old constitution dealing with the president and parliament with the new provisions. The edict put into effect another regulation on the election system to be used in December. The new regulations were to have legal force until a nationwide popular vote had confirmed the full text of the new constitution and until a new election law was adopted. His decree also instructed the constitutional assembly and the constitutional commission to convene and to produce a joint draft of a new constitution by December 12. It did not indicate how the constitution was to be adopted.

An English translation of the text of President Yeltsin's decree on constitutional reform will be found in British Broadcasting Company, Summary of World Broadcasts, SU/1801 C/1, September 23, 1993.

27. Wendy Slater, "Russia's Plebiscite on a New Constitution," RFE/RL Research Report, January 21, 1994, 1.

28. Slater, "Russia's Plebiscite," 2.

29. S. A. Avak'ian, "Vybory 1993–94 v Rossiiskoi Federatsii: Pravila i Protsedury," (Moscow: International Charitable Foundation for Political-Legal Studies "Interlegal," 1993), 4.

30. Below I will describe the powers of each chamber more fully.

31. The impeachment procedure was a check on presidential autonomy, although a crude and ineffective instrument. Removal of a president through impeachment must clear six hurdles. First, at least one-third of the members of the Duma must agree to initiate the procedure. Second, by a two-thirds vote the Duma must agree to form a commission to investigate the charges. Third, upon the report of the commission that the president has indeed committed "state treason or other grave crimes," which are the only grounds given by the constitution for removing a president from office, the Duma must approve an accusation against him by a two-thirds vote. Then the Supreme Court must concur that the actions of the president constitute a crime. Fifth, the Constitutional Court must find that the constitutionally prescribed rules of procedure have been observed. Finally, the Council of the Federation must approve the decision to remove the president by a two-thirds vote, and it must do so within three months of the Duma's formal accusation. Moreover, under the constitution, if the Duma does vote formally to accuse the president of treason or high crimes, the president cannot dissolve the Duma in the event it votes against confidence in the government. The procedure therefore gives the members added protection against the threat of premature elections.

32. *Sobranie zakonodatel'stva Rossiiskoi Federatsii,* no. 19, May 6, 1996.

33. See Thomas F. Remington, Steven S. Smith, and Moshe Haspel, "Decrees, Laws and Inter-Branch Relations in the Russian Federation," *Post-Soviet Affairs* 14, no. 4 (October-December 1998): 287–322.

34. Vladimir Ryzhkov, "Mify i skazki sovremennoi politiki," *Nezavisimaia gazeta,* May 30, 1997.

35. Yeltsin avoided calling the vote a referendum, no doubt because a 1990 law on referenda had set a very high threshold for passage of an issue (50 percent plus one of *all eligible*

voters had to approve the item) and Yeltsin calculated, reasonably enough, that he was unlikely to be able to win under those rules. Instead, his decree provided that the vote would be valid if half the eligible voters in the country participated, and of them, 50 percent plus one voted to approve the draft constitution. Thus, in principle, the constitution could be put into force by 25 percent plus one of the eligible electorate.

36. No one has ever satisfactorily explained how it happened that the number of registered eligible voters reported by the CEC fell from 107.31 million in April 1993, the time of the April referendum, to 105.28 in December. Nor did the CEC ever explain the wide discrepancies in turnout across districts. The CEC never could explain the discrepancies between the absolute numbers of votes and the percentages it reported for pro and con votes. And it destroyed all the ballots to prevent a recount. Alexander Sobyanin and his associates, in particular, using both mathematical estimation procedures and the analysis of discrepancies and abuses in particular districts, concluded that the referendum had been conducted with massive fraud; that actual turnout had been on the order of 46 percent; and that the percentage of voters supporting the new constitution was actually considerably higher than that reported. If Sobyanin was correct, the vote was not legally valid. See Slater, "Russia's Plebiscite," 4–6; Vera Tolz and Julia Wishnevsky, "Election Queries Make Russians Doubt Democratic Process," RFE/RL Research Report, April 1, 1994, pp. 1–6.

37. Slider, "Federalism, Discord and Accommodation," 261–62.

38. RFE/RL Daily Reports of September 27 and October 1, 1993.

39. "Izbiratel'nyi zakon: Materialy k obsuzhdeniiu" (Moscow: n.p., June 1993). This pamphlet was prepared by the Sheinis group and contains a text of the draft they proposed in June 1993 to the constitutional assembly, together with several articles explaining their thinking.

40. Sources include a memorandum written by Alexander Sobyanin, Eduard Gel'man, and Oleg Kaiunov, "O vozmozhnoi rasstanovke sil v Federal'nom Sobrianii, pri ispol'zovanii mazhoritarnoi, proportsional'noi i razlichnykh variantov smeshannoi sistemy vyborov," a typescript dated June 22, 1993; the article by Alexander Sobyanin and Viktor Sukhovol'skii, "Itogi vyborov 12 dekabria 1993 goda i budushchii federal'nyi zakon o vyborakh," in *Konstitutsionnoe pravo: vostochnoevropeiskoe obozrenie* (fall 1993/winter 1994): 2–10; and interviews with many of the principals in 1993 and subsequent years.

41. B. A. Strashun and V. L. Sheinis, "Politicheskaia situatsiia v Rossii i novyi izbiratel'nyi zakon," in "Izbiratel'nyi zakon," 55.

42. Ibid.

43. Ibid., 55–56.

44. On compensation as a means of winning other actors' agreement to institutional arrangements that place them at a disadvantage, see Jack Knight, *Institutions and Social Conflict* (Cambridge: Cambridge University Press, 1992).

CHAPTER 7. ORGANIZING THE FEDERAL ASSEMBLY

1. The term "party" is used for convenience. Not all electoral associations were registered as parties. The electoral law provided that registered "electoral associations" (*izbiratel'noe*

ob"edinenie) that collected 100,000 valid signatures could both nominate candidates in single-member districts and run candidates on party lists. Some of the electoral associations that ran candidates in the 1993 elections did constitute themselves as parties, while others, such as Yabloko, constituted themselves as "blocs," and still others as "movements." For simplicity, I shall refer to all electoral associations as parties.

2. Elections were not held in Tartarstan and Chechnia in December 1993, and an insufficient number of candidates running invalidated the Council of the Federation election in Cheliabinsk. Consequently, a total of 444 seats in the Duma and 171 seats of the Council of the Federation were filled when the Federal Assembly convened in January. Tartarstan and the Cheliabinsk held elections later in spring 1994. The Central Electoral Commission refused to publish a full tally of election results, providing a list only of what it declared were the elected deputies, so the exact vote totals for party candidates in single-member district races remain unknown, at least officially.

   On the effects of the mixed election system on the representation of parties in the Duma, see Robert G. Moser, "The Impact of the Electoral System on Post-Communist Party Development: The Case of the 1993 Russian Parliamentary Elections," *Electoral Studies* 4 (1995): 388–91; and Moser, "The Electoral Effects of Presidentialism in Post-Soviet Russia," in John Loewenhardt, ed., *Party Politics in Post-Communist Russia* (London: Frank Cass, 1998), 54–75.

3. G. V. Belonuchkin, ed., *Federal'noe Sobranie pervogo sozyva: Sovet Federatsii. Gosudarstvennaia Duma. 1993–1995-Spravochnik,* 6th ed. (Moscow: Panorama, 1996), 113.

4. Moshe Haspel, Thomas F. Remington, and Steven S. Smith, "Electoral Institutions and Party Cohesion in the Russian Duma," *Journal of Politics* 60, no. 2 (May 1998): 427.

5. *Nezavisimaia gazeta,* October 9, 1993.

6. Interview with senior staff aide to Mitiukov, May 1994.

7. *Segodnia,* January 18, 1994. The account presented here is also based on interviews with several of the principals at these meetings. A *Washington Post* article of January 8, 1994, quoted Egor Gaidar as saying that his faction, Russia's Choice, was planning to withdraw from these early negotiations because it was appearing that the communists, agrarians, and Zhirinovsky parties were forming a coalition and dividing up the major committees among them. In retrospect, it is clear that the differences between the communists and agrarians, on the one hand, and Zhirinovsky's LDPR, on the other, were too great for such a coalition to succeed. The communists were nearly as reluctant to cede control of the foreign affairs and defense committees to Zhirinovsky as the democratic factions were. The communists found it preferable to let Yavlinsky's Yabloko faction have the foreign affairs committee.

8. TASS, January 4, 1993.

9. Technically, a faction was the parliamentary organization of deputies elected from a party list; since to have won seats on the party-list part of the ballot required that the organization win at least 5 percent of the party-list vote, the smallest faction would in principle have received 5 percent of the 225 seats allocated to party list candidates, or 12 seats. Because victorious parties were given "bonus" votes that had been cast for parties that failed to clear the threshold, all of them gained a small additional margin of seats, but they also lost members as deputies decided to deaffiliate from their faction.

10. See Steven S. Smith and Thomas F. Remington, *The Politics of Institutional Choice: Formation of the Russian State Duma* (Princeton: Princeton University Press, 2000) for a detailed analysis of the voting on the threshold rule and other early institutional issues.

11. Russia's Choice refused to delegate any of its members to December 12. The communists seconded some members to Russia's Way, but not enough to bring it up to thirty-five.

12. RFE/RL Daily Report, April 29, 1994.

13. Under the rules then in place, a candidate required an absolute majority of the votes of all elected deputies to win. Six seats remained vacant after the December election, so 223 (50 percent plus one of 444 elected deputies) was an absolute majority. Deputies voted by secret ballot. Rybkin's opponent in this second round withdrew his candidacy in favor of Rybkin. Rybkin thereupon received 223 votes. One ballot was disputed because it had not been cast properly, but the voting intention was clear, and the floor voted by a substantial margin to consider it a valid ballot. Later, the Constitutional Court ruled that an absolute majority required 226 votes, that is, an absolutely majority of the total number of constitutional members of the Duma.

14. Moshe Haspel, "Should Party in Parliament Be Weak or Strong? The Rules Debate in the Russian State Duma," in *Party Politics in Post-Communist Russia,* ed. John Loewenhardt (London: Frank Cass, 1998), 192.

15. *Segodnia,* January 26, 1994. The procedure described in this newspaper article was more or less the procedure used, according to participants in the process whom I interviewed.

16. Shortly after the agreement was approved, the deputy chairmen devised a functional division of labor. The first deputy chairman became responsible for overseeing the orderly processing of legislation, preparing plans of legislative activity and presenting them for approval to the Council of the Duma and the floor. Another deputy chairman was given responsibility for overseeing liaison with the initiators of legislation, another for liaison with public associations, another for information technology in the chamber, and the fifth for economic issues and liaison with the regional associations. They take turns chairing the floor sessions. This is an informal assignment of responsibilities, at the behest of the chairman and by mutual consent, and has not been formally codified in the rules. More important than functional expertise has been the political balance among them.

17. Haspel, "Should Party in Parliament Be Weak or Strong? 192.

18. Ibid., 193; *Segodnia,* January 18, 1994.

19. For simplicity's sake, I shall refer to both categories as factions. Nonetheless, the distinction between them is real: factions are the parliamentary organizations of electoral associations that have cleared the 5-percent threshold, whereas groups are formed of any deputies who wish to associate for any reason. If they wish to be registered and thus acquire the same status and rights as factions, they must meet the thirty-five-member criterion. At that point, they are indistinguishable from factions in their activities and claims on Duma resources.

20. The Duma considered and rejected an "imperative mandate" rule that would apply to deputies elected on party lists. See Thomas F. Remington and Steven S. Smith, "The Development of Parliamentary Parties in Russia," *Legislative Studies Quarterly* 20, no. 4 (1995): 471–72.

21. The 1994–95 deputy survey was conducted in December 1994 and January 1995. The Center for Political Technologies interviewed 214 deputies of the State Duma with interviewers of the All-Russian Center for Public Opinion Research (VTsIOM). The sample includes 125 SMD deputies and 89 party-list deputies. The 1996 deputy survey was conducted in March and April 1996 by Center for Political Technologies with VTsIOM interviewers. There were 175 deputies interviewed, of whom 81 were elected from party lists and 94 were from single-member districts. For more details, see Steven S. Smith and Thomas F. Remington, *The Politics of Institutional Choice* (Princeton: Princeton University Press, 2000), appendix.

22. On the electoral law, see Thomas F. Remington and Steven S. Smith, "Political Goals, Institutional Context, and the Choice of an Electoral System: The Russian Parliamentary Law," *American Journal of Political Science* 40 (1996): 1253–79; also see Stephen White, Richard Rose, and Ian McAllister, *How Russia Votes* (Chatham, N.J.: Chatham House, 1997), 192–94; and Laura Belin and Robert W. Orttung, *The Russian Parliamentary Election of 1995: The Battle for the Duma* (Armonk, N.Y.: M. E. Sharpe, 1997), 22–30.

23. The new law raised the number of signatures that needed to be gathered for a party to nominate candidates to 200,000 but lowered the minimum number that could be obtained in any single region to 7 percent.

24. Parties hired agents to collect signatures, some of whom used dubious or outright illegal means to do so. Prices for signatures rose as the deadline for registration drew near, reaching as much as one U.S. dollar per signature.

25. See Sarah Oates, "Voting Behavior and Party Development in a New Democracy: Russian Voters, Parties and Campaigns in 1993 and 1995" (Ph.D. diss., Emory University, Department of Political Science, 1998).

26. White, Rose, and McAllister report that the percent of Russians expressing approval of the current political regime was 28 percent in 1996 while 59 percent approved the old communist regime. Approval of the current economic system stood at 22 percent and of the old communist economy at 72 percent (p. 182).

27. Yabloko and the agrarian group objected to the arrangement, but a position was held open for Yabloko and was later filled by a Yabloko deputy. The package passed on the floor by a vote of 359 to 56 with one abstention. (RFE/RL Newsline, January 19, 1996.)

28. RFE/RL Newsline, January 23, 1996.

29. *Segodnia,* January 24, 1996. Note that the distribution of committee chairmanships in a package in proportion to the strength of factions in the chamber is a purely informal and largely unenforceable arrangement. Several episodes have demonstrated that factions do not "own" their committees; when a committee chairman leaves his post or a faction expels a member who is a committee chair, it has no automatic right to replace him with another faction member. Rather, it must negotiate each new appointment separately with the other factions, typically through piecemeal deals involving two or three leadership positions simultaneously. More firmly established is the rule of interfactional consultations on major political decisions.

30. On the relation between committees and factions, see Joel M. Ostrow, "Procedural Breakdown and Deadlock in the Russian State Duma: The Problems of an Unlinked,

Dual-Channel Institutional Design," *Europe-Asia Studies* 50, no. 5 (July 1998): 793–817.

31. *Segodnia,* June 30, 1998.

32. Moshe Haspel, "Committees in the Russian State Duma: Continuity and Change in Comparative Perspective," *Journal of Legislative Studies* 4, no. 1 (spring 1998): 188–205.

33. According to Ivan Rybkin, during the first year of the Duma's work, committees typically had fifteen to seventeen staff members assigned to them, less for smaller committees and more for larger ones. Factions had roughly the same number of staff members. Each deputy was also assigned a paid staff assistant for work in Moscow and could hire more for work in his home district out of a limited pool of funds; deputies are also free to recruit volunteer aides. See I. P. Rybkin, *Gosudarstvennaia Duma: Piataia Popytka* (Moscow: Znanie, 1994), 67–68.

In some cases, an outside organization that wants to see a particular piece of legislation sponsored takes on itself the expenses of hiring a team of experts to draft the bill. This practice, while not illegal, lends credence to the belief that powerful lobbies often control lawmaking.

34. Moshe Haspel reports that most committee recommendations to adopt and to reject packages of amendments are accepted on the floor the first time they come up (73.7 percent of the sets that committees recommended for acceptance; 70.5 percent of the sets of amendments recommended for rejection). Individual deputies may demand that some particular amendment be voted on separately and the chair generally puts such motions to a vote, but only 10.6 percent of the amendments that committees wanted to reject are passed on the floor. Haspel also finds that the more balanced the partisan makeup of a committee, the greater its success in winning approval on the floor that it has voted out, in part because members themselves are more likely to support their committees' products in plenary session. Haspel, "Committees in the Russian State Duma," 199, 201.

35. The Council of the Federation does not have to consider all bills. Article 106 of the constitution requires that the Federation Council consider all legislation only in certain matters: budget and taxation issues; financial, customs, credit and currency issues; the ratification and denunciation of international treaties; status and defense of state borders; and matters of war and peace. Also all constitutional laws must be voted on by it, as must any matter falling into the joint jurisdiction of the federal government and the subject units of the federation. In practice this covers the vast majority of bills passed by the Duma. Of course, the council is free to take up any other bill passed by the Duma and consider it. But, in the case of other legislation, if the Federation Council fails to act on it within fourteen days, it is sent to the president. Disputes have arisen over the power to define whether particular legislative measures fall under the constitutionally enumerated categories or not, and if so whether the fourteen-day rule applied. The Constitutional Court ruled that the fourteen-day limit did not concern legislation where Federation Council action was constitutionally mandated. The Federation Council has also asked the Constitutional Court for a decision on the question of whether the Federation Council could itself determine whether a bill fell under the mandated categories. This question arose in late 1994 when the president signed part 1 of the Civil Code into law even though the Federation Council had rejected it; the president's justification was that

the Federation Council had failed to act within the required fourteen-day period. Before being considered on the floor, each bill that is sent to the council is considered by its appropriate committee, which makes a recommendation to the floor. If it concerns a matter the committee believes can be approved without floor action and sent directly to the president for his signature, and if the chairman concurs, and if there is no objection by the members or the government or president, then consideration by the full membership can be bypassed. On the other hand, the Council of the Federation has only fourteen working days in which to act on legislation; if it fails to act within this time period on a bill where council action is not required by the constitution, the bill is considered to be automatically approved by the chamber. Therefore a committee that fails to report a bill out in time may prevent the chamber from acting on it. In January 1997, accordingly, the chamber amended the rules to give the chairman the power to bring a matter to the floor even if the responsible committee has not completed action on it.

36. The initial Standing Orders were adopted February 2, 1996, and subsequently amended a number of times by the 1994–95 chamber. The 1996 Federation Council adopted a slightly revised version of the Standing Orders on February 6, 1996. Since then the chamber has amended the rules slightly on several occasions. The rules themselves are published in *Sobranie zakonodatel'stva Rossiiskoi Federatsii* (henceforth *SZRF*) no. 7, February 12, 1996, item 655. The amendments may be found in *SZRF* no. 16, April 15, 1996, item 1774; *SZRF* no. 27, July 1, 1996, item 3204; *SZRF* no. 1, January 6, 1997, item 45; *SZRF* no. 1, January 5, 1998, item 8; and *SZRF* no. 12, March 23, 1998, item 1389.

37. In the case on which the court ruled that Yeltsin must sign a law when both chambers of parliament have overridden his veto (the case concerned the celebrated law on the restitution of cultural artifacts seized by the Red Army in World War II), the court invited Yeltsin to seek a separate ruling on the constitutionality of the law itself and the constitutionality of its manner of passage. Yeltsin immediately submitted appeals on both points to the court. He pointed out that the Duma had passed the law by the (very common) expedient of allowing members to vote for the absent colleagues. This practice is winked at for practical reasons. Article 85 of the 1998 rules states that "for every item a deputy of the State Duma has one vote" and "He exercises his right to vote personally."

   In July 1999 the court ruled on the president's appeal. The court struck down some provisions of the law but allowed others to stand. The result was to give the president some discretion to negotiate with foreign governments over the return of particular cultural artifacts while not challenging parliament's right to pass legislation in this area. As to the Duma's informal practice of allowing deputies to vote for absent colleagues, the court rendered a Solomonic judgment. It held that for deputies to vote for other deputies was indeed unconstitutional. But the court refrained from striking down the trophy art law on the basis of the irregularity of the Duma's voting methods because this would have required the court retroactively to overturn most of the legislation passed over the past several years on the same grounds. Instead, the court warned the Duma that if proxy voting was needed in the future, the Duma should formalize it in the rules of procedure.

38. Chechnia has yet to send any members to the Federation Council, although an election of sorts was held in 1995 for a deputy to the Duma.

39. See Table 7.8 for a breakdown of the number of each type of federal subject.

40. Note that the term "member" is used in connection with the Council of the Federation after 1995 because it is composed on an ex officio basis. The term "deputy," signifying a popularly elected representative, was used for the first contingent in the Federation Council and continues to be used in the case of the State Duma.

41. The definition of the chief executive's position varies from region to region. In ordinary oblasts and krais, the chief executives are termed "governors" (*gubernatory*). In the cities of Moscow and St. Petersburg, which have the status of federal subjects, the city mayors are the chief executives and thus have seats in the Federation Council. (Note that the cities of Moscow and St. Petersburg are administratively separate and autonomous of the regions that surround them, Moscow oblast and Leningrad oblast. Each of these oblasts is also a federal subject and thus is represented in the Federation Council by its chief executive and the head of its legislative assembly.) Most of the ethnic republics have established executive presidencies so are represented in the Federation Council by their presidents. As of March 1996, there were twelve presidents, four heads of republics, four chairmen of republic governments, one chairman of the state council of a republic, two mayors, nine elected governors, and fifty-four appointed chiefs of administration. (Information from G. V. Belonuchkin, ed., *Federal'noe Sobranie: Sovet Federatsii. Gosudarstvennaia Duma: Spravochnik,* 6th ed. [Moscow: Panorama, 1996], 35.) By the end of 1996, nearly all positions of chiefs of administration had been filled through elections. Representative bodies vary considerably as well across the subjects of the federation, but most are relatively small, weak, part time, and dominated by the executive branch in the region.

42. *Nezavisimaia gazeta,* April 7, 1994.

43. Belonuchkin, ed., *Federal'noe Sobranie,* 64. This volume is an invaluable reference source on many aspects of the first Federal Assembly.

44. On the PPO of communist deputies in the Duma, see Viktor Zorkal'tsev, "Zavtra nastupit bez ukaza," *Pravda,* June 7, 1994; on the PPO in the Council of the Federation, see Belonuchkin, ed., *Federal'noe Sobranie,* 67.

45. Belonuchkin, ed., *Federal'noe Sobranie,* 67.

46. Ibid., 78.

47. Ibid., 49.

48. Ibid., 71.

49. Ibid., 260–63.

50. According to one expert, for council members who have to fly from the Far East and are therefore exposed to high levels of radiation during the flights, the council leadership allows them to attend less frequently. Attendance continues to be a problem, as in the past, but many members of the council make use of their trip to Moscow to make the rounds of the government ministries on questions concerning financial and other decisions affecting their territories.

51. Belonuchkin, ed., *Federal'noe Sobranie,* 38–39.

52. *Segodnia,* January 24 and 25, 1996.

53. This account is based on interviews with members and staff of the Federation Council.

54. This information is based on interviews with several of the strategists and participants in these efforts.
55. This is the major theme of Rybkin's book. Rybkin emphasizes the urgent need for conciliation, harmony, and cooperation among all the political actors, particularly following the debacle of October 1993. He portrays his own role of chairman as an instrument for achieving constructive agreement within the Duma, and between Duma and president. Rybkin, *Gosudarstvennaia Duma,* esp. 105–6.
56. Interview information, June 1998.
57. Article 117 of the constitution, paragraphs 4 and 3; Articles 149 to 154 of the 1998 Standing Orders of the Duma.
58. Note, though, that since Yabloko supported the Chechen war-related charge, Zhirinovsky's forty-nine-member strong faction could have ensured its passage had it chosen to do so.
59. See RFE/RL Newsline, May 19, 1999; *Segodnia,* May 20, 1999.
60. *Segodnia,* July 1, 1998.
61. Ibid., July 29, 1999.
62. Ostrow, "Procedural Breakdown and Deadlock," 796, 806, 807, 809.
63. Likewise, if the Duma ran the way the Russian Supreme Soviet did, with a strong chairman to manage proceedings, we might expect the Duma to be more effective at getting bills passed than getting them signed. A depiction of the Russian Supreme Soviet along these lines is provided by Joel M. Ostrow, "Institutional Design and Legislative Conflict: The Russian Supreme Soviet—A Well-Oiled Machine, Out of Control," *Communist and Post-Communist Studies* 29, no. 4 (1996): 413–33. Ostrow describes the Supreme Soviet under Khasbulatov as relatively efficient in its internal processes of lawmaking, thanks to the ability of the committee chairs to use the Presidium to work out agreements on legislative priorities and agendas; but in its external relations, Ostrow finds, the centralized, committee-dominated structure of the parliament allowed an errant, ambitious chairman such as Khasbulatov to engage in destructive conflicts with the president.
64. *Segodnia,* December 25, 1999.
65. The president issued 210 normative decrees in 1998 and approximately 160 in 1999.
66. Cf. Thomas F. Remington, Steven S. Smith, and Moshe Haspel, "Decrees, Laws, and Inter-Branch Relations in the Russian Federation," *Post-Soviet Affairs* 14 no. 4 (October-December 1998): 287–322; Thomas F. Remington, "The Changing Balance between President and Parliament in Russia: The Evolution of Constitutional Practice since 1993," *Slavic Review* 59 no. 3 (Fall 2000): 499–520.
67. Note that a small percentage of bills passed by the Duma in third reading—about 8 percent—were rejected by the Federation Council and were never subsequently passed through a veto override by the Duma or following negotiations by the two chambers. In 1996–99, 23 percent of Duma-passed bills were rejected by the Federation Council, and of these, 34 percent were killed by the Federation Council's action.

A German political scientist has argued that during the first two Dumas, President Yeltsin and his parliamentary opposition found it advantageous to publicize their conflicts and conceal their readiness to strike deals. Thus they postured publicly over their differences, while seeking backstage agreements. See Silvia von Steinsdorff, "Kalkulierter Konflikt und begrenzte Kooperation: Zum Verhaeltnis von Praesident, Regierung und Parlament in Russland," *Osteuropa* 1 (1999): 16–34.

68. Source: Federal'noe Sobranie—parlament Rossiiskoi Federatsii. Gosudarstvennaia Duma. Analiticheskoe upravlenie, *Gosudarstvennaia Duma vtorogo sozyva v vesenniuiu sessiiu 1999 goda. Informatsionno-analiticheskii biulleten',* no. 6 (Moscow: 1999), p. 4; Federal'noe Sobranie—parlament Rossiiskoi Federatsii. Gosudarstvennaia Duma. Analiticheskoe upravlenie, *Gosudarstvennaia Duma vtorogo sozyva v osenniuiu sessiiu 1999 goda. Informatsionno-analiticheskii biulleten',* no. 10 (Moscow: 1999), p. 4.; and Federal'noe Sobranie—parlament Rossiiskoi Federatsii. Gosudarstvennaia Duma. Analiticheskoe upravlenie, Analiticheskii vestuik, vyp. 3. *Statisticheskie kharakteristiki zakonodatel'noi deiatel'nosti Gosudarstvennoi Dumy vtorogo sozyva (1996–1999)* (Moscow, 2000), pp. 6–8.

69. Gosudarstvennaia Duma, *Gosudarstvennaia Duma vtorogo sozyva v vesenniuiu sessiiu 1999 goda,* p. 5.

70. See note 21, above.

71. See discussion in chapter 5, where I called attention to Yeltsin's and Khasbulatov's use of such Presidium acts to grant privileges to particular regions and industries. Between the end of the Sixth Congress in April 1992 and November 10 of the same year, the RSFSR Supreme Soviet passed a total of 1,073 legal acts. Of these, 53 were laws and 268 were legislative decrees. The rest of the actions consisted of: 390 decrees and edicts of the Presidium of the Supreme Soviet; 281 orders (*rasporiazheniia*) of the chairman of the Supreme Soviet and his deputies; 10 appeals and declarations of the Supreme Soviet; 49 decrees of the Council of the Nationalities; 22 decrees of the Council of the Republic. *Rossiiskaia gazeta,* November 14, 1992. In all, parliament took around 180 actions per month in session but fewer than 9 of these were laws.

CHAPTER 8: DOES PARLIAMENT MATTER?

1. A systematic attempt to measure the impact of these overlapping influences on deputy behavior is carried out in Steven S. Smith and Thomas F. Remington, *The Politics of Institutional Choice: Formation of the Russian State Duma* (Princeton: Princeton University Press, 2000).

2. William Riker, "Political Science and Rational Choice," in *Perspectives on Positive Political Economy,* ed. James E. Alt and Kenneth A. Shepsle (Cambridge: Cambridge University Press, 1990), 175.

Index

Other Books By:

Linda Dockery & Jolene Giordano

Three Little Words; Comedy/Romance

An Angel for Christmas: Inspirational

[Nominated for a Pulitzer Prize]

Due Out in 2004:

Once Upon a Time: Comedy/Romance

Tangled Web: Suspense

Jaded Lady: Adventure/Romance